THE ELDER IERONYMOS OF AEGINA

THE ELDER IERONYMOS OF AEGINA

By Peter Botsis

With

MEMOIRS OF THE ELDER IERONYMOS

Translated from the Greek by the
HOLY TRANSFIGURATION MONASTERY
Boston, Massachusetts
2007

The Elder Ieronymos of Aegina

✠

DISMISSAL HYMN
Plagal of First Tone. Let us worship the Word

REACHING forth with thy whole soul unto the Lord thy God,
thou didst attain to the stature of the great Fathers of old,
striving after their humility and love for God;
and as a sharer in their grace,
thou dost cover with thy prayers
the faithful that seek thy succour.
Hence ever pray to the Saviour,
O blest Hieronymus, that we be saved.

KONTAKION
Fourth Tone. Be quick to anticipate

LIKE Moses, thou spakest face to face with God as a friend,
and thou wast thyself a fiery pillar of ceaseless prayer,
O Father Hieronymus;
wherefore do thou lead us from the Egypt of passions,
out of thickest darkness to the light of salvation;
for thou possessest boldness with Christ,
Who was well pleased in thee.

MEGALYNARION

UNTO thee, O Father, the hearts of men,
like a book, lay open,
where thou readest their secret thoughts.
Wherefore, we acclaim thee,
Hieronymus our Father,
who wast like a great Prophet,
guiding new Israel.

Copyright © 2007 by the
Holy Transfiguration Monastery
Brookline, Massachusetts 02445
All rights reserved
Printed in the United States of America
ISBN 13: 978-0-943405-14-8
ISBN 10: 0-943405-14-9
Library of Congress Control Number: 2007921639

Contents

	Introduction	9
Chapter 1	*Testimony of Sanctity*	21
Chapter 2	*The Great Mainland*	25
Chapter 3	*God-Pleasing Upbringing*	49
Chapter 4	*Deacon*	60
Chapter 5	*At the Holy Places*	67
Chapter 6	*Constantinople*	73
Chapter 7	*Greece*	91
Chapter 8	*Aegina*	95
Chapter 9	*A Priest Called by God*	105
Chapter 10	*The Angelic Life*	117
Chapter 11	*Suffering the Things of Men*	121
Chapter 12	*To the Mountain that is Holy*	135
Chapter 13	*Experiences of a God-seer*	138
Chapter 14	*Spiritual Solicitude*	143
Chapter 15	*No Man on Earth Loves Me Like Father Ieronymos*	149
Chapter 16	*Example of Humblemindedness*	153
Chapter 17	*Lover of Tradition*	159
Chapter 18	*In Mine Affliction Thou Hast Enlarged Me*	164
Chapter 19	*The Hermitage*	169
Chapter 20	*Daily Ministry*	181
Chapter 21	*My Strength is Made Perfect in Weakness*	229
Chapter 22	*Last Struggles*	242
Chapter 23	*Departure*	249
	Epilogue	253
	Appendix	257
	Memoirs of the Elder Ieronymos of Aegina	263
	Miracles of the Elder Ieronymos	333
	Service to the Elder Ieronymos of Aegina	337

Pantocrator in the eastern cupola of the eleventh-century Karanlik Kilisse (Dark Church) in the Göreme region of Cappadocia.

Introduction

In the Name of the Father, and of the Son,
and of the Holy Spirit. Amen.

> *Praise ye the Name of the Lord;*
> *O ye servants, praise the Lord,*
> *ye that stand in the house of the Lord,*
> *in the courts of the house of our God.*
> *Psalm 134:1–2*

BELOVED CHRISTIANS, you are about to read the biography of the Elder Ieronymos the Cappadocian of Aegina, one of the two great Elders of the Jesus Prayer in the twentieth century in the land of Greece, the other being the Elder Joseph the Hesychast of the Holy Mountain. Both were very strong in the interior prayer of the heart.

They were contemporaries and knew each other; from time to time they exchanged notes on their experiences of the Jesus Prayer. Actually, Mother Eupraxia, who served the Elder Ieronymos, was the sister in the flesh of the Elder Arsenios, the Elder Joseph's fellow ascetic. Before the Second World War, both the Elder Ieronymos and the Elder Joseph would visit each other; but for the last two decades of their life both were cloistered and rarely left their cells.

The Elder Ieronymos was a very amazing man, like one of the ancients, the great Desert Fathers. Wherever he lived—in his beloved Cappadocia, at the Monastery of Saint John the Baptist by

The flight into Egypt, fresco in the Church of Qeledjlar in the Göreme Valley, 1911.

the Jordan, which was his domicile during his prolonged pilgrimage in the Holy Land, in Constantinople where he served as deacon and preacher to his Cappadocian and Anatolian compatriots who were merchants, or in Aegina where he lived the last four decades of his life—he praised the Name of the Lord in the depth of his heart and mind in deep stillness. He perpetually stood in the "house of the Lord, in the courts of the house of our God."

Father Ieronymos was wont to say that the mind of man is a very amazing thing. One can stand in one place physically, but his mind can be found in many places. A man can be found in prison, but his mind cannot be bound. It is free and can soar to the very throne of Divinity. "In one's heart and mind one can always be found at the feet of our Christ," he often said. The Elder loved the Holy Land exceedingly; he lived and experienced the Holy Shrines to the uttermost, being at the very places where our Saviour was born, baptized, transfigured, crucified, buried, arose from the tomb, ascended into Heaven. He often told his listeners, "In my mind I am now found in the cave in Bethlehem where our Saviour was born," and he would begin to chant the Sessional Hymn of the Feast of the Lord's Nativity, "Come, ye faithful, let us see where Christ the Saviour hath been born; let us follow with the kings, even the Magi from the East, unto the place where the star doth direct their journey..." And he would weep from compunction. He so loved the Holy Land that he often said, "Every Christian should visit the Holy Shrines at least once in his lifetime. After he has visited the Holy Land, his heart and mind will often be found there."

Thus, in a very real way, the Elder throughout his life stood in the "house of the Lord, in the courts of the house of our God."

Often while speaking with an individual or a group of pilgrims he would say, "I am tired now. Could you step outside for a little? The Eldress Eupraxia will bring you treats. I'll rest a little and then call you back." Those present always complied, and a quarter to half an hour later he would ring his little bell and receive his visitors again. At the time, we thought that because he was old and weak he really wanted to rest a little, to catch his breath. Only after his blessed repose did we learn that the prayer at such times became strong in him and he wanted a little time of stillness and quiet to immerse himself in prayer. He could not carry on two conversations—one with God and one with men—at the same time.

On other rare occasions, when we went to visit him we were told that the Elder was not in and would only be back late in the evening. Wondering where he could have gone, we contented ourselves with visiting the chapel and his cell, accepted Mother Eupraxia's hospitality, and then left to visit the other shrines of Aegina, the foremost being that of Saint Nectarius. It was only after his repose that we learned that on such occasions he took refuge and hid in his workshop, praying in darkness and deep stillness. His "workshop" consisted of a semicircular cavernous corridor not unlike the caves of his native Cappadocia. It was built at a later period and connected to the back of a previously built structure. The

The Elder Ieronymos's "workshop" where he prayed in secret.

floor-level was some feet below the original building, so that at the end of the corridor one had to climb four high steps to enter a little cell with a cot and a few icons. Another tiny cell was to the right. He could thus spend the whole day in his "workshop" at his special work (the prayer of the heart) and even take a little rest without ever coming out. It was in this "workshop" that he spent as much as fourteen hours in deep continuous prayer, mentioning to us

End of corridor with steps to hidden cell; door on left opens into the "workshop."

that he knew of a monk who prayed for fourteen continuous hours of undistracted prayer.

The Elder built three churches on Aegina: at the Hospital of Saint Dionysius; the Church of the Annunciation, at Mother Eupraxia's hermitage; and the Church of the Holy Unmercenaries Cosmas and Damian, which serves as the parish church of the Traditionalist Christians of Aegina. After he had retired to the hermitage of the Annunciation and entered into deep *hesychia* and given himself up to noetic prayer, he used to say, "I squandered the best years of my life building churches. If I had known the sweet-

Interior of the "workshop" where the Elder prayed in secret.

ness of *hesychia* and the compunctionate prayer and tears of the heart, I would have entered into stillness earlier in life."

The Elder Ieronymos was a serious man of few words—a real Cappadocian. His utterances were like the sayings of the Desert Fathers—a few words with much depth, chiselled in stone. His pronunciation was clearly and unmistakably Anatolian.

If the great Catastrophe of Asia Minor had not taken place in

Secret cell with a cot where the Elder rested.

1922, he probably would never have emigrated to Greece. He would have lived and reposed in his beloved Cappadocia, hidden in the mountains of Anatolia, unknown to the world at large like so many contemporary compatriots of his, a few of whom are mentioned in this book. It was a great blessing from our Lord that this magnificent light was not hidden from us in these latter times.

Now with the publication of his life in English, this lamp is put upon the lampstand and will shine to many that thirst and hunger for things spiritual.

Of late it has come to our attention that in certain church circles in Greece and elsewhere it is claimed that the Elder Ieronymos reposed in communion with the innovating State Church of Greece. This is erroneous, to say the least. Father Ieronymos went to Greece as a refugee in 1922, two years after the repose of Saint Nectarius, and settled on Aegina. He lived at the hospital of the island and was responsible for the building of the hospital church of Saint Dionysius, Bishop of Aegina and Wonderworker of Zakynthos.

He was ordained to the priesthood on the eve of the change of the calendar (1924), served for a very short time, and then ceased to serve the Holy Liturgy. Something happened while he was serving Liturgy and this was the cause for him not to serve again. All this was before the calendar innovation. Thereafter he would hear confessions, would chant, would preach, but would not liturgize.

At the time Father Cosmas, his compatriot and fellow refugee, was living on Aegina; he served the Liturgy, and Father Ieronymos chanted and preached. This took place in the 1920's and 30's and till the beginning of the 40's. They would hold vigils and celebrate in the various chapels of which there is a multitude on Aegina (some say there are 365 chapels throughout the island).

Father Ieronymos was by nature a quiet man who avoided controversies and demonstrations. He was like the saintly Papa-Nicholas Planas of Athens, who celebrated Liturgies in the chapels of Athens and environs—mostly at night; and like him, he also continued celebrating the feasts according to the Church Calendar quietly but steadfastly without making an issue of it. This was so until August of 1942, when someone informed the Metropolitan of Hydra and Aegina that Father Ieronymos was celebrating the feasts according to the Julian Calendar. It was then that the Metropolitan said that he would come to Aegina and force the issue by compelling the Elder to concelebrate with him at the

Cathedral according to the Papal reckoning. Whereupon Father Ieronymos sent in his resignation in writing, officially separating himself from the State Church (see pages 160–63.)

It was at this time that he left the hospital, where he had erected the Church of Saint Dionysius, and built a small cell next to the Church of the Annunciation, which he had also built at Mother Eupraxia's hermitage. A little earlier in 1935 three Bishops of the State Church came over and led the resistance of the faithful in keeping the traditions of the Church.[1] Thus from 1942 he belonged to the jurisdiction of Metropolitan Chrysostom of Florina and his successors Archbishops Akakios and Auxentius. He was visited twice by Archbishop Auxentius during his last illness, once at the hospital and the second time one day before his repose at the apartment of the late Eleutherios Koumbis. At his funeral in Aegina, Bishop Akakios of Diavlia, of the Synod of Archbishop Auxentius, presided with other clergy.

Since the repose of the Elder Ieronymos, many miracles have been reported, miracles of healing and other cases of assistance through his holy prayers. In reading his life in Greek, many Christians have reproached themselves, saying, "We lived right next door in Athens and Piraeus—just an hour by ferryboat to Aegina. We even frequently visited Aegina and didn't know that such a man existed in our days." Yet after reading his life, many exclaim that his presence becomes so strong that they think they have met him.

The Elder Ieronymos is a giant among the recent Saints of our Church. We have been told that several inhabitants of Aegina who knew him have had the same dream independently. In the dream, three clergymen appeared: Saint Dionysius of Zakynthos, who was Bishop of Aegina in the late sixteenth and early seventeenth centuries, Saint Nectarius, and the Elder Ieronymos. The first two

1. *The Struggle Against Ecumenism*, The Holy Orthodox Church in North America, Boston, 1998, documents the origins and history of the True Orthodox Christians of Greece in detail.

were conversing between them and pointing to the Elder, they said, "He is higher than we are." Now, Saints Dionysius and Nectarius are great wonderworkers and were both Bishops who lived in retirement as simple monks—but the Elder Ieronymos was a true hesychast who progressed in mental prayer of the heart to a rare and great height, like that attained to by the great Desert Fathers of the first centuries. It seems that for this reason he is acknowledged as being greater. We were informed of the above dream by Mrs. Amalia Serelis of New York, a native of Aegina whose husband comes from a prominent family of the island.

Dear Christians, when we printed the life of Papa-Nicholas Planas, we mentioned in the introduction that our monastery was obligated to do this, since our brotherhood had received so many blessings and instructions of the Elder through his spiritual daughter Mother Martha. We never met Papa-Nicholas, since he reposed in the early 1930's, before we were born. But the Elder Ieronymos we knew well. Both our Founder, Father Panteleimon, and our Abbot, Father Isaac, knew him, and so did other of the senior Fathers. To his blessings, prayers, and instructions, we owe much. Thus, it was even more fitting, and we were under greater obligation, to translate and publish the present book.

We are indebted to Mr. Peter Botsis of Athens for composing and printing the original biography in Greek, and we thank him for the permission to print it in English, and for supplying many of his own photographs for this edition.

We thank the Library of the University of Newcastle upon Tyne for kindly providing us with the photographs of Kelveri on pages 30 and 35–7, which were taken by Gertrude Bell in 1907 while the Elder Ieronymos was still living in Kelveri. The photographs on pages 27 and 61 were also taken by Miss Bell in 1907, and appear in *The Thousand and One Churches,* which she published with Sir William Ramsey in 1909. The University of Newcastle is currently scanning and archiving all of Miss Bell's photographs of Asia Minor, the Holy Land, and elsewhere, and many of them can be seen at the library's web site, www.gerty.ncl.ac.uk.

The Sweet-kissing icon on page 148, from page 44 of *Sacred Art of Cappadocia* by Ahmet Ertug, is copyright 2005 by Ahmet Ertug and is used by his kind permission. We have retouched it to reduce the damage it has suffered over the centuries.

We also thank the sisters of the Holy Nativity Convent in Brookline and the second Mother Eupraxia of Aegina for generously supplying us with many photographs of Aegina, of the Elder Ieronymos, and of the first Mother Eupraxia, who had served the Elder until his repose.

The photographs of Cappadocia on pages 8, 10, 32, 38, 40, 44, 45, 50, 52, 53, 58–9, 112, 139, 158, and 286 were taken in 1911 by Father Guillaume de Jerphanion and printed in Paris in three volumes between 1925 and 1934 under the title *Les Églises Rupestres de Cappadoce.*

We are blessed to have here in our monastery the walking-stick of the Elder Ieronymos gifted by him to our founder Archimandrite Panteleimon on his last visit to his hermitage a few months before his blessed repose. We also have his monastic cowl and *skoufaki* made of cloth, together with other items from his cell (i.e., his hand bell, Mount Athos back scratcher, etc.). After the recovery of his holy remains we have been blessed with many of his holy bones. We treasure all these blessings and have them as a staff and consolation in these troubled times. May his holy blessings be with us always.

Remember us, dear Christians, and pray that we find mercy in the day of the Lord. Amen.

HOLY TRANSFIGURATION MONASTERY
Beginning of the Indiction
Saint Symeon the Stylite
September 1, 2006

*Street Entrance to the Elder Ieronymos's Hermitage in Aegina.
The road was unpaved in the Elder's day.*

CHAPTER ONE
Testimony of Sanctity

A CONVERSATION WAS IN PROGRESS in the office of a certain religious organization in Athens. Four or five young people had gathered, among them a deacon from the provinces who was a student in the theological school. They were discussing general subjects of spiritual edification, when suddenly the deacon interrupted the gathering and, addressing himself to all, said, "I often wonder, friends, what the Saints were like. How did they live? What wouldn't I give to know a holy man at close range! But where can you find one nowadays, when all of us have become depraved?"

But one of those present answered, "Saints still exist even today. I've even met one."

"You've met a Saint? So where is he? If what you say is true, I wouldn't hesitate to travel to the ends of the earth to make his acquaintance."

"You don't have to go quite so far. Just make the effort to get as far as Aegina, and you'll meet him there."

"Where does he live? What is his name?"

"When you get off the ferryboat to Aegina, ask where Father Ieronymos lives. Everybody knows him there, and they'll tell you how to find him."

After a short while, the gathering broke up and each went his way. A few days later they met again, and he who had told the deacon to visit Father Ieronymos asked him, "So what happened, Father, did you go to Aegina?"

"Yes, I went," answered the deacon, his face beaming with joy.

"And what did you see? Were you satisfied?"

"My brother, you sent me to see a Saint. And I, when I met him, I experienced such joy that I thought I found Christ Himself. What a man he is, my brother! I felt such comfort, such gladness and strength entered me, that I thought my heart would burst from joy. My emotions can't be described. In his presence I felt like an ignorant child. All my theological knowledge was annihilated before his simple and prophetic word. He really is a Saint. My brother, I can't find the words to thank you. Nothing I could say would ever be enough. You could not have given me greater joy. May the Lord reward you."

S∪CH ARE THE IMPRESSIONS of one of those fortunate people who were deemed worthy to meet Father Ieronymos, the renowned Elder of Aegina. Nor was he by any means the only one who was so impressed by meeting him. All who came to know him, one this way and another that, speak of their encounter with him with the same enthusiasm and the same love, with the same devoutness and reverence. With his simplicity, his humility, and the holiness of his life, he was able to touch the souls of all who visited him and became for them father, brother, good friend and, above all, their wise and unerring guide. It was because of this that the people of God, who are able to perceive the odor of sanctity, flocked to him to enjoy his divine teaching. They found refuge in their misfortunes, comfort in their afflictions, and help in facing the trials of life. And he, always affectionate, always long-suffering and magnanimous, would receive them all, giving peace to one, consolation to another, courage to a third, guiding yet another in the path of repentance. All were able to fit in his small and simple cell, because his love was large enough for all. And all departed from this spiritual infirmary changed, healed, peaceful.

Who then was this venerable elder, who made so many people run to him? From whence did this swallow of the wilderness spring up and was found amidst us, to water with his tears the earth made desolate by our sins, and to transform it into a spiritual oasis, wherein every sort of wayfarer found refreshment and rest?

Let us closely follow the path of this terrestrial angel, who came with his holy life to inspire a multitude of people in Aegina, in Greece, and in Orthodoxy in general, and to show that even in our days it is possible for a person to reap the fruits of sanctity, if he will dedicate himself completely to God.

Houses carved out of the rock cones, Cappadocia, c. 1919. Note people at right.

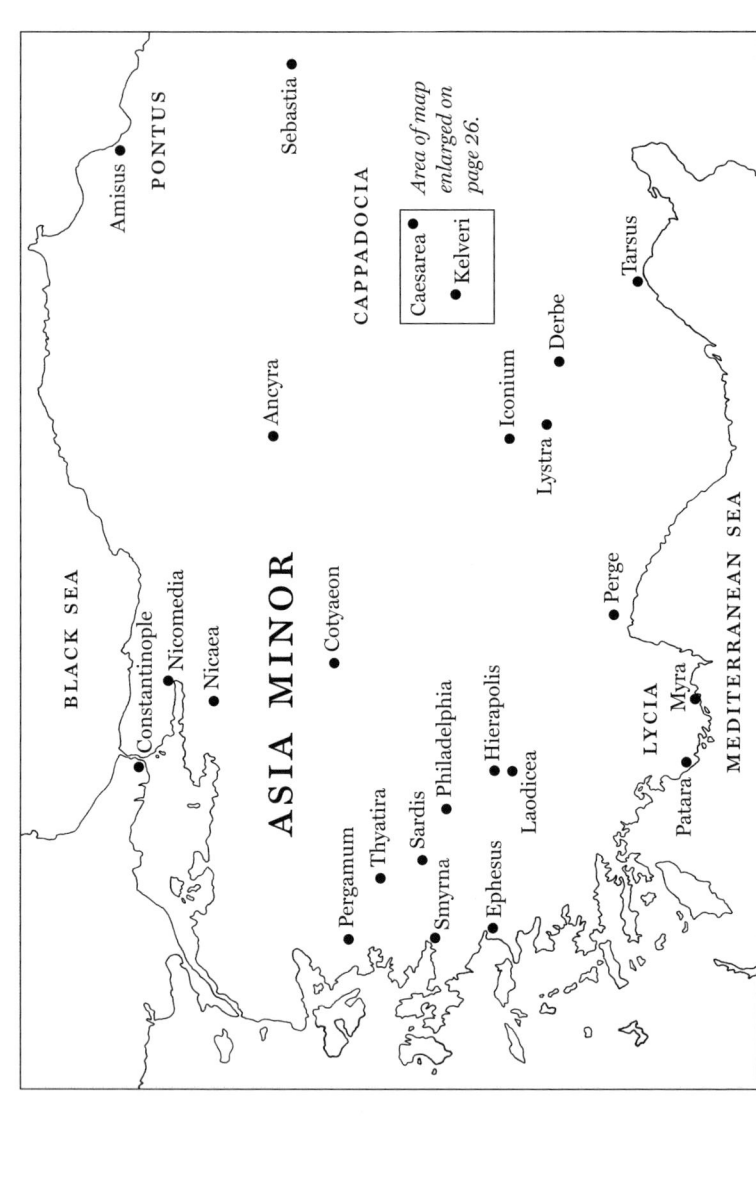

CHAPTER TWO
The Great Mainland

FATHER IERONYMOS, whose secular name was Basil Apostolides, was born in 1883 in Asia Minor, the "great mainland," as Kontoglou so aptly put it, that fountainhead of holiness. His place of birth was Kelveri of Cappadocia, a region which showed forth some of the greatest Saints of our Church (Saint Basil the Great, Saint Gregory the Theologian, Saint Amphilochius of Iconium, etc.).

Kelveri, at the time that Father Ieronymos was born, was a small town of some 4,000 inhabitants. It was considered one of the major commercial centers of the area. Ecclesiastically, it was subject to the diocese of Iconium.

According to trustworthy testimony, Kelveri[1] in ancient times was the site of a series of cells and monasteries, some perched like eagles' nests high up on the rocks, others carved out of the mountains round about. Ascetics lived there like herons in their nests,

---

1. Many are of the conviction that Kelveri (also spelled Gelveri) is identical with the ancient Karvali, with its ancient monasteries. The people of Kelveri seem to be of the same opinion, because after the destruction of Asia Minor in 1922, its inhabitants who came to Greece were settled in a district near Kavala and they named their village New Karvali. The people of Kelveri were not alone in this; the official authorities also held this opinion. Below (see page 74) we will include a letter of Sophronios, Metropolitan of Iconium, to the Ecumenical Patriarch, in which, among other things, Father Ieronymos is referred to as, "... hailing from Karvali..." A letter from Saint Gregory the Theologian to the Emperor Valentinian begins by mentioning Karvala, PG 37:336.

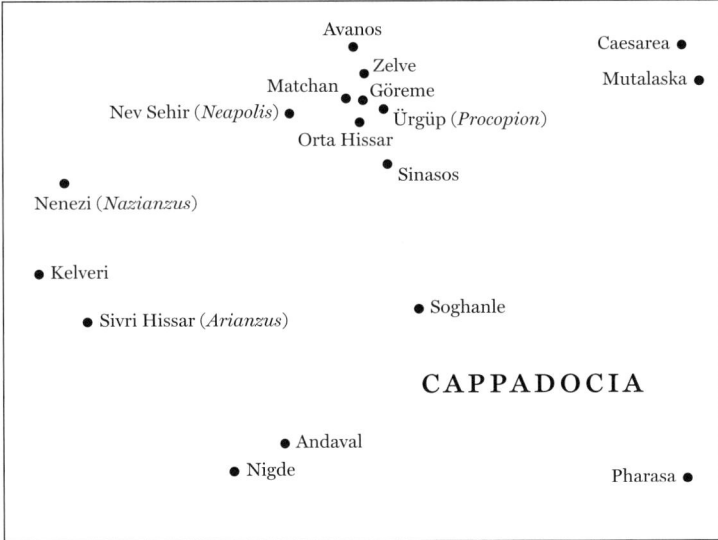

or like otherworldly beings in the dens and caves of the earth. The very name of the place confirms the above assertion: Kelveri is a corruption of the older "Kelivara," a mixed Greek-Turkish word signifying "a place of many cells." This view is supported by the fact that there used to be many churches at Kelveri: the evidence shows that last century there must have been over two hundred.

With the passage of time, the angel-like ascetics of the monasteries became fewer. And later, from fear of the persecutions and oppression of a conqueror holding to a different religion, the monasteries and hermitages closed down one by one. The *rassa*-clad occupants of the cells were replaced by layfolk, until finally what had been a monastic republic was reduced to a village.

The Saints, wherever they may be found, are not sanctified for themselves alone; they sanctify creation around them also. The power of their prayers, and the sweat of their ascetical struggles, affect all things around them and transmit to them their holiness. Even as we have icons that work miracles, because they were

Ruined Church in Sivri Hissar, identified with Arianzus,
the hereditary estate of Saint Gregory the Theologian.
Photographed in 1907 by Gertrude Bell.

painted by holy men, in like manner the entire area where holy men lived is sanctified and their descendants live by their tradition and under their influence.

Kelveri was considered the most important Christian center of the whole region. From extant historical testimonies, and also from narrations and recollections of the blessed Elder Ieronymos, we shall mention a few details that will help us to come somewhat closer to the spiritual atmosphere that prevailed there in the Elder's day and age.

Tradition in Anatolia

EVERY HOME IN KELVERI had a separate room, which was the special place of prayer. On the eastern side of this room they would make a niche, where they placed the icons, the censer, the religious books (the *Synopsis*,[2] the *Psalter*, the Gospels, the lives of the Saints), holy water from the feast of Theophany, and so forth. It was here that they all prayed together. They prayed privately also, when any felt the need. But there were also the prescribed hours of common prayer: in the morning, at noonday, in the evening when the church bell rang for Vespers, and in the evening for Compline. Many were they who awoke at midnight in order to read the midnight service, because at this time, they said, "the gates of Heaven open up." And, of course, there was always prayer before and after meals. It is noteworthy that before they commenced any work whatsoever, their lips whispered the prayer, "Lord, Jesus Christ..." Such was their zeal for prayer that many said the Kelveriotes were the spiritual descendants of monks, and thus a sort of legend took hold.

The keeping of Sundays and the other Christian feasts as non-work days was something sacred and inviolable. Not only would the stores and workshops remain closed, but even the women at home would stop every kind of work. It was the same with the fasts, which were observed with great strictness. They even made the little children, as soon as they were weaned, to begin keeping the fasts.

Many of the people of Kelveri, chiefly women, were in the habit of going in groups to country chapels to pray. This usually took place at night, early at dawn, or in the evening, especially during the period of the Great Fast. One of them would kneel in the middle of the church and would relate to the others, who stood, narrations from the Birth, the Crucifixion and whatever else they knew, whereupon all began to pray with tears. They attached special significance to tears. They would endeavor not to rise from prayer without shedding at least one teardrop because, as they said, tears have great power; "they put out the fire of hell."

---

2. A prayer book providing morning and evening prayers, Vespers, Compline, etc.—TRANS.

The monastic tradition of the Orthodox Church was maintained very energetically in Kelveri. Many abandoned the world and became monks. The women took the lead here also; once they had decided to consecrate themselves to God, they would go to a convent or would put on monastic clothing and live in a monastic way in the village, occupying themselves exclusively with the study of spiritual and ecclesiastical books, with prayer, with vigils and good works.

Almost all the inhabitants of Kelveri nourished within a deep desire to visit the Holy Places. Every year, around fall, small groups of men and women would gather, and once they had prepared all that was needed for their journey, which usually lasted for six months, they all set off together. These journeys had a festive character. And when the pilgrims returned to Kelveri, the inhabitants awaited them at the entrance of the village, in the so-called "ravine of the monastery." There they would have a doxology to God and then return all together.

Of the village's two hundred churches or so, those of the Holy Unmercenaries Cosmas and Damian and Saint Gregory the Theologian stood out, because of the special reverence which the Kelveriotes had for these Saints. On the feast of the Holy Unmercenaries[3] in particular, the first of November, a great festival took place in Kelveri which was attended by the whole village. The Holy Unmercenaries, the "doctors without money," were their pa-

---

3. The Holy Unmercenaries (*Anargyroi* in Greek, lit. *without silver*, i.e. without payment) are very beloved and popular among the Orthodox. There are some 24 saints with this description in the Church calendar. Saint Panteleimon the Healer is the exarch of the Holy Unmercenaries and three sets of brothers, named Cosmas and Damian, are favorites of the faithful: Saints Cosmas and Damian of Rome, celebrated on July 1; Saints Cosmas and Damian with their brothers Leontius, Euprepius, and Anthimus of Arabia, celebrated on October 17; and Saints Cosmas and Damian the sons of Theodota of Asia Minor, celebrated on November 1. All were physicians in the world and healed all who came to them freely by the power of God, without payment.—TRANS.

Church of Saint Gregory the Theologian in Kelveri. Photographed by Gertrude Bell in 1907, while the Elder Ieronymos was still living in Kelveri.

trons. Even the few Turks living in Kelveri believed in the miraculous power of the Saints. There are many incidents demonstrating the faith that the Turks nourished towards the Holy Unmercenaries and Saint Gregory the Theologian. We shall mention two characteristic incidents.

During World War I, in 1914, a certain Kelveriote Turk took part in a major battle, which lasted for two days. The battle was fierce and his life was endangered. In those difficult hours he found no other refuge except in the Holy Unmercenaries, whom he knew to be great wonderworkers. He implored them to save him and he would give whatever they requested of him. Then during a respite in the battle, when he had been overcome by a little sleep, he saw the Holy Unmercenaries who said to him, "We will save you, but as soon as you return to Kelveri offer our church a vessel of oil." The Turk in fact was saved and he immediately gave his wife word to fulfill his vow to the church.

Another Turk related that before the exchange of populations in 1924, a certain young girl fell from her house into the void and was not harmed. During her fall Saint Gregory held her by her hand and saved her. After the exchange, the daughter of a certain Turk fell from the same house and was killed.[4] According to the refugee Turk, "Saint Gregory had become a refugee in Macedonia (the place where the Christian inhabitants of Kelveri were resettled after the exchange) and was no longer there to save her."

The Church's presence in Kelveri was conspicuous; not only did it have the spiritual leadership, but it was also foremost in preserving the Greek language, and it endeavored to keep the national consciousness thriving and flourishing. In the rough and trackless path that the Greek faithful of Asia Minor traversed, in their

---

4. In Kelveri and many other villages of Cappadocia, the inhabitants lived in cave houses dug out of the rock. Most of these "houses" were formerly monks' cells and were perched up high on the cliffsides. It was therefore not uncommon for people to fall and be maimed for life or even killed.—TRANS.

The Village of Tchaouch In, located between Matchan and Zelve in Cappadocia.

life-or-death struggle for their religious and national survival, it was their attachment and devotion to the Church, their worshipful and sacramental life, their prayers and seething faith in their miracle-working Saints that helped them preserve their tranquillity of soul and the hope for a better tomorrow.

Angel-like Ascetics

WE SHOULD MAKE SPECIAL MENTION of certain holy persons, who towards the end of last century[5] extraordinarily helped in the spiritual uplifting of the inhabitants of Kelveri and deeply influenced the formation of Father Ieronymos's personality. Two of these persons were:

1. MISAEL

Misael, a patriarchal personage, was an ascetical type, one of those whom we only encounter in the lives of the Saints. Austere

---

5. The original edition was printed in 1991; such references have been left intact, even though at the present time "the last century" etc. refers to the twentieth, rather than the nineteenth.—TRANS.

yet meek, he was like unto a Prophet who bears in himself a whole age-old tradition. He combined the type of the austere Prophet with the introspective ascetic who spends all his days and nights in prayer. He was a dynamic personality who played the part of spiritual guide to all the inhabitants of the village. As the Elder Ieronymos used to say, "Misael was another Abba Isaac.[6] So much had he progressed in prayer."

Misael was married but he did not live with his wife; they were like brother and sister. He worked for his family and provided for them, but did not live with them. By day he worked alone in the fields, not wishing to work with others lest they observe him as he prayed. The nights he passed praying at some country chapel,[7] or if he returned home he remained by himself. He had a great love for stillness and a burning desire for prayer. When he prayed, his heart was so enflamed that he forgot himself. He had the strength to remain kneeling in prayer with his hands upraised for two days.

He had especially given himself over to so-called "compunctionate" prayer. This "compunctionate" prayer, as they called it in Kelveri, was nothing other than noetic prayer (that is, prayer of the heart). He would kneel before an icon or in the open air outdoors and set his soul free to overflow before God. He would bring to mind his sins and pour forth abundant tears, from which he awaited deliverance. He often went up into the mountain and remained there praying till nightfall. And when he finished, the sweat of his agony was so great, that as the Elder Ieronymos would say, "If you wrung out his undershirt, you'd get three pints of water."

When he went to church, during the Divine Liturgy, he would

---

6. That is, Saint Isaac the Syrian.—TRANS.

7. Ἐξωκκλήσι in Greek, literally "outside church." All Orthodox countries abound in these small chapels and churches usually found in the fields and countryside outside the towns and villages or on mountains and hills. Many were built as the fulfillment of a vow or in thanksgiving to a certain Saint for a benefaction rendered. In the present instance these chapels were usually cave churches carved out of the rock by monks many centuries before.—TRANS.

Rock-cut Church of the Panagia in Kelveri, in the Ravine called *Monaster-deresi*.
Opposite page: the entrance, photographed in 1907 by Gertrude Bell.

not enter the nave, but stood in the narthex or behind some column. He would have his head resting on his chest and prayed noetically. Oft-times when the priest made the exclamation "Especially our all-holy, immaculate, most blessed, glorious Lady Theotokos and Ever-virgin Mary," he would quietly leave and disappear. As it became evident later, he would go to some chapel to continue his prayer into the night.

Many seeing him leave before the Divine Liturgy ended thought it strange and wondered where he went and what he did. One Sunday, therefore, as soon as Misael left the church, some women followed him discreetly from a distance in order to see where he went. He took a footpath and in a short time arrived at one of the

many chapels. A little later the women following him arrived also and stood quietly outside. Misael, who had not noticed them, began to pray aloud with sobs, tears, and groanings that cannot be uttered. He prayed different prayers, known and extemporaneous, whatever helped to bring his heart to compunction. In this manner, with Misael praying aloud inside with tears and the women outside listening to his divine occupation, several hours passed with holy exaltation and contrition of heart.

As soon as Misael finished, he came out. When he saw the women, he was very upset, almost angry. He left without speaking

Kelveri: Rock-cut Church of Saint Euthymius, built, according to local tradition, by a certain Saint Symeon in the year 690. Opposite page: another entrance to the same. Both were photographed in 1907 by Gertrude Bell.

to them. But they, transported by this divine mystagogy which they experienced so many hours near him, were envious, and they said among them, "Does God hear only Misael? Why don't we try to pray like him too?"

And they gave themselves over to the endeavor of prayer. But it is not as easy as that to devote yourself to noetic prayer without someone to teach you. The women soon understood this and began to approach Misael beseeching him to teach them the art of prayer. Though he taught them, and told them what to do, he would not show them, and would not pray with them. They then began to pray to God that He enlighten Misael to reveal to them the secrets of prayer by actual deeds.

The answer was not long in coming, and even came in a wondrous manner. Soon after, a monk appeared to Misael and said to

him, "Misael, take the women who followed you to the chapel, and as many others as you wish, and at night come to such and such a house which is suitable and spacious. Only do not invite indifferent and superfluous people. I shall be there also and I shall teach you compunctionate prayer."

The Village of Orta Hissar in Cappadocia, 1911.

Misael, although he avoided people and did not wish to pray with others, obeyed. He invited the women and a few others, among whom was also the Elder Ieronymos, then a small child, and at night they all assembled at the appointed place. The monk then began to pray with sobs and many tears, which made everybody else weep also. He uttered various prayers and compunctionate sayings, which came from his heart with yearning and faith and revealed the great love that he had for God. This lasted all night and was repeated for a second time and a third. Towards the end of the third night, as soon as he had finished his prayer, and was counselling Misael to continue to teach the Christians, he disappeared before their eyes. Evidently he was an Angel of God or a Saint. From that time on Misael began to teach "compunctionate" prayer and at night all would gather at different houses and pray.

Misael had a daughter, who had a great calling to the spiritual life. Her father's genuine child, she inherited from him all his virtues and had a special devotion to compunctionate prayer. And even though she was quite young, little by little various women began to gather around her, and she taught them, she guided them, and all together they prayed with compunctionate prayer. With time, when this assembly gathered in a certain house to pray, it separated into two groups. Misael with the men would pray in one room, and his daughter with the women in another. And so Misael's daughter was the consolation of all the women of Kelveri, even as he was for the men.

When Misael's daughter reached the age of eighteen or twenty, she fell seriously ill. All the inhabitants of the village, especially the women, began to be alarmed. If something happened to her, they would lose their only consolation. What could they do? They all began to pray. They implored God day and night to make her well, because in the difficult times in which they found themselves, she was their singular consolation, the person who instructed and guided them, their bond with God. But her condition only worsened.

In their despair they thought to have recourse to her father, Misael. They knew well the power of his prayer and the audience he had before God, and they pleaded with him to pray for his daughter.

"We implore you," they said, "pray to God that He make her well. We're not asking you to make special supplication because she is your daughter, but for our own sake, because if we are deprived of her, we'll be left without any consolation. We have so many woes and so many troubles, that if we lose our only help and our support, despair will overwhelm us."

Entrances to the Church and Chapels of Qeledjlar in the Göreme Valley, 1911.

Misael at first did not wish to yield to their entreaties, lest it be misconstrued that he had a special weakness for her as his daughter. His mind was bound exclusively to God; all other people he held equal in his heart. Nevertheless, to the women's insistent pleadings, his heart at last inclined. Thus, according to his custom, one Thursday morning, before it dawned, he went up into the mountain.

He knelt, lifted his hands on high and began his prayer. Set afire with divine love, he remained in "prayer and supplication," from "the morning watch until night." While the sweat was running down his face, he spoke to God, and among other things, he spoke about his daughter also, not that he was pained for her as a father, but because they told him that she was the support and consolation of the Christians.

Suddenly, as he stood absorbed in prayer, estranged from all that is worldly, and his soul was caught up into things celestial, he heard within himself a gentle voice, a divine voice saying, "Do you give surety for your daughter?"

"No, Lord, I am not able to give surety. I am a sinner and I know the fickleness of man. Today my daughter is struggling and working Thy will. But tomorrow? How can I give surety? May Thy will be done!"

This visitation, which God deemed him worthy of receiving, calmed him. He was entirely flooded with a heavenly tranquillity and continued his holy pursuit with even greater zeal. Towards the end of the day a messenger came to inform him that his daughter had reposed and he should hurry back for her burial.

Having been previously informed, Misael received the message calmly and even with a certain relief. He had deep faith in God and in the resurrection of the dead, and he did not permit himself to mourn for the temporary separation of his daughter. His joy for her salvation, which God had revealed to him in a wondrous manner, gave him the strength to transcend even this sorrow over her death. After offering a prayer of thanksgiving to God, he set out with the messenger for the village.

This in short was Misael, from what the Elder Ieronymos related to us about him from time to time, and for whom he cherished a very great reverence. "Such men you do not find today," he would say, "he was another Abba Isaac. He spoke little, was humble, loved silence, and had a deep consciousness of his sinfulness. He never allowed anyone to praise him. And if anyone made bold to say a flattering word to him, it was likely that Misael would never speak to him again."

2. FATHER JOHN

In one of the churches of the village there served a priest named Father John. He was a family man. On weekdays he went to the fields, on Sundays and feast days he served in church. He was very simple, humble, unkempt in appearance. If you met him in the road, you would not pay much attention to him; but if you came to know him personally, you would see that this was a spiritual man with rare gifts. He was especially distinguished by the gift of

The height on the horizon is the village of Uch Hissar, near Matchan, c. 1919.

Note toe- and finger-holds cut in the side of the cone. Photograph c. 1919.

Entrance to the Chapel of Saint Barbara in Göreme, 1911.

prayer. It seems that in the parts of Anatolia, prayer was a flower that thrived exceedingly.

Concerning this Father John, the Elder Ieronymos narrated to us marvellous things, which one could only encounter in the ancient ascetics who had a burning faith. The characteristic event, which typified his presence in Kelveri, was the following:

When he served the Liturgy, he almost always wept, and sighed, and often could not hold back his sobs—such was his faith, and to such an intense degree did he live the mystery of the divine Eucharist. But when he reached the time of the consecration of the precious Gifts, his fervor would reach its peak. The chanters would finish the "We praise Thee...," which they chanted as slowly as possible, and from within the sanctuary there would still be heard the prayers and sighs of the priest. They would begin "We praise Thee..." again. They would have to repeat it often, five or six times, until Father John would finish and say the exclamation "Es-

Monastery near Karanlik Kilisse, 1911.

pecially..." When this delay for the exclamation, "Especially..." had been repeated for a few Sundays, the chanters became perplexed, not knowing what to do. They could not chant anything else—the *Polyeleos*, for example—since the sacredness of the moment did not permit it. All the same, they did not have the boldness to complain to the priest, for they reverenced him greatly. One day, therefore, they told their problem to the church wardens.

"The priest takes a long time to finish the prayer at the time of the consecration of the precious Gifts, and we have no idea what to do. We chant the 'We praise Thee...' over and over, but in so doing, it seems to us, confusion is created. Couldn't you please tell him to hurry a little?"

The wardens conveyed the chanters' request to the priest. He answered them, "How can I finish any sooner? It doesn't depend on me. As soon as I begin to read the prayer, the holy table is surrounded by divine fire, which reaches two or three yards high, and

I am not able to approach. I fall upon the ground and pray, until God in His good pleasure withdraws the divine fire: or many times it divides in two, and then I enter and continue the prayer, 'and make this bread...' and so forth."

When the chanters heard this, they marvelled at the holiness of their priest, and did not dare to bother him on this account again. So they continued to chant "We praise Thee..." as slowly as they could, and repeated it as many times as needed for him to finish the prayer, endeavoring to feel some contrition at what was being enacted in the sanctuary.

Father John, even though he was simple, made his presence felt with his holiness. Crowds of the faithful began to gather at his church. Often Christians from other neighboring hamlets came to attend his Liturgy. There were instances when over a thousand Christians gathered at his church. All came to compunction and wept profusely. When the Liturgy finished, it was not rare to see the floor of the church wet with their tears.

I N ORDER TO COME CLOSER and enter more deeply into the spiritual climate that prevailed in Kelveri, let us permit the Elder Ieronymos himself to speak to us of the people of his epoch:

"The people in my homeland had very much zeal for divine things. They were pure and very pious. They had fear and great love of God. During vigils the pavement would fill with tears. We children had reverence, love, and obedience to parents, and respect for strangers. In school, the teachers taught us reverence and love of God and fatherland first, and then letters. Our religious holidays had grandeur. And all of us eagerly waited for them to arrive. I loved all this, and from my childhood I had great zeal, especially for the things of God. When we came to Greece, after the exchange of populations, we were deeply scandalized. We had the impression that there weren't even any Christians living in this

Landscape between Procopion (Ürgüp) and Avanos.

country. People swore, sang worldly songs, dressed immodestly, did not keep the fasts, and didn't go to church. *Aman*,[8] we said, where did we come to? Had it been possible, we would have immediately taken ship and returned to Anatolia. There our villages were like monasteries. All fasted, prayed, and ran to the churches. The young men in the fields and the young maidens at home doing their work quietly chanted various psalms, instead of singing indecent songs as they do here. You never even saw women with uncovered head and short sleeves. But here everything is different. And the more time goes by, the worse it gets."

8. An expression often used by speakers of Turkish, meaning "Woe is me!" "Alas!" "Oh, my goodness!" It is not related to "Amen."—TRANS.

Modern view of Kelveri, with the Church of Saint Gregory the Theologian.

CHAPTER THREE
God-Pleasing Upbringing

THESE WERE THE SURROUNDINGS and such was the spiritual atmosphere in Kelveri at the time the Elder Ieronymos was born. His parents, Anestis and Elizabeth, were very pious. They had six children altogether: John, Barbara, Despina, Basil (Father Ieronymos), Alexander, and Olga. His father was a potter. His children helped him in his work, especially his first-born son, John. Pottery was a traditional craft, and the earthenware of Kelveri was renowned for its beauty and was much sought after by both Turks and Greeks.

His father's work often compelled him to be absent from home for long periods of time, sometimes up to six months. During these periods the whole care of the house and, more important, the upbringing of the children, was undertaken by their mother. She was a woman of deep faith in God and conscious of her calling as a Christian mother, who never tired of counselling and instructing her children to walk in the path of virtue. Her anxiety for the children was very great and often it would manifest itself in prayer.

She spent hours in the prayer room which had been made in a special place in the cellar of the house.[1] There, by night, after the labor and anxiety of the day, she let herself express all her worries and poured out her heart to God, seeking His help for herself, for

---

[1]. Most of the homes of Kelveri were converted cave cells of the monastics of old. Many times the houses were built out of the caves. Thus the store-rooms and cellar were usually the caves themselves.—TRANS.

Entrance to a chapel at Göreme, 1911.

her husband, and for her children. Prayer brought her relief; and her deep faith revived her and gave her strength to continue the difficult work of rearing the children according to God, to which she had given herself over with such conscientiousness. Especially during the times that her husband was absent, "sleep would overtake her kneeling in prayer," as the Elder told us.

That deep faith and burning love for prayer that she possessed, she sought to plant in her children. Every day she would assign them by turn, today one and tomorrow another, to read the six Psalms, a Supplicatory Canon, Vespers, and Compline, besides other soul-profiting readings. They said their prayers together and then went to bed, so that very early next morning at the crack of dawn they would hear: "Get up now! Time for prayer!" She endeavored to instill this sacred pursuit in them from childhood, so that they would become accustomed to it and progress in the spiritual life.

Basil stood out from his brethren. He had curly black hair, a cheerful countenance, and dark, lively, and intelligent eyes, and even from childhood was distinguished by the seriousness of his thoughts, his prudence, and his diligence. A sensitive lad, he was endowed with a deep and instinctive faith in God. The Church was his abode. There, besides the Liturgies, Vespers, and so forth, he spent many hours each day in prayer and the reading of the books of the Church.

This inner predisposition and love for the Church, God's temple, often led him to the various country chapels scattered in the surrounding area. He would spend most of the day there "occupied with God." He would clean the chapel, read, and pray. It was by no means rare that, after these divine occupations, sleep would overtake him next to the Holy Table. And when he awoke and returned to the village, often at a late hour, he would find his family worried by his absence. He, however, felt joyous, and met their gaze with calmness and tranquillity, as if telling them: "How is it that ye sought me? Knew ye not that I must needs be about the things of my Father?" (Luke 2:49).

His contact with the Church filled him with joy; he was "eaten up by the zeal of His house." Even from his tender years, he had only God in his heart, and he felt joy only close to Him. He was in the habit of saying to us later, "I grew up in churches, I slept next to the holy tables." One could say that from a little child he was "temple-bred." He grew up in the Church, with her waters was he reared spiritually, and there he felt was his foreordained place. He had all the indications of one "consecrated from his mother's womb."

He was diligent in school. He also had a beautiful and melodic voice; from the age of seven he frequented the chanting stand and would quietly chant along with the chanters. He was quite bright and assiduous. He had learned even from that time the whole order of the Church. Once, in fact, when they sent a certain newly

Rock-cut cell of a stylite, near Zelve, 1911.

ordained priest to the church who did not know the typicon well, they commissioned little Basil to instruct him how to serve.

His pious mother beheld all these activities of her son, she divined his calling, and "kept all these things in her heart" (Luke 2:51).

"This child shall be a great man," she would say.

She began to increase her prayers for the whole family and above all for Basil, whom both she and her husband loved especially. "We were six brothers and sisters, but my parents loved me more," the Elder would tell us. Her prayers had no end: "As she was kneeling in prayer, sleep would overtake her." Her tears never ran dry, they formed "two continuous furrows" on her cheeks. When later the Elder was counselling a certain mother who was anxious about her son, because he had "fallen away from the path," he said to her, "Unto God you will present either your son saved, or the calluses on your knees from prayer."

Chapel at Belli Kilisse, near Soghanle, 1911.

Evidently he was inspired to say this from the experience of his own mother, who passed the nights till dawn in her prayer room.

Little Basil would see his mother continuously pray and weep, and his sensitive soul would be shaken, it would bleed. So he prayed also and wept, and asked God to comfort his mother. One day he approached her and said, "Mother, what's wrong, why do you weep? Is it because of our poverty?"

"No, my child, I do not weep on account of our poverty. It's for all of you that I weep, for your father and for you, my children. I entreat God to keep you all well, and that you might not depart from His path."

Basil heard all this and fell to thinking. He would secretly observe his mother who sighed and wept, and he himself persisted in weeping. Often he would not even go out to play with the other children at school when it was time for recess. He would stay in the room and think of his mother. He would lay his head on the desk and cry. Once his teacher noticed this. Seeing him crying, he asked him, "What's wrong, my boy? Why do you stay inside and don't go out to play with the other children?"

"My head hurts," answered Basil.

On another occasion when he asked him the same thing, he answered, "My stomach hurts."

When this had been repeated many times, the teacher visited his mother and said to her, "What's wrong with this boy that he's continuously sick? Why don't you take him to a doctor? He always sits in the classroom during recess and cries, now he tells me his head hurts, now that his stomach hurts, and so on."

His mother did not answer. She prayed all night long and on the morrow she took the ten-year-old Basil and went to one of the chapels outside the village. There she asked him, "What's wrong with you, my child, that you're always crying? Tell me the truth."

"Mother, nothing ails me. I only think of you, and how you're always weeping, and I can't control myself, and I weep, too."

"Listen, my child. I weep for my sins and for all of you, as I told you before—but especially for you. I see certain signs in you and I entreat God to make you steadfast. I, as you see, entered the world, I married, I have a family: you know our woes. I will tell you just one thing. I want you to become a monk or a priest, and dedicate yourself completely to God. You are foreordained for this way of life. Do you give me your word, here before the icons, that you will follow in this way?"

Basil was a little thoughtful and then answered with a firm voice, "Yes, Mother, I give you my word."

Who, truly, can grasp the magnitude of this offering on the part of his mother, reminiscent of the Emilys and Nonnas,[2] or that of the resolute decision of Basil who, from the age of ten, decided to embrace the monastic life? Surely this scene in no way falls short of the service of the monastic tonsure, where the candidate vows to remain "in the monastery and the ascetic life until his last breath."

THEIR HOUSE was close to Misael's. Basil, even though he was still young, had understood the great value of this man and he visited him often. Misael, even though he avoided people, discerned the faith and zeal of his young neighbor, and welcomed him. He conversed with him on spiritual subjects, he counselled him and taught him the secrets of "compunctionate" prayer. Basil listened to him with attention. He drank in every word that came out of the mouth of this experienced monkish layman, and he assayed to assimilate everything in active deed. He imitated him in everything: in his posture, in his gait, in his speech, as all children of his age do their heroes—their paragons.

As the days went by, Basil visited Misael more regularly, and with the passage of time he as good as became his shadow. He also began, like Misael, to go off to chapels near and far and to spend not only his days but also many nights praying before the icons or at some prayer-stall. As he himself told us, the joy he felt in these chapels cannot be described. Here the psalmic verse is fully applicable, "the zeal of Thy house hath eaten me up." At a time of life when others of the same age occupied themselves with games and mischievous pranks, he was running from monastery to chapel and from chapel to some ascetical cell and was spending his time in prayer. All marvelled at the zeal and faith of this child. Even the few Turkish women of the village would say to his mother, "What's

---

2. Saint Emily (July 19), mother of St. Basil the Great, and St. Nonna (August 5), mother of St. Gregory the Theologian. Both were from Cappadocia.—TRANS.

wrong with this boy, Elizabeth, that he is always running and sleeping in churches? Has he lost his mind?"

Even from before his adolescent years, he was careful and never spoke without a reason. An idle word never came out his mouth. He would only speak about spiritual topics. And although he was very sensitive and shy, he had an astonishing boldness and amazing courage in anything pertaining to spiritual things. Once during a religious feast in which his school was to take part at the church, someone had to give the oration. Basil, who was then eleven years old, asked his teacher if he could give it. His teacher tried to dissuade him, saying that he was too young and would not be able to handle it. But Basil insisted, and in the end the teacher permitted him to read the speech from the pulpit in the presence of two thousand people. This was the first, albeit from a manuscript, of his sermons in church.

As the years passed, little Basil strove to increase his struggles in prayer. And the passage from childhood to adolescence found him with the same goals, the same irrevocable decision to dedicate himself entirely to God. He was a model of piety for young and old. Never did anyone hear him sing. When he was merry he would chant. He would always counsel us likewise. "If any be merry, let him chant." (cf. James, 5:13) He even once said to us in jest, "A man should be part doctor, part musician, and part madman. Part doctor, so that he can give himself some help, should he get sick. Part musician, so that when he's merry, he'll know how to chant some hymn. And part madman, so that when he falls into despondency, he will be able to say: Let's go on an outing to such and such a monastery."

In the meantime, he finished school and began giving assistance in the workshop to his father and his older brother John, who also distinguished himself in love of work and piety. He was a lover of labor and continued to work into deep old age. Basil turned the shop into a missionary center. He had the gift of speech, and whoever entered the store he would engage in conversation on spiritual subjects. He endeavored to strengthen his piety and to tighten his bonds with the Church. But this was not enough for him. So he began to visit various homes and start conversations, especially with the women, and tried to draw them to the spiritual life, and to teach them piety and the life in Christ. And his word had such power, that many of these women were transfigured, they experienced the "change wrought by the right hand of the Most High" (Ps. 76:10) and began to live as nuns. Some of them even experienced a certain friction with their husbands, because the latter would be upset when they returned from work on Wednesday and Friday and found the table set with a fasting meal prepared without oil. It quickly became known who was the cause of this conversion, and in the village they began to call Basil, who was then sixteen or seventeen years old, The Priest. "That priest changed you," they would say to their wives, whom they saw suddenly manifesting a great turn and love for the Church. But he was a man of high integrity, and very careful and prudent, and in spite of his youthfulness, all respected him.

From this age, that is, about sixteen or seventeen years old, he began to preach in church.[3] As some of his compatriots remember, who also came to Greece after the exchange of populations in 1924, he spoke well and to the point and drew people like a magnet. All marvelled and were perplexed at this youth, who although he was so young, yet had great zeal for the things of God, great boldness, and, besides all this, great understanding.

F OR THE HOLY UNMERCENARIES, whom all honored at Kelveri, little Basil had a special devotion, which was made even

---

3. Lay preachers are not uncommon in the Greek church; usually they are appointed by the local bishop. Each diocese has a group of preachers who go throughout the parishes and preach during the Divine Liturgy.—TRANS.

The Western Quarter of the village of Matchan, 1911.

stronger by the following incident. It was the eve of the Saints' feast and Basil, according to his beloved habit, had gone out of the village to some chapel to pray. He had taken the mule with him to let it graze. He often used this as an excuse, to allow him to go off and be alone to pray. In the evening he took the animal and started for the village, to be in time for the Saints' Vespers. But suddenly a thunderstorm broke out; heavy rains began to fall, and the rivers flooded. On account of his great desire to be in time for Vespers, rather than stopping anywhere to take cover, he forced the animal to run. As he was fording a river, he fell off the animal and the water flowing down with great force carried him off. He attempted for a long time to stand up but it was impossible. The water continued to carry him downstream, until he caught onto some large rock and managed to hold on there. But to get to shore was impossible.

After he had come to himself a little, he began to pray to the holy Unmercenaries to save him from the terrible plight he was in.

Note group of people standing on the roof at lower right.

And God, Who always attends to the prayers of His faithful servants, was not long in answering. Four Turks who happened to be passing near saw him and ran to help him. They stood high up on the bank of the river, tied their belts one to another, and threw them to the youthful Basil. He caught hold of them, and with great exertion got out of the river.

They brought him to the village in a wretched state. His whole body, but especially his right hand, was full of wounds. They cared for him and his wounds were healed, but a small disability remained in his hand. He lost the full movement and flexibility and the palm did not completely close; the movement of the wrist was also hampered. But Basil, who believed that "without God nothing happens," glorified God and thanked the holy Unmercenaries for their miraculous intervention. They saved him from the danger he had passed through. And, as we shall see in what follows, the Elder had the holy Unmercenaries as guardians and helpers his whole life long.

CHAPTER FOUR
Deacon

H IS WHOLE SPIRITUAL MINISTRY, which as the years passed became more intense, made him beloved and respected throughout the village. Many encouraged him to become a priest. They believed that he "was made to be a priest." Basil also desired it. For in this manner he would be able to live the mystery of mysteries, the holy Eucharist, more closely. But he did not venture to ask for it on his own. As he would say to us, he believed that "the priest has to be either God-called or called by the people, never self-called. There are many impediments to the priesthood; I add one more—to seek it of oneself."

Kelveri was subject ecclesiastically to the diocese of Iconium. His compatriots, therefore, seeing his unwillingness to go himself to the Metropolitan and seek that he ordain him, went themselves and besought him for this purpose. The Metropolitan then was a certain Athanasios, who had heard much of Basil's piety and energetic activities and held him in high esteem. So he called him and proposed to ordain him deacon. Basil considered this a divine calling and accepted it with joy. He even expressed his desire to remain a deacon in his own village, since he had already formed a bond with the flock which he had created even before he became a pastor. But there was one additional reason; he wished to be close to Misael, in order to be fortified by his words and prayers.

But he had not yet entered into clerical rank and officially undertaken his pastoral ministry when the trials began. "My son, if

Church of Saint Amphilochius in Iconium (modern Konia), c. 1907.

thou come to serve the Lord, prepare thy soul for temptation," (Wisdom of Sirach, 2:1) warns the divine scripture. These temptations are unavoidable and impossible to foresee.

Whereas almost all the inhabitants of Kelveri rejoiced to hear of the impending ordination, there were a few, four or five in number, who did not see it with a good eye. These four or five were notable citizens of the village, rich and powerful. The reason was the spiritual atmosphere that prevailed in their families, and they feared lest their children, under the influence that Basil would exercise as a clergyman, might forsake the world and become monastics. So they raised up a great war against him. They asked the bishop not to ordain him, at least not in their area.

The Metropolitan surmised the cause of the hostility and was saddened, because he loved Basil. But he did not wish to create a scandal. For this reason he asked him to go to his friend the Metropolitan of Colonia, Sophronios, who had his seat in Amisso,[1] to be ordained deacon by him. Basil had certain reservations after the tumult that was stirred up, but at the Metropolitan's insistence, he accepted, and having received an introductory letter he departed for Amisso. There he was ordained deacon by Metropolitan Sophronios.

After his ordination, in order to avoid the disturbance and tumult created by his enemies in his own country, he departed for Caesarea. He was thinking of staying there for a while to allow things to quiet down. On the way to Caesarea, he stopped a short time at Nigde, where he was offered hospitality for three days in the home of an acquaintance.

The affair of these few enemies of his had distressed him greatly and he prayed continually to God to help him and enlighten him what he should do. The three days that he stayed at Nigde, he did not sleep at all, but prayed continually. He did not even unmake the bed which they had prepared for him to sleep in. But the acquaintance who was giving him hospitality was a friend of his enemies, and they sent him word to turn him out. On the third day, in the morning, he visited him in his room, and seeing him sleepless and tired he felt sorry for him. When he asked him why he hadn't slept, Father Basil answered that he was unable to sleep because he was anguishing over something and was continuously praying that God reveal to him what he should do. And God revealed to him that he should leave.

He left Nigde the same day. Later he learned that his enemies had so much hate against him that they were plotting to kill him, but they were not in time. God warned him and he fled.

Father Basil stayed in Caesarea for a long time, during which he especially gave himself over to prayer. The things that had come to pass in his village had wounded his sensitive soul.

---

1. The ancient Amisus, in Pontus.—TRANS.

Prayer was his singular consolation. But he missed the cave chapels and the hermitages of Kelveri, he missed Misael, as well as his other compatriots who loved him. So he decided to return and offer his services to his own people, believing that time would have helped to calm down the tumult that his enemies had created against him, and that their hatred would have subsided somewhat.

Thus, he returned to Kelveri, now a deacon. His compatriots, who—apart from the few exceptions mentioned above—loved him greatly, formed a committee and went to the Metropolitan (Athanasios had now reposed and been succeeded by Procopios) to beseech him to ordain him a priest. The Metropolitan had already heard about Father Basil and gladly agreed to make him a priest. But the enemies of Christ and of the truth again raised up an implacable war against him. They were the same four or five men who had enmity against him from the beginning, and they moved heaven and earth, if only they might utterly destroy him. Having nothing else to bring against him, they accused him to the Metropolitan of being illiterate.

The Metropolitan was put in a difficult position. One day, therefore, he called the young hierodeacon and said to him, "Please chant a doxasticon for me in Second Tone."

Father Basil, who had a melodic and compunctionate voice, chanted the Second Matinal Doxasticon, "The women who were with Mary…," which he particularly loved.

The Metropolitan was satisfied as much by the beautiful rendering of the hymn, as by his reverent composure, and he asked him, "Do you want me to make you a priest?"

"No, Your Eminence, because certain people in my village do not want me."

"Since they don't want you in your own village, come and I'll ordain you and place you in my village."

Father Basil did not consent.

In the meantime a disturbance had erupted in Kelveri. Those

who loved him, and were the majority—"all the people," as those who remember the events relate—got up and went to the Bishop demanding that he make him a priest. They could not bear that the opinion of four or five persons, who had no involvement with the Church, should prevail, and that the will of the believing people, who had a high regard for him and wanted him as their pastor, should not be taken into account. They even conscripted his mother. They exhorted her that she also should endeavor to convince her son to yield to the will of his pious compatriots and that of the very Metropolitan. But Father Basil was unyielding.

"If even one does not want me," he answered, "I will not become a priest."

Such was his fear of God, and so great his sensitivity, that it sufficed that the negative voice of one only, of his fanatical and unjust enemies, would cause him not to accept the priesthood, even though his conscience did not convict him in anything.

Father Basil remained in Kelveri and continued his previous energetic activities, despite the opposition and war his enemies had raised against him. The faithful recognized him as a shepherd and flocked to him. And he taught them the secrets of "compunctionate" prayer and counselled them how to live "according to Christ." On Sundays and on feast days he chanted and preached at the Church of Saint Gregory the Theologian. And the people ran to hear him.

But his enemies did not rest either. Darkened by the hatred nestling within them, they tried to convince the priests and church-wardens not to allow him to preach, nor even to chant at the analogion, just as the scribes and Pharisees threatened to cast out of the synagogue anyone who followed Christ.

Father Basil was patient in all this with Job-like patience and fortitude. He would go to church and follow the unbloody Sacrifice in the sanctuary, praying and shedding copious tears of contrition and compunction. But his enemies, blinded by their passion, could not bear to behold him even there. They feared that simply his modest presence in church, even without his speaking or chanting, would of itself have an influence on the people. And they thus reached the extreme recourse of attempting murder. One Sunday they waited for him to come out of the sanctuary so they could beat him up. But divine grace covered him, and he passed through their midst without their perceiving it, just as once the Divine Teacher passed through the Jews.

Metropolitan Procopios, who saw his compatriots' evil and unjust intentions against Father Basil, called him one day and suggested sending him to the Holy Mountain for a certain period of time. He believed that this would profit him spiritually and would also help to calm the spirits and quiet down the noise of the storm that had been roused up around his name. Father Basil greatly longed to go to the Holy Mountain. He had heard much about it and believed that there he would find holy elders who would profit him spiritually.

The Holy Mountain belonged to the jurisdiction of the Ecumenical Patriarchate and the pertinent permission had to be obtained from thence. For this purpose, on the fifth of August, 1911, the Metropolitan wrote a letter to the Patriarch "requesting the consignment of Hierodeacon Basil for a certain period of time to one of the Sacred Monasteries of the Holy Mountain for his practical training." The Patriarch answered "that he send him to him for this purpose."

But while the Patriarch's answer was still on the way, Father Basil, saddened by the unjust and irrational conduct of his enemies, decided to depart for the Holy Places. For many years he had desired to go there to worship the sacred shrines. Later his compatriots who came with him to Greece said that Father Basil loved his homeland so much that he probably would have never left it, had it not been for the evil and envy of his enemies which drove him away.

The Holy Sepulchre
Photograph by Felix Bonfils, c. 1880.

CHAPTER FIVE
At the Holy Places

WHEN HE ANNOUNCED to his parents his decision to depart for the Holy Places, they received it with reservation. They feared that he might possibly never return to them. But Father Basil was determined to accomplish his journey, and in the end his parents consented and allowed him to leave with their blessing. Before leaving, he gave word of his pilgrimage to the Holy Places to a certain widowed aunt of his in Constantinople, Despina, who was a very faithful soul and very strong in prayer and the word of God. A little later she also travelled to the Holy Places, and they met there.

Father Basil reached the Holy Land in 1911, at 28 years of age. His first concern was to worship at all the holy shrines, to kiss the places where the feet of Christ had trodden. He went first to the All-holy Sepulchre, then to Golgotha, to the Praetorium, to Bethlehem. After that, he visited all the other shrines: Cana, Tabor, Hebron, Jericho, the Well of Jacob, and so forth. Wherever he went, he experienced the presence of God. He would bring to mind the great events that took place at each shrine he visited, endeavoring to delve deeply into the mystery which each of these events had hidden within itself, and his heart was pricked with contrition and his eyes flowed with tears. He experienced such spiritual exaltation and ascents in the heart, that some fifty years later when we made his acquaintance and he spoke to us of the Holy Places, he would weep. His prayer, or rather his supplication and admonition, which he gave to all who visited him, was that they all go to worship at the Holy Places.

"I pray to God that He will not permit you to die, before you worship at the Holy Places," he would tell us. "People come from the whole world to visit the Acropolis, and here in Aegina, the Aphaia,[1] which is nothing but broken pieces of marble. And shall we who are Christians not go to worship at the place where our Christ was born, was reared, was crucified and rose from the dead? Even now I often go noetically and worship those sacred places. I stand in Bethlehem, and I hear those most compunctionate Troparia: 'Why, O Mary, marvellest thou, amazed at that which is in thee? Because I have given birth in time unto the timeless Son...' Is it possible for anyone to grasp this, the most supernatural event mankind has ever known?'"

And saying these things, the Elder would dissolve into tears. When one saw him at such moments, he appeared totally estranged from all things earthly, as if he hadn't the least perception of his surroundings, while on his face shone a divine light reminiscent of the Transfiguration.

Father Basil visited all the sacred shrines under conditions which, as he described them himself, were not at all pleasant. He had no money, oftentimes he did not even have bread to eat, and on many occasions during his long journeys he met with unexpected trials and temptations. But the sacredness of the place and his piety enabled him to overcome all obstacles. "Who can separate us from the love of Christ?" he would say. And he would continue with ever-increasing faith and strength of will.

After he had gone the round of the holy places, he wished to remain for a time in one of the monasteries of the area. And since he did not know himself where it would be best to go to be profited,

---

1. The temple of Aphaia in the northeast part of Aegina, built c. 500 B.C.—TRANS.

he asked the advice of a certain spiritual father, named Anthimos. He sent him to the Monastery of the Venerable Forerunner close to the Jordan River.

Before he left for the Monastery of the Venerable Forerunner, at Jerusalem he met his Aunt Despina, who had come from Constantinople to worship in the Holy Land. He rejoiced at seeing her, because she was a spiritual person, with an ascetical mind and a special love for prayer. She also had the gift of speech and profited many souls with her teaching. When Father Basil left for the Monastery of the Venerable Forerunner, his aunt went to stay for a while in one of the women's convents.

Father Basil remained at the Monastery of the Forerunner for nine months and the abbot entrusted him with the duties of secretary of the monastery. At the same time, and for the same reason, Father Anastasios was also present at the monastery. He was a monk from Pontus in Asia Minor, who later went to the Holy Mountain and joined the synodia of the Elder Joseph the Cavedweller. There he received the Great Schema and was renamed Arsenios. He reposed a few years ago at the age of ninety-eight at the sacred Monastery of Dionysiou, having lived as a monk some eighty years.[2] Father Anastasios was distinguished by an almost childlike simplicity, but also by a flaming faith and strong love for prayer. At the Monastery of the Venerable Forerunner the abbot entrusted him with the obedience of steward of the storehouses.

There the two men met and were united with a close bond of friendship. In the evenings, after the obediences of the day and the church services, they would meet and discuss various spiritual subjects, exchange experiences, and pray. Both considered their acquaintanceship to be a blessed coincidence.

One day the two befriended monks were visited by Father Basil's Aunt Despina and Father Anastasios's sister, who was then

---

2. The Elder Arsenios reposed on September 3/16, 1983.—TRANS.

The Elder Arsenios, fellow-ascetic of the Elder Joseph the Cave-dweller, and brother of Mother Eupraxia.

about twenty years old. She had become a nun at the age of sixteen in the Convent of the Holy Mother of God Theoskepaste at Trebizond in Pontus, and had now come as a pilgrim to the Holy Places. Father Anastasios's sister was none other than she who would afterwards be the venerable Eldress Eupraxia, who later came to live in obedience to the Elder Ieronymos on Aegina, and faithfully served him during the latter years of his life, after his disability, as we shall see further on.

The abbot permitted the two women to remain as guests in the monastery for one week. This whole time they all gathered every evening and Father Basil taught them "compunctionate" prayer until midnight. The nun Eupraxia forged a spiritual bond with Father Basil, and also with his aunt, who had it in mind to found a convent, and she followed her to the women's monastery where she was staying temporarily.

During his stay at the Monastery of the Venerable Forerunner,

Father Basil had the opportunity to visit various other monasteries in the surrounding area. He especially loved to visit the place beyond the Jordan where Saint Mary of Egypt struggled, for whom Father Basil had a very great reverence. He marvelled how a weak woman had such endurance as to live for forty-seven years in this desert without seeing a human being. "The mind of man is unable to comprehend what the righteous Mary accomplished," he would say. "She made the decision to die if necessary, and God helped her to achieve that which appears impossible." Every week he would take the small rowboat of the monastery, would cross the Jordan, and go to the chapel dedicated in her honor. He would light the vigil lamps and pray that God strengthen him in his struggles even as He had strengthened our righteous Mother of old. He would spend the whole day there praying and at night would return to the monastery.

After living in the Monastery of the Venerable Forerunner for nine months, Father Basil decided to leave. He was enflamed with the desire to visit other shrines also, and was thinking of going to Constantinople, to Saint Sophia, the center of Orthodoxy. He had the thought that since in his country, where people had little or no education, there were spiritual people like Misael and Father John, how much more would this be the case in Constantinople? He believed that there he would find experienced spiritual people, who would be able to teach him what he did not know.

The abbot and the fathers of the monastery had come to love him, for they all had been profited by his presence, his piety, and his conduct in the monastery in general, and they entreated him to stay with them for good. But Father Basil gave first place before everything else to his spiritual profit: and at the time, he reasoned, this was to be found in Constantinople. Because of this, he thanked them all and departed.

Constantinople from the Galata Bridge, c. 1890.

CHAPTER SIX

Constantinople

FATHER BASIL left the Holy Land for Constantinople. On the way he thought of passing by for a short visit to his own country, Kelveri, to see his kinsfolk. He believed the hatred of his enemies would have abated. But it is evident that this hatred was the work of demonic activity, and instead of finding that with the passage of time his enemies had been appeased, as soon as they saw him they became worse and threatened to make trouble. The sweet and meek Father Basil, even though many entreated him to stay and said that they would take it upon themselves to protect him, did not wish to remain. He was a lover of quietude and tranquillity, and as he used to say, "didn't want contentions." He therefore decided to leave for good. He bade farewell with tears to all his acquaintances, and venerated for a last time the churches of the holy Unmercenaries and of Saint Gregory the Theologian, where his holy relics were also treasured, and he departed.

On his way to Constantinople, he passed by Nigde to bid farewell to Metropolitan Procopios, who loved him and had stood by him like a father in all his trials. The latter consoled him, counselled him, and gave him the following letter of introduction to the Patriarch.

Nigde, October 13, 1912
No. 193

All-holy and most divine Master,

In my letter of August 5, 1911, I humbly submitted to your Divine All-holiness the facts concerning a certain hierodeacon, Basil Anestis Apostolides, a native of my humble community of Karvali, and ordained by our brother beloved in Christ, the Most Reverend Metropolitan of Colonia, Kyr Sophronios, and I requested that he be sent for a certain period of time to one of the Sacred Monasteries of the Holy Mountain to be trained in practical matters. Your Divine All-holiness, accepting my entreaty, requested by the letter dated September 21 of the same year that I send him to You for further instruction. But since the abovementioned deacon Basil in the meantime had left for Jerusalem, Your command to send him to the Reigning City was not fulfilled immediately. In May of the present year, having returned to his native land for a change of climate, he remained inactive till now. Now he is coming in order to avoid persecution by his compatriots and to be put under the protection of Your Divine All-holiness, to remove himself from the disturbance that was raised up here for no reason, and on account of which it was not possible either to enroll him in the list of clergy in my humble Metropolis, or to make use of him in any capacity. Reverently submitting the present request and kissing Your All-holy hand, I reverently sign,

Your lowly brother in Christ and all-willing
✚ Bishop of Iconium, Procopios

Father Basil arrived in Constantinople, received the blessing of Patriarch Joachim III, and gave him the letter from Metropolitan Procopios. Then he set off to worship and pray at all the sacred shrines. He went to Saint Sophia, to the holy springs of Blachernae and Baloukle (the Life-giving Spring), he venerated the relics of Saint Euphemia, he visited the Great School of the Nation, the Monastery of Chora, Pammakaristos, the ruins of the Monastery of Studium. His soul exulted. He glorified God and thought that here, in this holy place, where there were so many churches, so many hierarchs, the Great School of the Nation, there should also be an intense spiritual life. If in his country—where people did not know letters, hardly even knew Greek, and had no patristic books to read—a certain level of spiritual life prevailed, then Father Basil believed here he would find holy persons of a high spiritual level,

The Monastery of Chora, c. 1890.

from whom he would be able to learn what he did not know. He asked around, and wherever he heard that there was any good spiritual father he would run to meet him. But he was quickly disappointed. "Wherever I went, a man like unto Misael I found not," he told us. Many, when they heard him ask about "compunctionate" prayer of the heart, began to look upon him strangely as if he were deluded.

Father Basil was very distressed over this lack of experienced spiritual guides. Having no one to confess his pain to, he sat down and wrote a letter to Misael. He related to him all the marvellous things he had seen and venerated in "The City," but bewailed the tragic spiritual poverty. Among other things, he wrote to him, "No matter where I looked, I could not find a man like you to profit me spiritually."

All the profit that the spiritual fathers of Constantinople were unable to give him was accomplished by one austere answer that came to his letter to Misael. After the letter began with courteous and warm words to him in his sorrows, it ended, "You, my child, undertook to hurl me down into the depths of hell. If you write to me again that you cannot find a man like me, I will not write to you again, neither shall I pray for you, and even your very memory I shall blot out of my mind and my heart... But I set before me all my sins, and I was not shaken."

"What men these were!" the Elder would say. "I only said one word to him and he, in order not to be tempted, brought to mind all his sins. Where can you find such men today! If you do not say a word of praise to them, they seek it from you. They delight and rejoice in praises."

Father Basil understood well the sense of Misael's answer, and his whole life long he endeavored by every means to avoid praises. An incident similar to that which took place between him and Misael, to give another example, is the following:

On one of my visits to Aegina, at a certain lull in our conversation, I had gone out into the courtyard so that the Elder could rest a little. After a short time he came out with a fountain pen in his hand and said to me. "Perhaps you know how this works?"

"Yes, Elder," I answered. And I showed him how to fill it with ink.

"I'm not familiar with these things, therefore I give it to Peter[1] as a gift. And he should remember that it is from a sinner."

"The sinner is the man who receives it, Elder, not he who gives it," I made bold to say.

And the Elder who was always sweet and meek suddenly became serious and answered me in a stern tone of voice, which brooked no gainsaying, "Listen, my beloved, this is how I see my-

---

1. That is, Peter Botsis, the author.—TRANS.

self, and this is how I wish to see myself. And if you wish to see yourself likewise, I do not hinder you."

From other incidents also it was evident that he did not permit anyone to speak to him even one word of praise. Many times, services which he himself rendered, he attributed to others, in order to avoid praise, whereas he put down to his own account the mistakes of others.

INITIALLY THE PATRIARCH settled Father Basil as a deacon at the Patriarchate. The Elder always told us good things about Joachim III,[2] that he was faithful, devout, educated, energetic, and very compassionate. It is evident that the Patriarch also loved Father Basil, which is why he kept him at the Patriarchate.

Father Basil served at the Patriarchate for some time, the length of which we are not able to determine exactly. When he did not take part in the Divine Liturgy, he chanted and oftentimes preached. He did not receive wages. He subsisted on very little money, from that which the Christians would put in the knapsack he always had with him, and which he never counted. He used only what was absolutely necessary, and the rest he distributed to the poor.

As time passed, the Christians who got to know him began to leave their own churches and attended the Patriarchal Cathedral.

---

2. Joachim III (1834–1912). Born in Constantinople, he served as Patriarch 1878–84 and from 1902 to 1912, the year of his repose. Known for his almsgiving and compassion, he strengthened the bond of the Church of Constantinople with the other local Orthodox Churches, especially that of Russia. He was greatly esteemed by the last Sultan, Abdul Hamit. During his exile between his two tenures as Patriarch, he resided on the Holy Mountain where he was loved and esteemed by the fathers of the monasteries and sketes. His family name was Demetriades and according to some he was one of the greatest Patriarchs after the fall of the City (1453), characterized as "of great mind, majesty, and great accomplishments." (See *Encyclopedia of Religion and Ethics*, in Greek, Vol. 6.)—TRANS.

Patriarch Joachim III of Constantinople.

As eyewitnesses attest, multitudes of the faithful would fill the church of the Patriarchate to overflowing. In the spiritual dryness prevalent in Constantinople, this young deacon, who had come from the soil of Cappadocia, caught them by surprise with his fiery faith, his simplicity and humility, his love, and especially with his ascetical and mystical ways. He reminded them of other epochs, such as one reads about only in the lives of the Saints.

Father Basil continued to live as he had been accustomed to when he was around Misael, with prayer and vigils. He struggled against his passions and cultivated the virtues with exceeding ardor. He lived the essence of Orthodoxy, "he suffered things divine" and he endeavored to transplant into his own life the experiences of the holy Fathers. And this "suffering things divine" transfigured him, it sanctified and illumined him, and inundated him with love for his brothers, whom he saw running to him like sheep "without a shepherd."

So it was that he began to preach evening sermons, to which many people went to hear him. His words were simple, to the point, and aphoristic. They had immediacy, directness, and a great impact on his listeners, because they came from a heart ablaze with love for God and neighbor, and chiefly because they sprang from spiritual experience. He made no attempt to enrich his speech with rhetorical formulas or insipid and sententious generalities. He spoke of "our Christ," of "compunctionate" prayer, of tears and humility. He spoke of his elder Misael and Father John, and he would narrate to them all the spiritual experiences which he lived when he was close to them. And the faithful people listened to him with riveted attention. They understood that "this cleric was not like the many." For, besides his sermons, he provided them with every other assistance possible, both spiritual and material.

His cell at Constantinople was without whitewash and full of cracks. He covered the cracks with cardboard, but the wind entered unhindered and in winter the cold would pierce him through. But he was totally indifferent to himself. His entire concern and care revolved around others.

At Katikioyi in Chalcedon he was able by his exertions to erect a five-storey building, which served as a school.

At Constantinople, especially at the churches of Saint George and Saint Spyridon and at Halki, he often held vigils. Many people would attend, usually more than three hundred.

It would be useful here to mention a few incidents which have reached us, either from things alluded to by the Elder himself, or from narrations of eyewitnesses and those who heard them themselves, who came to Greece after the catastrophe of Asia Minor in 1922. These incidents bear witness to the great love that he had for God, which guided him to the love for neighbor, as well as to the integrity of his Christian character and his total dedication.

O NE OF THE FAITHFUL, a follower of Father Basil's, had his own store in Constantinople. He was a good family man and a faithful Christian. One day his store caught fire and the damage was extensive; it was appraised at some 600 Turkish banknotes. Crushed with despair, he wept and rained blows upon himself, because he had lost his whole livelihood and could not feed his children. Father Basil, finding him in such a state, comforted him as well as he could and asked him to follow him. They went to his cell and there Father Basil said to him, "Take that knapsack hanging on the wall. It has money in it. Take it and be on your way."

"How much money does it contain, Father?"

"I don't know, I don't ever count it. However much it is, take it all. It's yours."

The poor storeowner was beside himself. Such behavior, such kindness he had never encountered before in his life—not only not to know how much money he had, but also to give it all to him so generously!

He took the money and left doubly gratified, above all because he had verified that there existed people who, above money and other material values, lived in a way consistent with their calling.

But his astonishment was even greater when he got home and discovered that the money which Father Basil had given him was exactly 600 banknotes. He could not contain himself and dissolved in tears. From then on he became one of his most devoted disciples.

O NCE FATHER BASIL was informed that his brother-in-law J. Panagiotopoulos, who had a grocery store in Kelveri, used to open his store on Sunday. He was very grieved by this and sent him a letter filled with humility and love. Among other things he wrote to him:

"... My much beloved brother-in-law, how many weeks does the

The Church of the Holy Peace in Constantinople, c. 1890.

year have? Fifty-two. Fifty-two Sundays in the year—how much money do you make? I ask you kindly to write me, and I will send you double what you make, only, *aman*, do not open your store on Sundays, and God will give you every good thing. Sunday belongs to God, it is the Lord's day, and we ought to go to church, to pray and beseech the mercy of God. This with much love."

The Elder's brother-in-law was so moved by this letter that he never opened his store on Sunday again.

T**HE ELDER** lived God intensely and completely. He did not wish that anything in the world should disrupt this love and devotion of his for God—neither his love for parents and relatives, nor any other power.

Once a young man visited him who was intensely preoccupied with certain problems to the point of being dejected. As soon as the Elder saw him, he asked him, "Do you have a father?"

"Yes, Elder."

"Do you have a mother?"

"Yes."

"Your attitude indicates that you have neither father nor mother. I have my Christ as father and our Panagia[3] as my mother. Whatever ails me I entrust to them, and I find peace in myself."

On another occasion the Elder was visited by a certain monk from the Holy Mountain. When Mother Eupraxia, who served the Elder in his latter years, saw him, she asked him if he knew her brother, Father Arsenios. The monk answered in the affirmative; the Eldress rejoiced exceedingly with childlike joy, and she ran to the Elder and enthusiastically said to him, "Elder, this monk here knows Father Arsenios!"

The Elder pretended that he hadn't heard her and the Eldress repeated her words. Then the Elder answered, "Well, what of it? See how she rejoiced when she heard about her brother! Here we hear about Christ and we aren't moved at all, and as soon as we hear about our brother we leap for joy. I rejoice only when I hear about Christ and our Panagia. Them do I have as father and mother and brethren."

On other occasions, because he saw our personal attachment to him, he asked us, "When you pray, do I ever come to your mind?"

If the answer was, "Yes, Elder," he would continue, "I am your greatest enemy. If between you and Christ some other person comes in between, whosoever it might be, you must reject him immediately. For he captivates your mind, which should undistractedly be given to God."

Whereas he loved all people, his love for God was so great that he did not want anyone or anything to disturb it.

During his stay in Constantinople, for example, his mother sent him a few letters. Father Basil loved his mother exceedingly, and he was afraid lest if he read them his love for her might be rekindled at the expense of his love for God. Therefore whenever he received a letter from her he would straightway tear it up without

---

3. Lit. "all-holy," *Panagia* refers to the all-holy Virgin Mary.—TRANS.

Constantinople, the Column of Saint Constantine the Great, c. 1890.

reading it. He would only write a few words to her to inform her that he was well and not to worry. Surely his heart would bleed at this practice of his, but it shows us the magnitude of his self-denial and his spiritual grandeur.

NO SAINT OF OUR CHURCH ever ascended to Heaven with ease. The life of the Saints was full of adversities and trials, which God Himself often allows, either to train them in patience, or to give them occasion to increase yet more in sanctity. The Elder's life also was full of hardships and trials.

As he pursued his spiritual struggles and his work in Constantinople, his left hand, which had been wounded in Kelveri on the eve of the Feast of the holy Unmercenaries, began to bother him. The doctors said that he had osteomyelitis and advised him to be hospitalized immediately. Father Basil, with the help of faithful men, entered a hospital and had all the necessary examinations. His condition was not good at all. The malady was treacherous and if his hand were not amputated it would spread to all his body. The doctors informed him of their decision, and had even appointed the day when the operation would take place. The persevering Father Basil, who was entirely submissive to the will of God, accepted it with patience and trust in Divine Providence.

"If the Lord suffers it, then let them cut off my hand," he said. "He knows best. May His will be done. Better with one hand in Paradise than with two in hell."

He prayed without ceasing to the all-holy Virgin and the holy Unmercenaries to intervene miraculously so that he would not lose his hand, but that, if it were not in the plan of God that it be saved, they give him patience and fortitude.

And his prayer was heard. On the eve of the day when the amputation was to take place, he was visited by the brother of a monk of the Holy Mountain. He knew certain folk-medicines and with these he healed various illnesses. He heard of Father Basil and the danger besetting him, and he made haste to visit him and encourage him not to consent to have his hand cut off, but to leave the hospital and he would heal him.

Father Basil considered this visit to be a visitation of God, Who hearkened unto his prayer. He left the hospital and verily, after a few months of treatment, his hand became well. He thanked God for the benefaction he had received and warmly entreated his benefactor to teach him how to prepare the medicine, so that he in turn also would be able to heal others. But the man did not wish to reveal to him "how to fix the medicine" because, as he said, he had a son who was a doctor.

Many years later the Elder, on one of his visits to the Holy Mountain, became acquainted with the monk who was the brother of this practical physician and also knew the secret of the medicine. That monk showed him how to prepare it, and the Elder, for the rest of his life, and especially during the period that he served as chaplain of the hospital of Aegina, healed without payment very many of the sick.

A FTER HE HAD SPENT SOME YEARS serving as a deacon at the Patriarchate, Patriarch Germanus V, who had succeeded Joachim III in 1913, appreciating his work and the influence it had among the people, one day called him and announced to him that he was thinking of ordaining him to the priesthood.

"I'm going to ordain you a priest," he said, "and will assign you to a church where you will have a sizable income, since many memorial services are held there."

Father Basil had a very great reverence for the priesthood. Having as guides such priests as Father John of his homeland, he never thought of becoming a priest just to satisfy some inner inclination of his own, far less when the priesthood was offered to him as an occasion to make money. He had espoused voluntary poverty since his youth and such a prospect not only did not attract him but even repulsed him. "The greatest sin of the priests," he was wont to say, "is the love of money." For this reason, just at hearing the Patriarch's words, he spontaneously and resolutely answered in the negative to his proposal. The Patriarch was annoyed with this negative answer, for he did not expect it, and countered him, "But why do you not accept it?"

"I don't want to consider the church a house of commerce."

"Then I will not assign you anywhere."

"It doesn't matter. I don't want money."

And so it was. He remained a little while without assignment, then the Patriarch placed him in the church of Saint George of the Seven Hills and later in the church of Saint George on the island of Halki.

Wherever he went, he created yet another new spiritual hearth. Himself living the mystical experience of Orthodoxy, he endeavored to pass on to the Christians the apostolic and patristic tradition of noetic prayer. He always recommended the study of patristic books, because thereby the patristic mind is conveyed to our own times. And this was the goal sought after by Father Basil, that we all might acquire the "mind of the Fathers." He was himself, according to the characterization of many, a contemporary Father, another Abba Isaac.

Little by little, without his seeking it, his fame spread. Everyone spoke of this new deacon who, although living in Constantinople, lived ascetically, made a great impression with his prayer and resounding words, and brought help to many.

Once he was visited in his humble cell by a Turk. He was sent, he said, by his master, who was a *cadi* [*judge*], to invite him to his house.

Father Basil became a little alarmed. He was not used to invitations for the sake of social visits, and the possibility of some unpleasantness, bringing with it some new trial, crossed his mind. But he said his prayers and went with the Turkish servant.

When they reached the house of the Turkish cadi, he was received by him in person and even with much warmth. They sat in the *müsafir onta* [*parlor*] and the cadi began the conversation.

"Effendi Papa, I am a Turk, a Moslem. But from the wages I receive, I keep what is necessary for my family and the rest I spend on alms. I help widows, orphans, and paupers, I give dowries to poor girls for their marriage, I help the sick. I keep the fasts strictly, I pray, and, generally speaking, I try to be just. I do not show partiality to anyone, no matter how high a position he has. What do you say—all these things that I do—are they not enough for me to gain the Paradise that you Christians speak of?"

Father Basil was impressed by all that the Turkish cadi told him, and the centurion Cornelius (Acts 10) immediately came to mind. He discerned between them a similarity in way of life. He understood that before him was a just and well-intentioned man, and that perhaps his mission was similar to that of the Apostle Peter to the centurion. So he decided to give witness to his faith.

"Tell me, Effendi. Do you have children?"

"Yes, I do."

"Do you have servants?"

"Yes, I have servants."

"Who fulfills your commandments better, your children or your servants?"

"Certainly it's my servants. Because my children, with the boldness they have, are often disobedient and do whatever they want, whereas my servants always do what I tell them."

"Tell me, Effendi. When you die, who will be your heirs: your servants who faithfully do your wishes, or your children who disobey you?"

"Why, my children, of course. Only they have inheritance rights, not my servants."

"Well then, Effendi, all the things you do are good. But the only thing they are able to do is to number you in the category of good servants. But if you wish to inherit Paradise, the Kingdom of the Heavens, you have to become a son. And this can only be done through Baptism."

The Turkish cadi was impressed with the illustration that Father Basil related to him. They talked some more, and in the end he asked him to catechize and baptize him. And after a little while the Turkish cadi was baptized and became a Christian.

During his stay in Constantinople, Father Basil underwent many trials. Summing it all up, he would tell us, "Often while in Constantinople I suffered deprivations, sometimes I didn't even have bread to eat, often I slept out of doors covered with lice. But, glory be to God, I endured it all. The only thing I besought of God, *aman*, was to gain my Christ."

Once, after an accusation by his old enemies back home that he had not done his military service, he was called by the Turkish authorities to serve in the army. Suddenly the young deacon found himself in a military camp in the midst of many other young men. His soul was afflicted exceedingly. It did not bother him so much that he would have to serve his time in the military; he could serve God wherever he was found. But he did not wish by any means to take off his *rasso*. He had a very great reverence for the *rasso*, the garment of repentance, and did not want under any circumstances to take it off, even temporarily.

But he did not despair. The deep faith he had made him turn his gaze towards Him Who is All-powerful, and towards His all-holy Mother, the quick help of all who call upon her. He prayed with hot tears and besought them to come to his aid and help him in this plight that was so exceedingly difficult for him.

And God did not tarry to show His wondrous intervention. After he had passed the first night praying on the top floor of a five-storey structure, where he had been assigned to stay before being dressed as a soldier, in the morning he came down and walked about in the compound. He endeavored to compose his thoughts and was thinking what he could do to avoid taking off his *rasso*.

Suddenly one of the guards, who saw him walking about among the other newly enlisted, called him and sternly said to him, "Hey, priest, what do you want in here? Get out of here quickly before I get into trouble."

Father Basil heard this voice as the voice of an angel. He was quick to understand the intervention of Divine Providence and he left the camp. He could not hold back the tears of compunction and thanksgiving that filled his eyes. Straightway he went to his parish and then on to the Patriarchate for protection. With tears he implored the Patriarch to intervene in any way he could, so that he would not have to take off his *rasso*. The Patriarch made a personal appeal to the Sultan and was successful in obtaining a decree which exempted all hierodeacons from the compulsory draft. In this way Father Basil was able to keep his clerical garb and continued to serve as a deacon in his parish.

A little while later, Father Basil visited the Patriarch and said to him, "Your All-holiness, I wish to leave and go to Greece. I fear that here the Turks will take off our *rassa*."

"Are you being funny?" answered the Patriarch. "It's impossible that such a thing could happen."

Yet his words were shown to be prophetic. Some years later, a bishop of the jurisdiction of the Patriarchate visited the Elder dressed in secular attire. He asked insistently to learn from what source he had derived the information that the Turks would legislate the abolition of the *rassa*. At the time they had been impressed at the Patriarchate by how he had been so "fully informed." They didn't grasp that the information he received did not have its origin from any secular source. It was the prelude of a gift which God later so richly lavished upon him, as the reward of a life full of sacrifices and love for Him.

AT THE PARISH of Saint George where Father Basil served, he was once visited by the nun Eupraxia, whom, as we have said, he met in Jerusalem, at the Monastery of the Venerable Forerunner. She was accompanied by her brother, the monk Anastasios. From Jerusalem the two siblings went to their homeland Pontus and from there to Constantinople. When they learned that Father Basil was there, they rejoiced greatly and went to meet him. They wished to go to Greece to enter some monastery there, because they feared that in Turkey the conditions would not remain normal.

Father Basil helped Father Anastasios to obtain leave from the Turkish rulers to go to Greece, after which he went immediately to the Holy Mountain where he lived till deep old age (he reposed with the name Arsenios in the odor of sanctity at the age of ninety-eight). As for the nun Eupraxia, because he was not familiar with any convents in Greece, he entrusted her to his widowed Aunt Despina, a very spiritual person and a worker of "compunctionate" prayer, who aspired to build a convent. The nun Eupraxia lived with her and under her protection for six years until she was forced to abandon Constantinople.

Refugees from Smyrna arriving at the Port of Piraeus.

CHAPTER SEVEN

Greece

WE ARE FOUND in the year 1922. A landmark year for the Greek presence in Asia Minor. Father Basil had already completed ten years (1912–22) in Constantinople—a decade filled with struggles and trials, which were not however to have their end there. The devastation of Asia Minor came for its Greek inhabitants like a lightning bolt, in an atmosphere that was already less than pleasant.[1] In the upheaval that followed, Father Basil sought to leave Constantinople and to go to Greece. His thinking was that in Greece, the "sweet fatherland," he would be able to work out his salvation with greater ease and under more favorable conditions. There he would at last find holy elders and experienced spiritual fathers. He would not be under the persecution of the tyrant. Perhaps the feeling he had (was it just a feel-

---

1. The victory of the Turkish Nationalist forces over the Greek army in August, 1922, caused a general panic among the Christians of Asia Minor that brought an estimated 150,000 refugees to the port city of Smyrna; after Smyrna also was taken by the Turks on September 9, it was set on fire, thronged though it was with such multitudes, and became, in the words of a Western observer, "a Titanic blast furnace"; at the time some considered it an atrocity without precedent in human history. In the wake of the destruction, the Treaty of Lausanne of 1923 provided for the exchange of populations: the Christians of Turkey were to be transplanted to Greece, and the Moslems of Greece, to Turkey. The exchange began after the Treaty of Lausanne was ratified in July of 1923, but it was not until 1924 that the Christians of Cappadocia began their exodus. The genocidal massacre of the Armenians had already taken place some years before.—TRANS.

ing?) that the Turks "would force them to take off the *rassa*" also confirmed his decision to leave Constantinople.

The Turkish judge whom Father Basil had made a Christian implored him to remain in Constantinople and he would undertake to protect and provide for him. He had him as his spiritual guide and did not wish to lose him. The Patriarch also had a special liking for him and wished to keep him in Constantinople, promising every solicitude on his part. But Father Basil did not accept. For him this was an opportunity to distance himself entirely from his relatives and acquaintances, to become "a stranger to the world" and to live dedicated entirely to God. Thus, in September of 1922, having received his passport dated September 16, 1922 from the Greek consul of Constantinople, he departed for Greece.

For the length of the journey, according to his beloved habit, he prayed continually. He felt that he had thrown himself into the abyss of the mercy of God, and he entreated Him to guide his steps in the path of salvation.

At last he reached Athens. Here he met his compatriot Constantine Basiliades, who loved him exceedingly. He assisted him as well as he could and introduced him to a certain priestmonk Chrysanthos, who served in the church of Saint Basil, at Callipolis in Piraeus. Father Chrysanthos was a spiritual man. Father Basil found in him a friend, and besought him to try to find a monastery for him to dwell in. Father Chrysanthos finally sent him to the monastery of the Enclosed [*Kleiston*] in Phyli of Attica.

Father Basil left with longing to go to pray and dwell in this monastery. His quiet and desert-loving soul, with his great experiences of the hesychasts of Anatolia, sought like a thirsty deer for some desert place and real ascetics to whom to entrust his spiritual guidance, that he might partake of their experience as tried ascetics. Being by nature a quiet and introspective soul, he desired complete quietude in order to give himself over to "compunctionate" prayer and the vision of God.

As he approached the monastery, he met two elderly monks outside. Father Basil bowed humbly and, transported on high as he was by his divine thoughts, he greeted them with the usual monastic greeting.

"Bless, holy Fathers."

"Welcome. From whence do you come to us?"

"From Athens. They sent me to your righteousness so that I might find my salvation."

"Have you brought a newspaper from the capital?"

"What would you do with it, holy Fathers? Newspapers don't contain anything but worldly affairs. We have left the world, shall we get involved with worldly affairs again?"

"It's to help us pass the time, blessed one. How will the day roll on if we don't have a newspaper to read?"

This dialogue threw Father Basil into various cogitations. His own mind went about in other realms, heavenly ones. He could not understand how it was possible that men who had left the world could think in such a worldly way, how their mind could be attached to things and affairs that they had not only renounced and abandoned, but had even promised with an oath that they would preserve themselves far away from them. Accustomed as he was to see men consecrated to God like incarnate angels, he refused to make compromise with the present reality. That very night he decided to leave, in order to safeguard his soul from every contamination and worldly thought, and to preserve his mind pure, given up only to God and to prayer.

Early in the morning on the next day he thanked the fathers for their hospitality and departed. This experience filled him with anxiety. Conditions in Greece were far different from what he had expected to find, and now he was troubled wondering where there might be a place suitable to struggle for his salvation.

With his deep faith and trust in the providence of God, he prayed continually that God would reveal to him His will. He had it as a custom before every work and every decision to pray earnestly to God and the all-holy Virgin, and it was there that he committed his every hope. He never trusted in himself. He never did anything that was dictated by his personal volition or some passionate desire. He possessed absolute trust, united with absolute obedience, in the will of God.

Modern view of the Port of Aegina.

CHAPTER EIGHT
Aegina

THANKS TO THE EFFORTS of Father Chrysanthos, Father Basil was appointed shortly as a deacon to the Cathedral of Aegina. In the beginning this was pleasing to him and at the first opportunity he took the ferryboat to that beautiful island in the Saronic Gulf. When he arrived, even before he appeared at the church, he made the acquaintance of Archimandrite Panteleimon Phostines (afterwards Metropolitan of Karystia and later of Chios), who at the time was serving in Aegina as a sacred preacher and had initiated praiseworthy spiritual and philanthropic activities. The two men talked at length on spiritual matters. They esteemed each another and were joined in mutual friendship.

When Father Basil visited the Metropolitan Cathedral to meet the clergy and inform them of his appointment, his soul was not at peace. Perhaps a certain coldness or indifference with which they received him contributed to this: and suddenly he decided not to remain there. When they called on him to give his signature that he undertook his responsibilities, he answered, "I don't know letters."

"Don't you know how to sign your name?"

"I don't even know A from B."

"Then how did they make you a clergyman since you don't know letters?"

"Even they who ordained me repented of it."

Later he met Archimandrite Panteleimon again and explained to him what had happened. The latter entreated him to remain on

Aegina, since he perceived Father Basil's spiritual depth and his virtues, and that in his person he would find a worthy assistant in his work. When he met with his persistent refusal, he suggested that he visit the Monastery of Chrysoleontissa [*The Golden Lion*]. If he found rest of soul there, he would himself obtain the necessary permission for him.

He spoke to him about the patron Saints of Aegina, Saint Dionysius of Zakynthos and the newly appeared Saint Nectarius, the sanctified bishop who had reposed only two years before.

At that time the memories of Saint Nectarius were still quite fresh on Aegina. The inhabitants of Aegina already believed in him as a Saint. They prepared icons of him, and prayed to him to intercede for them before God and to protect their island on which he had built his convent. Father Basil heard all this, and he both marvelled at and loved the Saint, and his heart was kindled. So he contemplated following the advice of Archimandrite Panteleimon.

Before he went to the Monastery of Chrysoleontissa, he passed by the Convent of the Holy Trinity. While there, he prayed at the Saint's grave and entreated him warmly with tears to help him and to reveal to him what the will of God might be. Later, he would say this to us regarding similar circumstances, "If you have to make a decision about something, either be obedient to your spiritual father, if the situation warrants it, or else make fervent supplication and then observe where your thought finds rest, and do that."

The same he also practised himself. He prayed fervently and departed for the Monastery of Chrysoleontissa. But he did not find rest there and did not long remain. His God-loving and desert-loving soul sought the "desert," to give full rein to his loving disposition for God and to fly with the light wings of faith and prayer to the heights of divine ascents and vision. He could not reconcile himself to the many cares and frictions over properties, which during that period devoured and squandered the monks' time. His soul desired the heavenly. His mind longed to be unbound by any earthly desire or pursuit, in order to be able to rise up undistracted to the throne of God and there to take delight in prayer. His main care till the end of his life was not to bind his mind, not only to things of the world, but in general to anything that was not necessary for his salvation. This brought him later—after he had occupied himself with the building of churches—to make that unsettling statement which, no matter how much of an exaggeration it might appear to be, reflects his stand on these matters: "Take care of your mind. Don't bind it to anything. I myself have repented even of those churches that I built. Why should I have bound my mind with so many cares and hindered it from prayer?"

It is evident that a soul with such heavenly thoughts and divine quests, which seeks perfection with all the will and strength that is in her, is not easily satisfied with whatever surroundings she might happen to find. Thus, Father Basil, having thanked the monks for their hospitality all the days that he stayed in the monastery, took his leave.

In the city of Aegina he again met with Archimandrite Panteleimon, who made superhuman efforts to convince him to remain on the island. Father Basil's soul had already begun to find rest on this island. He highly reverenced its patron Saints; he liked the place because it lent itself to quiet and was dotted with picturesque country chapels; he also esteemed its inhabitants, who appeared to him to be simple and pious people. He had the thought that later he would be able to build a hermitage in some isolated place, where he would be able—"alone, with God alone"—to give himself over to ascetical struggles, and so he accepted to remain as a deacon at the Metropolitan Church.

T OWARDS THE END OF 1922 began his diaconate in Aegina. He served at the Metropolitan Church, where oftentimes he chanted and preached. At the same time he pursued philanthropic work with Archimandrite Panteleimon. They both strove as much as they could to alleviate for the inhabitants the pain of their ailments and their poverty. And there were many things they were able to do. The times were difficult, poverty was great, the means were few, and the illnesses were many and often incurable. For this reason they were accepted by the inhabitants, who considered them their own, as their defenders and patrons. And this they had shown in very deed and many times with self-sacrifice.

In those years the most grievous disease people had to confront was tuberculosis. Not only was it incurable and led to certain death, but what they feared even more was that it was highly contagious. Fear and trembling would seize the family when they discovered that one of their relatives had been assailed by this disease, the curse of that epoch. They would be forced to send him away from home, and that unfortunate man had to live isolated far away. They would scarcely even come near him to leave him a plate of food, then depart as though chased off. And when he finally died, alone and with no one to help him, they even avoided burying him.

Once one such sufferer from tuberculosis died in a rowboat at Aegina. Fear and panic seized the people. On the one hand they feared to fetch him in order to bury him, and on the other they were troubled by the danger they risked from an unburied corpse. Not even his relatives could come to a decision and dared not approach.

As soon as Father Basil heard of it, he went immediately to see Father Panteleimon. They discussed the matter and decided to go together and fetch the dead man and bury him. The citizens of Aegina watched in astonishment and disbelief as the two clergymen, disregarding the danger, dared to do that which the dead man's very relatives would not do. This self-sacrifice of theirs raised them even higher in their estimation.

This event made plain to the two clergymen the urgent necessity of giving their help so that the newly instituted hospital of Aegina might be equipped the soonest possible to serve the islanders' needs in the best possible manner. To this end they turned their attention and their efforts, and soon the condition of the hospital improved significantly.

In the meanwhile another refugee arrived in Aegina, Father Basil's sister Barbara, who was a widow, together with her two young children. When she came to Greece and learned that Father Basil was in Aegina, she decided to go to be with him. Father Basil assisted her as much as he could. Thus, to his other cares he added the protection of his sister's family. And his solicitude was not confined to securing material goods only (finding work and so forth), but extended to their spiritual cultivation also. He was moreover so humble, so meek and sweet, of such integrity and attentiveness as a person, that simply his presence instructed.

T HE HARDSHIPS OF BEING A REFUGEE, his continuous agonies and struggles, had a grievous effect on Father Basil. He slowly began to feel exhausted, that his strength was abandoning him, and finally he was forced to take to bed. They put him in a single room in the hospital, fearing lest he was stricken with tuberculosis. Many argued that he had contracted the illness when he went and buried the man who died of the disease. In the end, with the help of God and the care of the doctors, his health was fully restored.

In the course of his hospitalization he was not content only to receive the doctors' attentions. He himself visited the other patients, comforted them and tried to raise their morale. His patience and fortitude, his kindly demeanor and the purity of his life impressed the other patients. The result of his endeavors were so marvellous, that when the time came for him to leave the hospital, both the directors and the personnel besought him to stay on as the father-confessor. Father Basil, who had forged a bond with human suffering and greatly loved the infirm, answered, "If you give me the room in which I was a patient to make it into a church, I accept."

"The room we grant you, but we have no money to give you."

"I don't want money, not even a dime. By myself, with the help of God, I will fix it up."

Thus, Father Basil began the work of raising up the church, which he dedicated to Saint Dionysius, Archbishop of Aegina. In the beginning he built a small church; he afterwards enlarged and renovated it four or five times, until it reached its present final form.

For the building and successive renovations of the church, Father Basil exerted tremendous efforts. He was himself an example of untiring labor and industry. He took part in all the manual work. As those who knew him in the old days would relate, whatever he undertook to make with his hands, he did impeccably. He worked as a carpenter, as a mason, and as a craftsman. He was also greatly helped by pious women who, seeing the righteousness of his life and his freedom from avarice, assisted him and gave him all that was needed for the building of the church. Even as of old with Saint Cosmas of Aetolia, so also with Father Basil, many besought him to receive their offerings for the building of the church.

Parallel with the building of the church, Father Basil did not neglect the work of the comforting and spiritual formation of the sick. This he considered his primary work. Every day he visited them like a loving father. He asked them how they were doing and gave them courage. He let his soul, which was rich in love, overflow and encompass them all with its sweet warmth. Like a good instructor he first bestowed his bountiful love and kindness; then he endeavored after that to transmit to them his fervent and steadfast faith, by which they were able to acquire patience, which was so necessary if they were to suffer their sickness without mur-

The Church of Saint Dionysius, attached to the hospital of Aegina, built by the Elder Ieronymos. Above, the front entrance; below, seen from the street.

muring. His entrance in the wards of the sick, with his sweet, tranquil, and imposing presence, was a pleasant change, a bedewing of the Holy Spirit that warmed their tormented soul and raised their morale. With the comforting words that flowed so bountifully, easily, and freely from his mouth, they ceased seeing their sickness as a trial and looked upon it as a gift of God, or as something allowed by His grace for their spiritual cultivation. All of them blessed the hour and the moment that they came to know this earthly angel, who had the power to lift them up to spiritual heights, formerly unknown to them, who was able to change even their most bitter trial into a blessing of God.

Alongside the consolation and spiritual edification he offered them, he never tired of tending to their physical healing also. The rich and unsparing love he bore for all moved him to occupy himself with the alleviation of bodily pain. The relevant experience he had in healing injuries, wounds, and so on, acquired from the things he had undergone himself, helped him in applying himself to the healing of the ailing with success and efficacy.

That which particularly characterized him in all his endeavors was his real, guileless, and unselfish love for God and his fellow man. He never allowed a thought of pride, self-projection, or ostentation to prevail in his soul. He performed the work of love because it had to be done, because he loved God and man, and not to win fleeting praise or to gain some transitory glory of dubious worth. For this reason, he never cared that his name be heard of in the accomplishment of a work of love, but only that the work be done. He knew well the destructive power that praises and glory harbor for the soul, and so avoided them with a passion. He strove to remain in obscurity, looking for recompense only from Christ, the Bestower of rewards, which is richer and more abiding. The following incident makes manifest his great humility and avoidance of human praise.

At the hospital he had once substantially contributed by word and deed to the complete recovery and cure of an ailing villager. On the day when this villager was released from the hospital he sought to find Father Basil to thank him, but could not. But one day he met him in Aegina and ran to meet him, to express to him with emotion his thanksgiving. Father Basil remained unperturbed and said to him, "Concerning what matter are you speaking to me? I don't understand."

"But are you not the priest who healed me in the hospital?"

"No, my boy, you are mistaken."

The man was confused. Could there be such a resemblance? Then curiosity began to torment him. Why was this priest trying to hide from him? Why, others seek by all means to appear as benefactors, and here he was running away from it.

He lost no time. He quickly went to the hospital and waited until he saw Father Basil cross the threshold with priestly dignity.

"Why, Father, did you hide from me when I met you down in Aegina?" he burst out plaintively.

"I? Oh, you must be mistaken. You must have seen someone else."

The villager's dismay was succeeded by admiration. This priest, he reasoned in himself, is a different manner of man; he isn't like ordinary people. And he returned to his village doubly benefited.

His humility and pursuit of obscurity was not confined to the avoidance of praises. Many times he went to the point of even assuming the responsibility for actions and damages done by others, in order to restore love and peace. On not a few occasions he presented himself before the authorities of the hospital and said that he was at fault for this or that damage, either at the request of the guilty party or without his knowing, in order to forestall the coming reproach or the imposition of some sanction. On account of the general esteem that he enjoyed they did not want to grieve him, nor did they seek who was guilty, and the matter stopped there, without any further seeking of punishment.

Although by day the hours were taken up with the work of building or adorning the church or with the sick, by night he gave himself over to his beloved prayer, to send up his deep sighs as fragrant incense before the throne of God and to pour forth abundant tears. Being a soul especially sensitive and given to quiet, he found rest only in prayer, through which he was raised up into the celestial realms; he touched the throne of God and there forgot himself in the sweetness of His presence. He had the rare gift of coming to compunction and weeping very easily. He never prayed without weeping. With the first "Through the prayers of our holy Fathers..." he said to begin Vespers or any other service, a breaking in his voice was noticeable, which betrayed sobbing, and tears would be rolling down his ascetical face.

Thus, while on his knees praying for himself, his patients, his spiritual children, and the whole world, sleep would overtake him for a little. Then he got up again and began the same struggles.

CHAPTER NINE

A Priest Called by God

IN THE MEANTIME Archimandrite Panteleimon Phostines was elected Metropolitan of Karystia.[1] But he never forgot Aegina and especially Father Basil, whom he had particularly esteemed and loved. He often invited him to his Metropolis and together they made various visits of spiritual ministry. The better he got to know him, the more his esteem for him increased. One day he said to him, "I think you should become a priest. The faithful have need of shepherds. Reflect on the responsibility you have before God for these people who have come to you. If those who have understanding don't become priests, then who will?"

Father Basil did not want to take up such a burden. He had a very deep understanding of the mystery of the priesthood and, as he later told us, he desired to remain a deacon till his death. He felt himself to be very sinful and could not imagine it possible that he, with his "sinful hands," should touch the Lord of Glory. So it was that he avoided the matter and answered the Metropolitan, politely but firmly, that he did not desire to become a priest.

But during one of his visits to the Metropolitan of Karystia, while they were liturgizing, on August 29, 1923, the Metropolitan was prepared to ordain him priest and he announced it to Father Basil during the Divine Liturgy.

---

1. A southern province on the island of Euboia. Kymi (mentioned in the heading of the letter given below) is a city of Karystia.—TRANS.

The Elder Ieronymos as a young priest.

"But, Your Eminence—"

"No buts. You are going to show obedience."

Father Basil was caught by surprise. He was not expecting this. Humble as he was, he did not want to resist and disobey the Bishop. He presumably thought that since things came about in this manner, it was the will of God; and he obeyed.

He came before the Beautiful Gate with his lips and all of his members trembling with emotion.

> "Divine Grace, which always healeth that which is infirm, and completeth that which is wanting, elevateth through the laying-on of hands Basil, the most devout deacon, to the Priesthood…
>
> "Receive This Which is entrusted unto thee, and guard It, until the Second Coming of our Lord Jesus Christ, when He shall ask It of thee."

Words and prayers that engraved themselves deeply in his soul and strengthened even more the feeling of responsibility which he felt so heavily within himself.

The Divine Liturgy ended with the Metropolitan bestowing on him the office of Archimandrite and advancing him to father-confessor in order to hear confessions.[2] The greatness of the gift and the grace of the priesthood made Father Basil, now a priest, send up supplications, entreaties, and thanksgivings to God, for having deemed him worthy to receive this great office.

Before he departed from the Metropolis of Karystia, the Metropolitan gave him the following "Directive."

> Protocol No. 638/510   Kymi, August 29, 1923
> THE METROPOLITAN OF KARYSTIA
> To the all-righteous Archimandrite Basil Apostolides
>
> Our mediocrity entrusts to you, the most pious priestmonk, the ministry of spiritual paternity. Wherefore you are obliged to receive

---

[2]. In the Greek Church ordination to the priesthood does not of itself confer the right to hear confessions; it is through a special prayer read by the bishop with the laying-on of hands that a priest also becomes a $πνευματικός$ (spiritual father or father-confessor) with a blessing to hear confessions.—TRANS.

the thoughts and actions and various passions of all that come to confession to you and to provide for their repentance and salvation, according to each one's strength and their differing sins. For you shall bind what needs to be bound, and shall loose what needs to be loosed, as the fellow worker and servant of the spiritual and apostolic grace given you of God, unto the salvation of men's souls. As for those who are brought to the dignity of the priesthood, you are obliged to examine everything about them exactly, as the apostolic and canonical injunction requires, lest you err through indolence or by some sudden mishap, and thus partake of other men's sins, as the divine Apostle says. For this reason the present directive letter, written by my mediocrity, is given to you for all surety.

☦ The Metropolitan of Karystia
Panteleimon

Father Basil returned to Aegina a priest. Shortly thereafter, by request of the administration of the hospital, he undertook the duties of rector of the church of Saint Dionysius, which he had built himself. But the great responsibility of the priesthood weighed on him very heavily.

"I was a deacon for eleven years," he told us. "I never desired to become a priest. They made me one by force."

He considered the work of being a father-confessor, with its responsibility for hearing confessions, both very heavy and dangerous spiritually. He often said, "Many become father-confessors without having the corresponding experience. Without themselves having applied, they teach and guide others. This is dangerous. When they made me a father-confessor, they gave me a book to read entitled *Confessor's Handbook*. There I learned of sins that I never imagined existed. After reading a few pages I closed it and gave it to an elderly priest. Take it, I told him. I don't need it, I don't want to hear confessions."

In Aegina there had already gathered around him a number of pious women, who were guided by and obedient to this ascetic, who was at once both otherworldly and filled with love for mankind, who came from the sanctified earth of Anatolia and brought to their land a spirituality hitherto unknown. As many as were able to enjoy him serving the Liturgy recount the majesty, the compunction, and the heavenly atmosphere that reigned in church during the Divine Liturgy. For Father Basil, the Divine Liturgy was not a formality, some obligation for the servicing of the faithful, but divine exaltation and participation. In it he lived in succession all the phases of the Lord's appearing upon the earth, the progression to Golgotha, and the very awesome and man-saving sacrifice, which finds its crowning in the divine changing of the holy elements. At this point Father Basil would stop and for a long time was unable to hold back his tears, remembering that blessed priest, Father John, whom he had known in Kelveri.

"How is it possible that God, Who is beyond touch and has no need, condescends to be touched by hands that are sinful and mortal?" he would later say and dissolve in tears.

The presence of God and the Angels was manifest to Father Basil. He felt this presence close to him, next to him, and he trembled with divine fear and emotion. He was so certain of this presence of the bodiless hosts, and so accustomed to it, that he once told a certain visiting clergyman, as something completely natural and matter-of-fact, "If you don't see your Angel next to you at the holy altar, don't liturgize. I fear the divine things greatly, I tremble."

A great crowd began to gather at the hospital church. The people left the other churches and came to attend the Divine Liturgy where the Elder served, drawn by his humble presence, his comely and modest voice, and especially his great piety, which he was able to impart to others. It was also his habit to preach. His words were like sayings, concise and clear; they touched the hearts of all.

The administration of the hospital, which followed all this activity of the chaplain, thought it worthwhile to propose to him a fifteen-year contract of service. The people saw how useful and profitable this priest was to them and they wanted to bind him to themselves. They feared that he might suddenly leave for the Holy Mountain, as in fact he had on occasion expressed the thought and desire to do, or that he might found some monastery and forsake them. For this reason the Administrative Council called an extraordinary meeting and made the following decision:

The Administrative Council of the Hospital of Aegina 'Saint Dionysius,' being called by its President to an extraordinary meeting, comprising the members listed below and according to Article 5 of the constitution, taking into account the President's proposal, that he who is serving as the priest of the church of the Hospital, Archimandrite Basil Apostolides—being the chief founder of the church, and having offered out of his own material means much for the building of the church, and not only this, but having gathered even more funds from various pious Christians—on account of his virtuous life and the faithful performance of his duties is the cause of the flocking together of many people into the church, from which the Hospital profits, and caring for the interests of the Hospital, judges it necessary that the said priest be legally bound by an agreement and thus remain in the Hospital in the future.

RESOLVED

To give to the President, Tasia E. Betra, the authority and right to proceed to draw up a signed contract either by a public notary or private agreement with Archimandrite Basil Apostolides by which he will be obliged to serve as the priest of the Hospital, as he is serving presently, for fifteen years. The Hospital undertakes the obligation to provide for him domicile, food, and a monthly stipend of 400 drachmas.

This contract may be drawn up for the duration of one year, with the clause that Archimandrite Basil Apostolides has the option to serve notice within one month after the signing thereof that he wishes the extension of the agreement for the duration of fifteen years, whereupon the one-year agreement automatically becomes binding for fifteen years for both parties by obligation. For which cause the present document is drawn up and legally signed, being deposited in the original in the Notary's office in Aegina.

                The President   The Members

FATHER BASIL'S TENURE as priest at the church of the hospital of Aegina lasted much less than what the administrative council wished and expected. After his ordination he served the Liturgy for forty days continually. These days Father Basil lived in a state of divine ecstasy and exaltation, something between Heaven and earth. Neither he nor those who lived with him were ever able to forget these heavenly experiences. Together with the priest of the Most High were also lifted up to celestial heights all who attended and observed him in these divine ascents.

These experiences increased his fear of God even more, which he so intensely felt within him. And the more his soul was lifted to the Heavens and approached the throne of the Divine Majesty, the more he felt himself unworthy to minister the immaculate Mysteries and to touch the King of Glory. Participation in the divine gave him the desire to escape from the things of men and to see "the things accomplished above nature" no longer as a man, with mortal eyes, but with the noetic eyes of his pure and chaste soul, which saw "this, the very body of the Lord, being slaughtered."

And while he lived in this state of divine participation and of the divine darkness, offering daily the unbloody Sacrifice, on the fortieth day after his ordination to the priesthood he was deemed worthy to see a terrible vision. This played a definitive role in his later course as a celebrant of the Most High.

During the Divine Liturgy, while his prayer, as was wont, had carried him away and lifted him on high, at the throne of the "slaughtered" Lamb, suddenly he saw the Precious Body and Blood of the Lord actually changing in the Holy Chalice and taking on the form of flesh and blood. Father Basil was terribly shaken at the sight of this supernatural phenomenon. For a long time he prayed in the presence of this divine mystery, shedding abundant and burning tears. Afterwards, with unsteady step on account of emotion, he came out at the Beautiful Gate and gave the Dismissal,

Fresco of the Mystical Supper, Karanlik Kilisse in Cappadocia.

without revealing to anyone the astonishing miracle that had taken place in the Sanctuary.

When everyone had left the church, Father Basil knelt and gave his pure soul free rein to be "emptied out" in the presence of his Creator. For many hours he prayed with tears and besought God to beckon that His Divine Body resume the appearance of bread and wine, so that he would be able to consume the holy elements. His humble soul saw in all this God's favor, in revealing to him, in such a visible way, his unworthiness; and this evoked contrition, and he besought God with greater fervor and superabundant tears.

Finally, after many hours of prayers and tears, which could be compared with the days which the God-seer Moses spent on the God-trodden Mountain of Sinai, the Immaculate Mysteries resumed their original form. And Father Basil literally "communicated" of the Precious Body and Blood of the Lord.

That same afternoon, shaken by this experience, he appeared to the administrator of the hospital and with evident emotion said to her, "I'm sorry, but I am unable to continue to serve as the chaplain of the hospital. Let us endeavor to find some priest to replace me. Until then, I will serve you."

"But why, Father? Are you not satisfied? Perhaps the money we offer you isn't enough? We can discuss this."

"No, that's not the reason. This work is very heavy for me. A certain priest confessed to me that, while he was serving, he beheld at the time of the consecration the bread and wine changing into flesh and blood. And it took many hours of prayer for the elements to return to their natural condition so that he could consume them. Yes—the work of a priest is very heavy. And I neither wish, nor am I able, to carry it."

At the first opportunity he visited the Metropolitan of Karystia, Panteleimon, who was his confessor. He related to him with tears all the details of the vision, and he besought him never to reveal it to anyone.

Later, nevertheless, the Metropolitan made it known, for the sake of spiritual profit, to the president of the administrative council of the hospital, Mrs. Tasia Betra, that it was Father Basil who saw this fearsome vision. She marvelled at Father Basil's great holiness and humility, and at a later date she related everything to the Eldress Eupraxia.

Father Basil continued to serve a little longer until, approximately six months after his ordination, a cousin of his arrived on Aegina, Father Cosmas, a very devout and virtuous priestmonk. Father Basil suggested to him that he undertake the position of priest for the church of the hospital and he accepted. Father Basil rejoiced not only because he found a replacement, but even more because Father Cosmas was very pious and led a righteous life. Many related that when he liturgized, they saw him in the sanctuary "a forearm's length off the ground." He also was a worthy son of Anatolia.

From that time on, Father Basil ceased serving the Liturgy. But at the request of the administration of the hospital, he continued to offer all the other services as rector. So Father Cosmas liturgized and Father Basil chanted and preached the word of God. He maintained and increased his contact with his spiritual children both within and without the hospital. He continued to occupy himself with the relief and consolation of the sick, to strengthen them, to fortify their patience, and never lost an opportunity to plant in them the seed of faith in Christ. His holy life alone was enough to inspire them all, for they saw before them the living example of a Christian brought to perfection. He was the personification of love—an uncompromising ascetic, and at the same time a quiet yet very active and efficient worker in society.

The Elder Ieronymos with Father Cosmas, his compatriot and kinsman.

The Athonite Monastery of Simonopetra
Wood-block print by Pol. Regos, 1934.

CHAPTER TEN

The Angelic Life

AFTER THE VISION he saw during the Divine Liturgy, Father Basil thought of making a pilgrimage to the Holy Mountain. He had already conceived this desire in time past, wishing to see the conditions that prevailed there, to decide if he should go to live in one of its monastic houses.

But now he felt an acute need to hasten this trip: not only to worship that holy place and appraise the conditions there, but to go to confession to one of the ascetics of Athos and seek his advice.

In the course of this first trip of his to the Holy Mountain, he visited most of the monasteries. He forged a special bond with the abbot of the Sacred Monastery of Simonopetra, Father Ieronymos, who was also from Asia Minor. He stayed there several days, he went to confession, and they exchanged spiritual experiences. Father Ieronymos saw the pure and guileless soul of the humble priestmonk Father Basil, so enkindled with divine love, and he loved him very much.

Father Basil left the Holy Mountain profited and maintained communications with Father Ieronymos. He often corresponded with him and sought his counsel in many spiritual matters. On his next trip to Athens, Father Ieronymos visited the "ascetic" of Aegina. He had been impressed by his great faith, his love of God, and his ascetical way of life. He thus suggested to him that he receive the Great Angelic Schema.

Father Basil desired his whole life long to become a monk of the

Great Schema, to be clothed with the garment of repentance. He only stated some reservations and scruples concerning how spiritually prepared he was for this. As always, he did not want to undertake this responsibility on his own, to do his own will. For this reason he answered that he had to mention it to his spiritual father and let him take the appropriate initiative. He wished to make the beginning of the monastic life with obedience. But when Father Ieronymos insisted, Father Basil humbly bent his head and accepted his decision as the manifestation of the divine will.

The date for his tonsure was set for December 13, 1923. Father Basil, accompanied by a few pious faithful, came to the little chapel of Saint Gerasimus, which was located close to the convent of Saint Nectarius, to receive the Great Angelic Schema. There, in the stillness of this solitary country chapel, were heard the awesome prayers and promises of the newly-ordained monk, the recollection of which would accompany him his whole life long.

> "Why hast thou come hither, Brother, falling down before the holy Altar and this holy Assembly?"
>
> "I am desirous of the life of asceticism, Reverend Father."
>
> "Dost thou desire to be deemed worthy of the Angelic Habit and to be ranked in the choir of the Monastics?"
>
> "Yes, God helping me, Reverend Father."
>
> …
>
> "Our Brother, Ieronymos, monk, is clothed with the tunic of righteousness and gladness, of the great and Angelic Habit, in the Name of the Father, and of the Son, and of the Holy Spirit. Amen."

Father Ieronymos gave his own name to the newly-tonsured monk, as an indication of the favor and great love that he nourished for him. He would later say to his acquaintances, "Do you see how, from a thorn, a rose comes forth?" In this manner he demonstrated both his own humility and his great esteem for his new namesake in Aegina.

In confirmation of the tonsure, he gave the following certificate:

SACRED CENOBITIC MONASTERY OF SIMONOPETRA

Certificate

The undersigned certifies that with the paternal blessing of the All-sacred Metropolitan of Karystia, Kyr Panteleimon, I tonsured as a monk of the Great Schema Basil Apostolides, renaming him Ieronymos, on December 13 of the year 1923 in the sacred chapel of Saint Gerasimus which is in the proximity of the Sacred Convent of the Holy Trinity on Aegina. His Righteousness, Ieronymos monk, remains under the guardianship of the Metropolitan of Karystia, Kyr Panteleimon, while residing in the Hospital of Saint Dionysius on Aegina. He was tonsured, as has been stated, into the Great Schema, and asked of me the present certificate, which I impart to his Righteousness to be used wherever need be.

The Holy Mountain, July 27, 1924
The Abbot of the Sacred Cenobium of Simonopetra
Archimandrite Ieronymos

"Village of Ascetics" on Athos, by Pol. Regos, 1934.

CHAPTER ELEVEN

Suffering the Things of Men

FATHER IERONYMOS took on a new position in the society of his faithful. Since he refused, out of exceeding piety and immeasurable humility, to continue to serve them as a celebrant of the Most High, he dedicated himself to their spiritual edification and became their spiritual director and instructor, the "Elder," as he was known to his flock in Aegina and later throughout all Greece.

He was for all an affectionately loving father, their good counsellor and dear friend, their encourager in afflictions, the great helper in their difficulties, their instructor in faith, and, in general, he was the example of kindness and love.

He had special concern for the poor and the sick. Wherever he heard that there was somebody who was sick or poor, he made speed and endeavored by all means to help him. And if he were not himself in a position to help, on many occasions he went about begging, that he might be able to alleviate the pain and destitution of his neighbor.

On account of his holy life, many people, among them even the affluent, reverenced him and had him as their spiritual father. Father Ieronymos, who had never asked even a dime for himself, often used his influence to assuage his fellow men's hardships. And this he did in a gentle and sweet way and with humility, which always brought about positive results. In this manner he was able to achieve two purposes simultaneously: to aid those who were in need, and to accustom the Christians to doing good works.

Once he visited his friend C. Basiliades in Piraeus. After they had had a cup of tea he said to him, "I want you to do me a favor. Let's go together to a certain house."

"Fine, Elder. Let's go."

They took a taxi and went in the direction of Tabouria (a poor section of Piraeus where refugees from the Asia Minor catastrophe of 1922 had settled). They stopped at a place that Father Ieronymos indicated, and rang the doorbell. When the door opened and they entered, the scene they encountered was horrible: a family scourged by poverty, the father sick in bed, without any money even for medicine, and his young children barefoot and hungry. They sat for a little while and spoke with them and afterwards, as soon as they were outside, Father Ieronymos said to his friend, "If I were in their place, would you not help me?"

"Yes, Elder, without fail."

"I earnestly entreat you therefore to undertake the care of them. Say that you do it for me. I ask this of you as a personal favor."

"Fine, Elder, may it be blessed."

On the evening of the same day the doorbell rang again and someone unknown (an employee of Basiliades') brought them some parcels full of food and a little envelope with money. The people didn't catch on who these strangers were who behaved towards them in such a Christian way, with such humanity.

In this manner did Father Ieronymos work. Quietly and with results. Human suffering tormented him, because he did not suffer the things of God only, but also the things of man.

He also displayed great concern for his compatriots, many of whom, since they had arrived from Asia Minor tormented and in dire poverty, suffered hunger, and were not able to endure the poverty and tribulations and therefore despaired. Some contemplated suicide and others gave themselves up to drinking. They themselves were suffering and their families endured hunger and afflictions. Father Ieronymos counselled them all, he strengthened their morale, made their faith steadfast, and provided for them as he was able. Wherever he learned that there were such who suffered undeservedly, he ran to their aid. He had care for all.

Very many are the incidents related by people who were helped by Father Ieronymos; and certainly those we do not know of are many more. The unlying witnesses are the widows and orphans who wept on the day of his funeral, because, as they said, they lost their provider. Father Ieronymos worked "in secret." His purpose was not self-projection but rather how to help the afflicted both in body and soul. And this poured forth from a soul inundated with love for God and neighbor.

Alongside the care he had for the "least" of his brethren, his little flock, he did not neglect his spiritual obligations. By day he was the untiring worker in society; by night he was the meditative ascetic, the exact observer of the spiritual life and man of watchful sobriety, who spent himself in prayer. He prayed for his sins, for his spiritual children, and for the whole world.

Prayer for Father Ieronymos was no dry formality; it was an integral part of his life. In an oblique way, as was his wont, he once said, "Some men, when a little time passes without praying, are not able to endure it, they suffer. The hours in which they want to pray and cannot seem to them as martyric torments."

These words give us to understand the measure of his love for God and the violent desire that impelled him to commune with Him in prayer. In confirmation of this assertion we mention the following: Without fail, when he spoke to his visitors, after about an hour's conversation, he would say, "Now go out a little so that I can rest, and afterwards I'll call you again. Nun, treat so-and-so to a cup of coffee. Give him some loukoumi. Whatever you have, give."

It was the time of his communication with God and Father Ieronymos was not able to endure any longer. And all the while that the kind Eldress Eupraxia, like another Martha, was occupied with serving the treats—usually fifteen to twenty minutes—he would give himself over to prayer. When, after this quick intermission of spiritual exaltation, the visitor was called back to his cell, he would see his face shining "as it had been the face of an angel." And he would immediately begin to give counsel on certain specific matters, which as a rule were of direct concern to his listener. And his prayer together with his words had such power that they gave the assurance with certainty that that which one heard was not only the product of his spiritual experience, but "the fruit of the Holy Spirit."

Here I ought to state one of my own personal experiences. After every visit to the Elder, no matter how troubled and run-down I was from various trials and difficulties, I always left so rested and comforted it was as if nothing whatsoever oppressed me. And I know not if the beloved reader has ever had such an experience, but personally I am obliged to confess that as I took the path leading from the hermitage to the town of Aegina, I felt so light that I just barely felt that I touched the earth. The remission of transgressions and the various temptations which I deposited with him and which he as a loving father lifted off of me, I felt had an effect even on my bodily weight. Such power did his prayer possess. The problem troubling his brother or his spiritual child was also his problem. That is why he often told us, "When I pray for my brothers, I spend something of myself, my heart bleeds."

IN THE YEAR 1927 the Eldress Eupraxia arrived in Aegina as a refugee from Constantinople. She was numbered among the exchange of populations and according to the regulations had to leave Constantinople in 1922. But the aunt of the Elder Ieronymos, who was her guardian, hid her in her house for five years. She believed that in the future things would improve and she would be able to found a convent there. But the events betrayed her and the Eldress Eupraxia left for Greece knowing neither where her relatives were to be found nor the Elder, in whom she hoped to find a guardian. When she arrived in Athens, she learned from some acquaintances that the Elder was on Aegina and she left to find him.

The Elder received her and gave her every kind of help possible. Because she was poor, without help, and unprotected, he thought of temporarily sending her to her relatives, until she could be settled in some convent. The Eldress Eupraxia had heard that after the exchange of populations in 1924 her siblings had settled in Thessalonica. As a good and loving father to all, he took her with him and went to Thessalonica. They searched everywhere, they gave notification to the Red Cross, they put ads in the newspapers, but they found no one.

"God has loaded you on my shoulders," he finally told her, and took her with him back to Aegina.

He rented a room for her and took care through his acquaintances that she always had food and good companionship. After a little while they were informed that her siblings were settled in Drama of Macedonia. But before she was able to visit them, she fell grievously ill from the sufferings and hardships of the Asia Minor catastrophe of 1922 and was forced to enter a hospital in Athens. The Elder took care for everything and primarily, because he feared lest under the sufferings and the illness she succumb and lose her patience, he took pains to strengthen her faith and reinforce her patience.

The letter that follows, which he sent to her while she was undergoing treatment in the hospital, shows his paternal anguish.[1]

---

1. The letter is translated in the way it was written, with abrupt sentences and peculiar grammatical syntax. This is the typical Cappadocian manner of speaking and writing. The Cappadocians would say a few words and the hearer was supposed to fill in the rest.—TRANS.

The Reverend Eldress Eupraxia.

Child in the Lord, Sister Eupraxia, Eldress, may divine grace protect you in all your hardships.

    I implore the All-good to take pity on us. Have faith in the Lord, Who governs the whole world and us. Have this mind: whatever good takes place, receive it with piety. I know that you must be very anxious. Since the Lord permitted, Sister, let us accept. Have this thought—all things are good. I am far away, but I am in your thoughts and I understand; our only consolation is God. Let Him try us, only let Him not abandon us. Beware: much sorrow poisons a man. This, God does not want. May we not sin; as genuine servants of His, let us be patient. The Lord above beholds and rules, let us be faithful to Him. He has given, that we may be patient. No one knows the mind of the Lord, have the patience of the Saints, do not search out what takes place, only have patience and courageous faith, from the depths of the heart shed a teardrop. He hearkens and makes trial and quickly He shall comfort you.

I received the telegram to send you the certification of destitution, but the person responsible says that he grants it only within Aegina, not outside—this is the order of the Ministry. I will send you, he told me, to Piraeus, to the office, they will give it to you, it will be good anywhere in the country and I will look into it. Write me what the administration and the doctors there say, because there are also persons there who grant it, he says, only locally. This will come to pass, God willing, do not be anxious, only write me the particulars and I will help you with all my strength. I had telegraphed you that if nothing can be done, come home, and God will be our helper.

Greetings to all, blessings to all.
Next year if I have health I will go to Drama.
Your continual supplicant to the Lord,
Archimandrite Ieronymos Apostolides

The Eldress Eupraxia remained hospitalized for a while and then came out of the hospital. After that, since she had need of attention and care, she went to her brethren in Drama, until she recovered completely. The Elder, even after she left the hospital, did not cease to have solicitude and concern for her, being afraid above all lest she lose her patience on account of the many hardships, privations, and sufferings she had undergone. He made every effort to strengthen her faith and patience. The following letter which he sent her at the time demonstrates his paternal care and anxiety on her account.

Sister in Christ, Eupraxia, nun,

I pray that our Panagia be always at your side and that Divine Providence gift you patience and perseverance in your faculties and consolation in your sentiments.

Today, Wednesday, I received your letter and rejoiced that you are well. Glory to the Most High that I am well also. Have it in your memory that we are monastics, that we should have great patience. You know this better than others and that through struggles we will be saved. Catechize your mind, that all the Saints were saved through struggles.

Let us not sin, by losing our patience. Unto this end was illness given by God, that you may be saved. Do not despair, lift up your mind to the invisible and behold the everlasting life, its happiness. Believe in all that our mother the Church teaches us, let us not fall short. Let us have a little patience, the Lord from above beholds, it suffices that all things will pass; you have suffered many things.

To all greetings, prayers, and blessings.
Your continual supplicant to the Lord,
Archimandrite Ieronymos Apostolides

AMIDST THE MANY CARES and concerns he had "for each and every one" of those in need, he did not neglect his duties at the hospital either. He had become "all things to all men," he spent himself, he anticipated all things. At the hospital church he chanted and preached. There he received all who came for confession. Nor did he stop his daily visits to the wards, to see the sick, to encourage them, to address to them a sweet word. And the sick awaited his visit as a visit from God.

In the meantime, the Archbishop of Athens and all Greece, who was the General Overseer of the hospital of Aegina, appointed Father Ieronymos his representative for the hospital, and a little later, he appointed him abbot of the sacred Monastery of Chrysoleontissa on Aegina. He valued the Elder's character and his work very highly, and because of this, even against his will, he burdened him with the above duties.

The help the hospital received from the offerings that came on his account, and the income from the faithful who filled the church, was great. The administrative council of the hospital, which observed this many-faceted activity of the rector and the related benefit resulting therefrom, acknowledged his contribution and out of gratitude decided to proclaim him a "Great Benefactor." Thus, on May 14, 1930, it sent him the following letter together with the relevant excerpt of the minutes of the Administrative Council.

HOSPITAL CLINIC "SAINT DIONYSIUS"
Aegina

Aegina, May 14, 1930

To Kyr Ieronymos Apostolides,
Archimandrite of the Sacred Church
of the Hospital Clinic "Saint Dionysius"

Holy Archimandrite,

Because you, as the representative of the General Overseer of the Metropolitan of Athens in the Hospital Clinic of Aegina "Saint Dionysius," and as a clergyman serving in the Sacred Church of the Hospital, have offered many spiritual and material benefits therein, an award in tribute of appreciation is granted by the Administrative Council of the Hospital which being assembled, signed Act No. 136 of March 27 of the current year, which being attached hereto is sent to you that you may be appraised thereof.

The President *The Secretary*
Tasia Betra L. Leouse

ACT 136

Today on Aegina, it being Thursday, March 27, 1930, the Administrative Council of the Hospital Clinic "Saint Dionysius" in an extraordinary meeting had as its main topic of discussion the activities of the representative of his Beatitude the Archbishop of Athens Kyr Chrysostom, the General Overseer of the Hospital Clinic, Archimandrite Ieronymos.

The President introduced in the council the subject of this clergyman's activities as the representative of His Beatitude in the Institution, and as a sacred preacher, and as the founder and builder of the

Sacred Temple of our All-venerable Saint Dionysius in the Hospital, and that the raising-up of this temple came about by funds that this clergyman alone gathered from various virtuous citizens with great labors, a thing most difficult for the present time wherein a very great recession prevails.

The council, having heard the President's report, acknowledges that the said clergyman is in truth a great benefactor, on account of his labors and sacrifices. Wherefore it declares and approves unanimously: first, that as a token of gratitude the clergyman's name be engraved on the marble plaque of the great benefactors of the Hospital Clinic; second, that there be sent him a congratulatory document and expression of gratitude on behalf of the whole Administrative Council; and third, that a copy of this decision be sent to His Beatitude the Archbishop of Athens, that he may be appraised of the activities of the said clergyman, who is his representative. Likewise, that a copy of this decision be given to the aforesaid Archimandrite Ieronymos Apostolides and present abbot of the Sacred Monastery of Chrysoleontissa "The Dormition of the Theotokos."

The subsequent matters are entrusted to Mrs. President.

The President   *The Secretary*
Tasia Betra   Lela Leouse

The Members
Koula Garoufale, Argyro Syriote, Marika Moutsatsou,
Spyros Rodes, George Heliotis, Panagiotes Zervas.

The Archbishop of Athens also gave him permission to preach at the Cathedral of Athens every time he came to Athens. And the Elder, for a very long period of time, went to Athens every Sunday evening and preached at the Cathedral. Many of his spiritual children and compatriots, Greeks from Asia Minor, would gather there to listen to him. Those who are still alive speak of these sermons with nostalgia. He spoke simply, with clarity, and with exceeding compunction. He never spoke without weeping during his talks. He strove to transmit his experiences to his hearers, to teach them noetic prayer and hesychasm, the ascetical life and the patristic discipline, which constitute the identity of Orthodoxy throughout the ages. After every talk, all awaited him in order to see him, to receive his blessing, and to hear some personally consoling word.

It was there that he learned of his compatriots' ordeals and trials, so that afterwards he might run to find them and encourage them. He had managed to combine, to an exceedingly great degree, the life of a hesychast with that of one who tirelessly works for the good of society. The great flame of his love for God flooded him also with love for his brethren. His life had become one continuous sacrifice. It was an inexhaustible fountain, from which welled up unending goodness and love.

O F THE LITTLE TIME LEFT from the exercise of his manifold activities and occupations, he devoted a significant part to the study of the Holy Scriptures and patristic texts, chiefly the ascetical writings. He especially had a very great weakness for the *Ascetical Homilies* of Abba Isaac the Syrian. He read them with regularity. A day did not pass in which he did not read at least one page, which he also recommended to his spiritual children.

"Let not one day pass without reading at least one page from Abba Isaac. I love the blessed one very much; I have him as my elder. And whatever you read, apply yourself, and say to yourself: Do I do this? In this way you will be prompted by the reading to cross over to accomplishing it in deed."

"Elder, I read him, but I observe that I am not corrected," I once said to him.

"Listen: the more you wipe a glass, the cleaner it gets. Read it; do not neglect it: and the profit will come. As often as you pour water into a glass, it will be cleansed, even if no water remains in it."

Once Father Th., then a deacon, who used to visit him regularly, asked him, "Elder, tell me, what spiritual books should I read to be profited?"

"Abba Isaac," was the Elder's answer.

"Agreed—you've often spoken to me of Abba Isaac, and I read him. But what other books should I read?"

"Abba Isaac."

"All right; and any other book besides Abba Isaac?"

"Abba Isaac. As for me, even if I am able to apply only one small part of Abba Isaac's words, I do not desire anything else. Thus with you also. Read even one page a day with attention and you will discover great gain. Only read him with attention. Have him like a mirror, in order to see your weaknesses."

So much had he come to love Abba Isaac, and had wholly espoused his writings, that he had himself become the express image of them. His life, his words, and his counsels reminded one of this great Syriac ascetic. This is why many spiritual people, when they met him, cried out: "I've met another Abba Isaac the Syrian."

He did not simply read Abba Isaac but, as he advised others, whatever he found in his words he strove to apply himself. Saint Isaac was his mirror. And he struggled continuously, his whole life long, to cleanse himself ever more completely, to purify himself even from the subtlest of thoughts, to pursue the illumination from above.

But from the other patristic texts which he read besides, like an industrious honey-bee he gathered whatever he found that was profitable and took care to stamp it upon his life. His speech was always sprinkled with references to such patristic texts. And whatever he considered most remarkable he had the habit of transcribing. There are many of his manuscripts with transcriptions of texts from Abba Isaac, Saint Symeon the New Theologian, and so forth. We offer a small text out of those which he copied, which also shows his own disposition for continual and unrelenting struggles.

"Run, therefore, brethren, run, in order to reach the Desired One. Make haste, make haste, lest the prey get out of your hands. Contend, contend, that others might not take your crown. Small is the labor, but great the repose. Temporary be the afflictions, but the good things that ye inherit are everlasting. Bitter is the cup of martyrdom, but sweet is the enjoyment of the Lord Jesus. A most profitable commerce is this, Beloved; ye give a corruptible body and ye receive it back incorruptible…"

The Athonite Monastery of Dionysiou, by Pol. Regos, 1934.

CHAPTER TWELVE
To the Mountain that is Holy

EVERY YEAR, without exception, from the time that he came to Greece, he made a pilgrimage to the Holy Mountain, and unfailingly saw his father-confessor, Archimandrite Ieronymos, at the Monastery of Simonopetra. Afterwards he would visit other monasteries to venerate the holy relics and to exchange spiritual experiences with the Fathers of the Holy Mountain.

Father Ieronymos was greatly profited by these visits, even as he also profited many. He often told us with nostalgia about his meetings with ascetics and hermits and the spiritual benefits he derived therefrom. He always spoke of the Holy Mountain with admiration. When he wished to relate examples of holy fathers, to show their great piety and their ascetical mind, he often made reference to the Holy Mountain and its ascetics. To emphasize the magnitude of the value of the priesthood, and the great responsibility thereof, he told of a certain hagiorite monk who, wishing to avoid becoming a priest because of his great reverence, cut off his nose and ears. Another time, desiring to make plain the grandeur of humility, he related concerning a certain bishop (perhaps he had Saint Niphon, Patriarch of Constantinople, in mind) who went to the Holy Mountain to become a monk, without revealing to anyone that he was a bishop. They assigned him the most menial jobs, and he not only tolerated everything, but even rejoiced inwardly, because he had put on the garment of our Christ, holy humility. And it was necessary for God to reveal in a wondrous manner that he was a bishop, perhaps for the edification of the monks; otherwise he would have passed his whole life without notice in obscurity and would have died as a simple monk.

Father Ieronymos considered the Holy Mountain to be a place where Saints lived in reality, an ark of Orthodoxy.

Once while in Karyes, the capital, he heard a monk shouting and using abusive language. He made frequent references to the Patriarch. He said that he was going to punish him, he was going to beat him up, and other incoherent talk. All this made the bystanders laugh at his expense and derisively shake their heads. Everyone thought him to be demented and laughed at him or just ignored him. Father Ieronymos, with the spiritual discernment that he had, saw certain signs in his speech that did not indicate an insane person. At a certain moment he called him privately and asked him, "Tell me, why do you say these things?"

"By golly, is he a patriarch? I'll fix him, I'm going to punish him..."

"Listen, I am a spiritual father and you don't fool me. Tell me the truth. Why do you act this way?"

"I'll tell you, Father. I am a sinful and weak man and am afraid of the praise of men, that pride not overtake me. In this way I humble myself and pretend to be crazy so that men will despise me. Maybe God will take pity on me and save me. I have not said this to anyone and I entreat you, at least while I am still alive, not to reveal this yourself."

And saying this he went away cursing and threatening the Patriarch and the rulers. Father Ieronymos glorified God that He had revealed to him a man with the rare gift and the power to disregard the glory of men and continually humble himself, that God might take pity on him and save him.

This monk was evidently one of those few who have appeared in the ecclesiastical realm and have broken with the world's way of thinking. Preferring the "foolishness of God," they do not conform to the acceptable forms of Christian behavior but become rather a "spectacle to the world." In essence their presence is a mocking of the world. Although they feign foolishness, their life is full of miracles and teachings with cryptic allusions which, for as many as have spiritual sense, help them to return to the right Christian way of life or strengthen and help them in their faith.

On another occasion, while he was walking from one monastery to another, he met a hermit in the way. "Bless, Elder. How are you?"

"The Lord bless you. What can we do, my Father? We struggle. I entreat you, please pray for us, because here on the Holy Mountain the devil mightily wars against us."

"But does he only war against you? Does he not go about in the world also?"

"In the world he has his representatives—women—which war against men, whereas here on the Holy Mountain, where women don't come, the devil doesn't stop even for a moment to war against us."

"No, Elder, I don't agree" the discerning Father Ieronymos answered him. "Women may be more easily susceptible to evil, but surely they are not representatives of the devil, they are images of God. I think your characterization is extreme."

The ascetic agreed with him. He justified himself by explaining that what he said was an exaggeration, on account of the war which the monks receive from the devil, not that he really believed it. It was simply a figure of speech which oftentimes the hagiorites use with a dose of humor. They exchanged the kiss in Christ and each went his way.

With such experiences was his life filled on the Holy Mountain. On his visits there, he profited some and was profited by others, but he always left rejuvenated spiritually. And certain thoughts he had of permanently settling there continually gained ground.

CHAPTER THIRTEEN
Experiences of a God-seer

O N AEGINA his fame had spread. Everyone spoke of him with admiration and love, considering him their own man. There began to gather around him a goodly number of young men and women, many of whom, being inspired by his way of life, began to manifest the proclivity for a total dedication to God, to be drawn to the monastic life. Many young girls implored him to start his own convent so that they could become nuns there. But Father Ieronymos always acted with prudence. He did not permit himself to be swayed by these urgings of the young. He prayed intensely that God reveal to him His will; yet he had an exceedingly great love for stillness and the monastic life, and he endeavored to make them feel this also.

Many times when young people gathered around him, he took them and they all went together to some field chapel[1] for Vespers and "compunctionate" prayer. These spiritual gatherings have remained unforgettable for those who had the special blessing to at-

---

1. Ἐξωκκλήσι in Greek. From two words *Exo* (*outside – without*) and *Ekklesia* (*church*). A small church or chapel outside of cities and villages, usually in the fields or on the hilltops and mountaintops, built by the pious throughout the centuries because of vows or a benefaction rendered by the Saints to whom they are dedicated. There are literally some thousands of such chapels dotting the landscapes of mainland Greece and the islands. They are usually celebrated on their feast day or whenever one wishes to honor or beseech a certain Saint for a favor. It is said that there are some 365 such chapels on Aegina.—TRANS.

Fresco of the Transfiguration in the eleventh-century Karanlik Kilisse.

tend them. Even though forty or fifty years have passed since then, they still remember them with nostalgia and compunction.

Behold how one of those fortunate souls describes the experience of one of these blessed gatherings. "We gathered early in the evening—about ten young people—and started out with the Elder to go to one of the field chapels, about a half hour by foot from the hermitage. The Elder was very cheerful and during the whole trip he chanted or counselled us. When we arrived, he entered the sanctuary and we cleaned the church and lit the icon lamps. Immediately afterwards we had Vespers, during which Father Ieronymos chanted with his melodious and compunctionate voice. Then he began to teach us compunctionate prayer.

"For one or two hours he prayed before us with tears, sobs, and sighs that cannot be uttered, evoking contrition in the hearts of us all. When he had finished we came out of the church, and he went into the sanctuary. We then started a conversation among us about the spiritual experiences that we had had in the presence of this blessed man and we waited for him to come out so that we could depart.

"That epoch was different from today, and the young people had to be home before it got dark. Four or five hours passed, it began to grow dark, and the Elder was nowhere to be seen. We began to worry, because if we were late our families would not permit us to go with him again. I then decided to go as far as the sanctuary, I opened the door carefully, and the sight that I beheld shook me. Father Ieronymos was on his knees with hands uplifted and his gaze set on high. Tears ran from his eyes, while his face was radiant with an unusual light. I immediately went out and related to the others that Tabor-like spectacle I had just seen. We all found ourselves in a dilemma. We did not want to disturb him in this divine state he was in, but we had to return home early, so that our parents would permit us again to make these sacred little excursions. We finally decided to speak to him. I went to the sanctuary again, very slowly opened the door, and touched him lightly on the shoulder. 'Elder, we have to go.'

"The Elder started a little, as if he were coming to himself from a dream, and answered. 'Oh! Yes, let's go.'

"Shortly he came out without saying a word, and all together we took to the road to return. One can easily understand the spiritual exaltation that we all felt after those celestial hours which we were deemed worthy to live at his side."

These sacred little excursions took place regularly. And what wouldn't the chapels of Aegina at Palea Chora, at Levadi, close to the Convent of Saint Menas, and so on, have to say concerning the prayers of Father Ieronymos! He also, as it would seem, was bound to these chapels and was nostalgic for them till the end of his life. I remember when, on the first day that he entered the hospital Alexandra, one month before he went to his rest, he asked me, "Does the hospital have a church?"

Wherever he was, his mind was on churches.

"Yes, Elder, and a very beautiful one at that."

"Why, do you know of any church that isn't beautiful? I feel the same in whatsoever church I find myself. Even should I go to a little field chapel, and even if it has only one icon, that's enough. God is present everywhere, and not only in large and imposing churches."

Evidently his mind ran to the numerous little chapels of Aegina and to the heavenly moments that he had experienced there.

His spiritual children besought him continually to go regularly on excursions to field chapels to have Vespers. And what didn't they devise in order to steal a little time, so that they could stay a little longer with him during these sacred and mystical meetings!

As one of those blessed souls who were deemed worthy to live these spiritual experiences with him relates, the girls would scheme among themselves to turn back the clock two or three hours before they left the house, because they promised their parents that they would return home early. People back then were simple and did not catch on to these tricks, and so the girls when they returned home would turn the clocks forward again. In this way they managed to prolong their stay with him for a few hours and so enjoy more of their divine devotion to prayer.

These were the unique occasions that Father Ieronymos allowed little white lies. Whereas he was always austere and counselled, "Do not tell lies, not even for a joke," when there was an occasion for spiritual profit he yielded somewhat. "Endeavor by all means to steal some time, so you can offer it to spiritual pursuits," he was wont to say. And to a certain soul who was not permitted by her spiritual father to read ascetical books, he once said:

"To all the sins you have, add one more. Buy Abba Isaac and read him every day. Maybe your spiritual father does not know, maybe he is against it. We don't know; do not judge. In any event, read Abba Isaac. You will profit much from it."

Wherever Father Ieronymos was found, whatever he was occupied with, he never abandoned prayer. Prayer was his main work and his delight. Everything else was secondary. And he was very industrious all his life and skilled in many trades. He knew how to build, he was a perfect carpenter, clockmaker, and so forth. He was never idle. Into his deep old age we remember him at his bench with his tools, tinkering with some clock he was repairing. But his mind was never bound by such things. His main concern was always prayer. He occupied himself with different employments in order to "bring under subjection" (I Cor. 9:27) his body, but simultaneously he prayed noetically to God. His mind was continuously cleaving to Heaven. There he found rest and rejoicing.

Once while he was walking in Piraeus, he saw two nuns on the opposite sidewalk. He called them and said, "How are you, Sisters? How do you fare? Is your mind in God? *Aman!* be attentive, your mind should always be in God. Do not become attached to transient things."

He gave the same counsel to everyone who visited him. The guarding of the mind was his continuous struggle and anxiety; prayer was the fitting means for this, and it was also his beloved occupation. Many times, as in a parable according to his custom, following the Apostle Paul's "I knew a man fourteen years ago," he related that he knew a man who "for fourteen hours prayed continuously and wept out of compunction." And again on another occasion, he said "There are people who, if a little time passes and they do not pray, they suffer, they can't endure it." There is no doubt that all this referred to himself, to his personal divine experiences. But out of exceeding humility he spoke of them as the doings and experiences of others.

CHAPTER FOURTEEN

Spiritual Solicitude

His spiritual children, who multiplied as time went on, began to entreat him to found their own convent for them in which to live the monastic life. They wanted him close to them as their elder and could not resolve to enter any other convent. Father Ieronymos, although he had planned to go to the Holy Mountain to pursue the monastic life, began to consider it seriously and prayed to God to reveal to him His holy will. But soon he changed his mind. He considered that a convent would entail many cares and concerns that would necessarily draw his mind away from prayer. And this for Father Ieronymos was an unbearable burden. Thus the thought of building a convent was abandoned. But he wished before leaving for the Holy Mountain to make arrangements for his spiritual children, and to this purpose they all made various trips together in the form of pilgrimages to many convents. He wanted to see the spiritual environment and then to recommend to them where to go to be nuns.

One of these convents which he liked and with which he formed a bond, was the Convent of the Life-giving Spring on the island of Andros. He went several times, either with others or by himself, and had many spiritual conversations with the Abbot, Father Panaretos. Among other things, he spoke to him about his purpose, that is, of sending his spiritual children to the convent and to remain there himself for a period of time, until they got accustomed to the environment and their new elder.

Father Panaretos, being a very spiritual person, understood the worth and holiness of Father Ieronymos, and became bound to him with a deep spiritual love. But he had certain reservations to what extent he should accept his proposal, which he expressed in the following letter. One is impressed as much by his humility as by his wonder and reverence for Father Ieronymos.

> The Sacred Convent of the Life-giving Spring,
> Mpatsi-Andros, September 4, 1938.

My beloved Brother in Christ and fellow celebrant in the Lord, Most Righteous holy Archimandrite Kyr Ieronymos, with all your brethren and children in Christ, rejoice in the Lord Jesus our common Saviour and God always and in all things. Amen.

Most sacred man!

By the grace and help of our Great Lady and Sovereign Mistress the Theotokos and Ever-virgin Mary, and by your holy prayers, we are all well, for which we the unworthy also pray for you daily.

My beloved Brother in Christ and Honorable Father Ieronymos, I have received both of your precious letters to me with much esteem, love, and thanksgiving. I gave thanks to our Lord Jesus Christ, Who keeps you and your children in Christ in health, and I reverently beg forgiveness for such great slowness in making answer to your brotherly letters to me. The cause is my inadequacy and it is not out of disdain, my Brother!

I greatly thank you, honorable Father, for your holy prayers and blessings, and for your so many truly Christian expressions of love for us the lowly, backward, and perfect strangers to the monastic way of life. But yet we, the worthless and unprofitable servants of our Lord Jesus Christ, hope in the infinite gulf of the mercy and love for man of Him Who has called us (on account of His goodness) to the lot of those who are sanctified through the intercessions of the Theotokos and Ever-virgin Mary and all His Saints, and also through your holy prayers, to have mercy on us in the universal day of the impartial judgment, for the sake of the glory of His Name. Amen.

We, on our part, pray heartily that with your spiritual children you will stand before the Tribunal of Christ all resplendent with the glory of Christ and equal in rank with the Saints. Amen. Amen. Amen.

Concerning the matter of which you have often spoken to me and of which you write, how and what can I answer, my Brother one in soul with me? You ask of me a thing that is unfortunately (in my estimation) very difficult, honorable Father. As it would seem, you reckon the thing with much naïveté and simplicity, without foreseeing what may later happen, to the very great harm of both you and us.

Your purpose is holy and blameless, without ulterior motive or self-interest—by no means, in very truth—this I know well and I testify to it before God and men, my Brother and honorable Father!

But experience has taught me that two rational flocks, consolidated into one while having two shepherds on an equal footing of rank and honor, can hardly succeed.

It is foreseeable that following this, sooner or later, some personal faction will arise—it could even happen right from the very beginning. What then? Should we keep silence, pretending ignorance? You happen to be a rational man with sufficient education, and are a very good and virtuous celebrant of Christ and a Spiritual Father; not only this, but you also have manifold kinds of knowledge, and Christian virtues, and skills useful to all.

But I (all to the contrary) happen to be naked of all virtue and Christian works and knowledge, totally incapable of every divine and human work. And not only this, but (woe to me, wretch that I am) while being filled with all evil and cunning, and burdened with crimes and great sins and the failings of the elderly, I manage (by the forbearance of Divine Justice) to hide beneath the veil of hypocrisy by supposedly being a worker of the mystical vineyard of Christ, and thus I convince the naïve and simple to reverence me as though I were a fervent servant of Christ (whereas I am a worthless sinner under heavy sentence).

This is not just humble talk, but I am making my confession, writing the above in truth, beseeching of God and of you the forgiveness of my manifold sins, miserable as I am.

How then is it possible that we collaborate? You being light, but I darkness! You being a faithful servant of Christ, but I of sin and hypocrisy! You verily being a worker of the mystical vineyard of Christ, but I, the miserable one, a worker feigned and false! You being a warrior and brave soldier of Christ, but I a coward and deserter! Yea, verily, my Brother and spiritual Father, this is how things are in very truth, such that we cannot work together, because from the start personal factions will be formed. And some, seeing rightly, will quite quickly discern the differences between us and will begin to express respect and reverence towards you, with spiritual love.

But the more simple and naïve, on the other hand, will ostentatiously begin to display towards me (the most worthless) their love and reverence, speaking out, assuredly, against your reverence and against the other sisters who will have expressed their reverence and respect and love towards you! Thus, while those who rightly see and discern the worthy shepherd will be called Ieronymites, those who do not discern aright—but rather blindly and without discretion fanatically respect and love me, who am but useless and sinful—will also be called by my name (which for me is just an empty name)[1]—that is, of Panaretos, or Panarites! From the start, they will begin by secretly confiding in one another, each one revealing her own thoughts and opinions, simply conversing among them about the gifts of each of us, their two spiritual fathers, until they come to disagree concerning our virtues. Then that evil-devising devil will find them divided and will thus contrive to sow in their hearts jealousy, bickering, secret gatherings, and the like.

As for me, your presence will assuredly be saving and profitable in manifold ways; but as you know, I am not alone, but have with me people of many different temperaments, who are not able as yet to put off the mind of their foremother Eve—even as I unfortunately also have not put off Adam's.

Therefore you will bitterly regret it, when new temptations, perhaps under another guise, unfailingly begin to appear—and not you only, but the people with you will also regret it: and then what shall we do?

Wherefore, that I might avoid being in any way misunderstood by your reverence, I counsel you with brotherly love to prefer rather to abide in peace and tranquillity in your own hermitage with your daughters in Christ, unto greater progress and profit for many souls. May the grace and blessing of the grace-streaming Life-giving Spring be with all of you now and always, Amen.

1. *Panaretos* in Greek means "all (or every) virtue."—TRANS.

These things I now write, asking your holy prayers and blessings for me, with the sisters that are with me.

✟ Archimandrite Panaretos, Your brother in Christ.

Father Ieronymos of course had no intention of remaining at the Convent of the Life-giving Spring; he only wished to make arrangements for settling his spiritual children, in order to leave after that for Mount Athos. But since he was very sensitive and discreet, after the letter he received, he did not pursue it any further. He preferred to wait a while, until God should show him His will.

The Elder Ieronymos with Father Cosmas (seated) and an unidentified priest.

Fresco in the tenth-century Tokali Kilisse (Buckle Church) in the Göreme Valley in Cappadocia. One of the earliest known icons of the type called "Sweet-kissing."

CHAPTER FIFTEEN
No Man on Earth Loves Me Like Father Ieronymos

During this interval he had, by his own efforts and endeavors, helped the Eldress Eupraxia to build a small hermitage to the northeast, about a kilometer from the hospital of Aegina.

The Eldress had long stayed as a guest in the homes of his acquaintances, until she might find some convent to enter; this hindered her from performing her monastic rule and prayer. The everloving Father Ieronymos, who always thought of everything and took care for everything, found this place that was appropriate for stillness and saw to it first that there be built two small cells, and later, a little chapel dedicated to the Annunciation of the Theotokos, for whom Father Ieronymos had a very great reverence and love. Here, outside the chapel and next to the cells, he installed a small workbench with various tools and used it as a workshop. Often, when there was some time left over from his spiritual ministry, he went to the hermitage to see Mother Eupraxia and give her guidance. After that, he occupied himself with various projects; he would repair clocks, lighters, and other objects which he later gave as gifts to monasteries and acquaintances. He always kept himself occupied. And, as with spiritual things, so also with the material, he did everything to perfection.

At one point the Eldress Eupraxia—when she perceived that Father Ieronymos had changed his mind and did not intend to start a convent—decided to go to Drama in Macedonia, to her relatives, and afterwards to find some convent where she could live as a nun. She had begun her monastic life in her youth in the Convent of Theoskepaste in Pontus of Asia Minor. Many nuns led the monastic life there, and now she longed once again to be found in a monastic environment, and live amidst nuns. Solitary life had wearied her.

She confessed all her longings and dreams, nurtured from her youth, to the Elder. She also revealed to him her thought to go visit her relatives in Drama, with the further purpose of finding some convent there close by where she could live as a nun. He heard her out without speaking, and wished her that with the help of God she might fulfill her desire.

After she had taken the Elder's blessing, she departed from Aegina for Piraeus and thence by boat to Thessalonica, in order to continue her journey to Drama. In the lengthy trip from Piraeus to Thessalonica, on board the ship she felt a great heaviness in her soul. She had suffered many hardships in her life. Journeys by foot, persecutions, expulsions, displacement from her homeland, poverty—all this had exhausted her. And now again she was marching off to the unknown with no certain destination. She was further tormented because when close to the Elder Ieronymos her soul had found rest. She considered him a loving and caring spiritual father and her guardian, and now that she had departed, she began to feel his absence intensely. Her thoughts were violently wrestling within her. On one hand, she wanted to be close to her spiritual father, that unerring, inspired, and illumined guide; but on the other, she was scourged with desire to be found in a monastic environment, to live in the midst of nuns and to attend the divine services with them. What was she to do?

There, in a corner of the deck, she bowed her head on her knees and dissolved in tears. She prayed intensely, imploring God and the Panagia to enlighten her what to do. Should she continue her voyage or return to Aegina? Many hours passed thus, with prayer and tears. At a certain moment, overcome as she was by the tension and her prayer, in a state which even she herself was not able to discern whether it were waking or in ecstasy, she saw that she found herself before the icon of the Panagia Quick to Hear and was entreating her to help her in this difficult moment. And suddenly she heard a voice coming forth from the icon:

> NO MAN ON EARTH LOVES ME
> LIKE FATHER IERONYMOS.

She jumped straight up, the words she had heard still echoing in her ears. Her soul calmed down, all her thoughts vanished. A deep tranquillity spread throughout her. That whole violent sea of thoughts which a short while before seized her soul had now become serene. It was as if she had received the answer she yearned for with such anguish. She bent down again, she put her head on her knees and dissolved again in tears; but they were tears of joy. How much consolation these tears now brought her! A few more hours passed like this, in this same position, with a prayer of doxology and thanksgiving. Upon reaching Thessalonica, she took the next boat for Piraeus.

When she arrived at Aegina, she found Father Ieronymos in his workshop occupied with various repairs. Endowed with discretion herself, she did not wish to reveal the vision, lest she harm him spiritually, fearing lest the demon of pride should trouble him. Nonetheless she approached him, and there as he was bent over at the workbench she said to him, "Really, Elder, you love our Panagia very much, don't you?"

He didn't answer; he only smiled enigmatically and meaningfully. Evidently he knew everything, but as always did not want to speak about himself.

"Once," Mother Eupraxia related, "I was about to travel to Drama; I was going to see my family. I had to pass a night in Athens and the Elder said to me, 'Go to such-and-such a church to receive Communion and then take your trip.'

"'Elder, may I go to this convent, where the nuns know me?'

"'No. Go to the church I told you.'

"I departed having decided to do as the Elder told me. But when I reached Piraeus, I thought, 'Wouldn't it be better to go to the convent where it will be more quiet and the services are read more carefully?' And without its even crossing my mind that what I was doing was a disobedience, I went to the convent. But things did not turn out as well as I expected. The nuns were very busy and gave me no attention whatsoever. I went the whole day on one cup of coffee. In the evening a family came whose daughter had left to become a nun and they made a commotion, yelling and threatening. They turned the world upside down. Suspecting that she had come to this convent, they rounded up all the nuns and took them to the police station for an investigation. I was frightened and left. I had a thought to go to an acquaintance who lived at Korydallo, a district of Piraeus, but alas I didn't find her there. I became very troubled and didn't know what to do. In the end, a certain woman from Pontus, seeing me in such a state of distress and so upset, took pity on me and invited me to her home. 'Have you eaten?' she asked me. And I, because of my disturbed state and my embarrassment, answered, 'Yes.' Thus I went to bed hungry. Then I understood that all that befell me was because of my disobedience. The Elder never made any remark without a reason, superfluously. Because he foresaw everything, he told me not to go to the convent. Whenever I disobeyed him, even in the smallest and most insignificant things, everything went bad for me. For this reason I decided never to disobey him again, not even in the least of his commands."

CHAPTER SIXTEEN
Example of Humblemindedness

FATHER IERONYMOS decided to remain a while longer in Aegina. Before he left, he wished to provide a spiritual roof for his spiritual children. So he continued to offer his services at the hospital in Aegina, as always, benefiting all his fellow men, both spiritually and materially. Everyone on Aegina, without exception, loved him and reverenced him exceedingly. It is rare for any to enjoy such honor and esteem from all men, and especially from those that live near him, those of his "own household." But Father Ieronymos accomplished this without even pursuing it. His holiness acted as a magnet. Whomever one might ask on Aegina concerning Father Ieronymos, they spoke of him in the best terms. Many related to us that when they visited him for the first time and asked the neighbors where the hermitage of Father Ieronymos was, they would receive the answer, "Ah, you want our holy archimandrite? There, a little further up is his hermitage. Go, he's a holy man, may his prayers be with us."

Many times when we were travelling to Aegina and expressed to some fellow traveller on the boat the reason for our trip, we heard from nearly everybody marvellous stories about the life of Father Ieronymos and personal experiences and benefactions they had received from him. One would say that Father Ieronymos had saved his family from certain destruction and led it to the Church; another, that he had healed his hand or his foot; a third would relate that he had stood by him in some difficult moment and saved him from the very gates of suicide; and generally all had something marvellous and astonishing to say of him.

He also regularly visited the various convents of Aegina. Everywhere he was beloved and all the nuns sought counsel from him in every difficult circumstance or about the spiritual concerns preoccupying them at the moment. He had a special reverence for the newly revealed Saint Nectarius and often went to venerate his holy relics. The nuns of the Saint's convent loved him greatly and always welcomed him with joy. In his person they beheld one who continued the work of their Saint and they had recourse to him to find solutions to problems in the convent.

I remember being very impressed when, on one of my visits to the convent of Saint Nectarius in the year 1967 (about one year after Father Ieronymos's repose), I heard the then abbess, Eldress Theodosia, say to me, "Father Ieronymos and our Saint changed the life of the island towards a more spiritual direction."

The Eldress Theodosia had known Saint Nectarius and had been his disciple; and it is a well known fact that all spiritual children have a special weakness for their elder—even more so when he is a Saint recognized by the Church. Often this weakness can influence his disciples to be partial to him, their own elder, and to disfavor others. Therefore this testimony of the Eldress Theodosia, which put the two (Saint Nectarius and Father Ieronymos) in the same rank of holiness and spiritual service, has special weight.

He also went rather frequently to the Convent of the Most Holy Mother of God Chrysoleontissa, where he had once served for a time as Abbot when it was a men's monastery. He often stayed there for a number of days and with his brother John taught the nuns how to make tiles and bricks. The nuns marvelled at Father Ieronymos's endurance. He worked hard all day long, and in the evenings, notwithstanding the labor and weariness, he spent many hours with them praying, and also chanted or spoke to them concerning the monastic life and prayer.

While all loved him and especially honored him, he remained simple and humble. He would never gainsay, never became angry, he never insulted or grieved anyone, nor did he criticize or judge anyone. If someone insulted him and acted badly towards him or berated him, he would endure it without answering. The higher he attained to the heights of sanctity, the more he felt himself a sinner and worse than all. He accepted all things with patience. The only thing that he could not endure was separation from Christ.

"I could wish to be a worm, that all might trample me underfoot, only—*aman!*—that I might not lose my Christ," he would say.

Once he was travelling to Piraeus on a ship named *The Enchantress*. As usual he sat somewhere off to the side and prayed. Suddenly he was approached by the captain who said to him, "Priest, get up from here and sit further on."

Father Ieronymos humbly and obediently conformed to his command. But shortly afterward the captain ordered him to change his place again. The same thing was repeated a third time. The captain's attitude was very provocative. The other passengers were indignant and made a remark to him about why he had behaved in such a manner to a venerable elder, who after all had paid his ticket. And the captain answered, "My mother told me that whenever I see refugees I should throw them into the sea."

Father Ieronymos was grieved when he heard this, but said nothing. He only decided never to travel on this ship again, in order to avoid temptation. But he prayed fervently for the captain and implored God to enlighten him. On another occasion, however, he had to travel to Piraeus and there was no other ship except *The Enchantress*. He said his prayers, boarded the ship, and sat in some corner. He hoped that the captain would not see him, so that he could avoid the pointless temptation. But eventually the captain passed by and saw him and approached him.

"Do you have a ticket?" he asked.

"Yes, I do."

"Give it to me and I'll return it."

He took the ticket and returned to him the amount that he had paid, saying, "My mother scolded me and told me never to take money from you again. From now on, come aboard whenever you want and travel for free." The humility and prayer of Father Ieronymos—and possibly some vision that his mother had seen—had subdued the proud captain.

On another occasion he was coming down one of the well-known narrow lanes to Aegina. It was the Feast of Saint Nicholas, and after the Divine Liturgy he was going into town for his accustomed ministry and in order to greet certain of his acquaintances who were celebrating their nameday. Passing by outside of a store he saw the proprietor, whose son celebrated for Saint Nicholas. He stopped a moment and greeted him, "Good morning! Many years! May Saint Nicholas be with us, and may you rejoice in your son."

The shopkeeper, for some unknown reason, instead of rejoicing at his blessings, answered with rudeness and in an exceedingly insulting way, "Get out of here, Priest, as fast as you can. That's right! Get going—bravo!—before I make some nasty remark to you."

Father Ieronymos went away in sorrow, not so much for the insult, but because he did not wish to grieve any man. Even if he was not at fault in the least, he felt obliged to comfort his fellow man. No one ever left him saddened; he always found a way to comfort and relieve whomever he saw in affliction. And in this instance he felt that he had to redress matters. Another in his place would likely have been angry, or at least would have avoided speaking with the offender again, or would await his apologies. But egotism had no place in Father Ieronymos's heart. For the meek and humble disciple of Jesus, that which was important was that the lost sheep be saved. As always, he left the matter to Christ, his Lord. He prayed all day and night and on the morrow he took the same path again. As soon as he came near the shop of his reviler, he saw him sweeping his courtyard. He approached him and with a great deal of sweetness and humility said to him, "Forgive me, my brother, if in any way I have grieved you. But won't you allow me even to bid you Good Morning?"

The shopkeeper was dumbstruck; he would never have expected such kindness and humility. He ran and fell on his bosom saying, "Forgive me, Elder. I don't know what satan put me up to speaking to you like that. I have repented over it bitterly and ask your forgiveness."

His prayer and humility had worked a miracle. In such a manner did Father Ieronymos conduct himself; he made use of all things, becoming "all things to all men," that he might gain men and guide them to repentance. This explains the fact that almost everybody on Aegina reverenced him as a Saint and loved him exceedingly.

Rock-cut cells and chapels of Tokali Kilisse in the Göreme Valley in Cappadocia.

CHAPTER SEVENTEEN

Lover of Tradition

THE REGION OF ANATOLIA, Cappadocia in Asia Minor, where he lived his childhood years, where he came to know the first spiritual stirrings, where he tasted the springing waters of Orthodoxy from the holy elders who lived there, and where he matured spiritually, remained unforgettable for him. He frequently referred to his homeland and waxed nostalgic for all the things he had experienced there. He never forgot the solitary chapels in the rocks, where one could go and pray in utter stillness, nor those simple people, those first-rate artisans, who, whatever they put their hand to, did it perfectly, with ardor, and with good taste.

Being a great lover of the life of stillness and prayer, he often recollected the beautiful days full of spiritual ascents and exaltations that he had passed in the chapels and abandoned monasteries of his homeland.

"Here in Greece you cannot find a quiet place to pray," he was wont to say. "In Anatolia there were many places where you could pass the whole day in prayer, without anybody seeing you."

This insatiable and never-silent desire for quietude and prayer, for undisturbed communion with God, never abandoned him. He never lost an opportunity to draw apart and give himself to prayer. Usually, even when he was speaking to his visitors, he would stop for a little and say, "Now let's chant something."

And he would begin with his imposing, deeply resounding, and melodious voice to chant "Let us worship the Word..." or "It is truly meet..." or some other hymn. These intermissions of prayer were indispensable for him, they were his life-breath, his spiritual supply-line. And at the same time, it was an excellent example for those who conversed with him, that they might form the habit of conjoining their every occupation with prayer.

He lived the essence of Orthodoxy, tradition, in all its breadth. Without rejecting any of the attainments of technological society, he had a special weakness, a passion we might say, for whatever was olden, ancient—from material things to the spiritual. He liked the ancient order of the services, the old books, antiques, because he believed that they carried the seal of their maker, they had been constructed with fondness and were not machine-made and in bad taste.

With such convictions and perceptions, having always lived his life within but also "outside this world," within the strict province of tradition, he felt a certain uneasiness from the time that the ecclesiastical Calendar was changed and the new was enforced. These anxieties of his increased as the years went by and he beheld many Orthodox customs changed. He did not like the abridgement of the church services, the secularization of the clergy, the abandonment of the Orthodox way of life. And although he always attended to the essence and not the dry outward form, he believed that these alterations in traditional usages and forms in and of themselves betrayed a certain indifference and slackness towards the Faith: that this was the beginning of a downhill slide whose end was unknown. For this reason, he often thought of following the Old Calendar, especially since he saw that the Old Calendarists faithfully followed tradition and would not tolerate innovations and transgressions in matters pertaining to the Faith. For some time he hesitated, and prayed continually and fervently to God, that He might reveal to him His will. He awaited some sign, some indication from God, that would make it clear to him what he should do.

In August of 1942, specifically on the 23rd of the month,[1] the eve of the feast of Saint Dionysius of Aegina, when the hospital church celebrated, Procopios, the then Metropolitan of Hydra, Spetsai, and Aegina, called him and told him to get ready so that on the morrow, on the occasion of the church's festival, they might concelebrate. Many priests of Aegina, who knew that Father Ieronymos was sympathetic to the Old Calendar, but were ignorant of the vision he had seen, were under the impression that he had stopped liturgizing at the hospital church on account of his Old-Calendarist sympathies. They reported this to the Metropolitan, and he, in order to ascertain the accusation, requested that they concelebrate.[2]

Men of God perceive the finger of Divine Providence behind every action and occurrence. Father Ieronymos, who had stopped liturgizing some eighteen years before, considered this invitation from the Metropolitan to be God's answer to his prayers. He prayed again all night long and finally decided not to go and concelebrate with the Metropolitan, but to follow the Old Calendar openly thereafter. He departed on the morrow from the hospital very early in the morning for the hermitage of the Annunciation of the Theotokos, where the Eldress Eupraxia was already staying.

---

1. That is, according to the New or civil Calendar; it was the tenth of August according to the Church (Old) Calendar. Since the feast of Saint Dionysius is August 24, the Elder Ieronymos was being asked to celebrate Saint Dionysius' feast according to the New Calendar.—TRANS.

2. The truth of the matter is that Father Ieronymos, like his contemporary the holy Papa Nicholas Planas of Athens (✠1932), quietly celebrated many of the feasts without liturgizing according to the Old Calendar. That he never liturgized or concelebrated according to the Papal Calendar since he had desisted from serving before the change of the calendar in 1924 was very convenient for him and somewhat eased his conscience.—TRANS.

From there he sent the Metropolitan the following notification of resignation from the hospital church.

> To the Most Reverend Metropolitan of Hydra
> Kyr Kyr Procopios
> Aegina
> Your Eminence,
>
> I beseech you to accept my resignation from the hospital, because since 1924 and henceforward, my yearning and also my zeal have been for the Orthodox Church and the Faith.
>
> Since my childhood I have reverenced her, having dedicated my whole life to her, being obedient to the traditions of the God-bearing Fathers.
>
> I acknowledge and proclaim the Patristic Calendar to be the correct one, as you also attest.[3]
>
> For this reason I request of you, that you yourself also pray that I abide till the end a genuine child of the Orthodox Church.
>
> Kissing your Eminence's right hand,
I most humbly remain
The servant of our Crucified Lord Jesus Christ,
Ieronymos Apostolides

Thus simply and quietly, without the beating of drums, excommunications, and fanatical manifestations, he followed the Old Calendar the rest of his life.

This event did not in any way influence his behavior towards his spiritual children. He received them all without distinction, whether they followed "the Old" or "the New." He never preached on the calendar issue. His foremost and principal aim was to instill into his visitors faith and love towards Christ; his chief care was how they progressed in the spiritual life, how they were united to God.

---

3. Many, if not the majority, of the bishops and other clergy of the State Church of Greece at the time privately acknowledged that the Julian Calendar used by the Church since the days of our Saviour was the correct calendar for reckoning the feasts as opposed to the innovating Papal New Calendar; but for fear of reprisals, they would not proclaim this publicly.—TRANS.

He never took part in fruitless and harmful conversations concerning the calendar issue, even when he was challenged to do so. He contented himself with simply confessing that he followed the Old Calendar since "that's the right one," and that from the time the Church put the New Calendar into practice "things just have not been going well at all." He never permitted immoderate and harmful fanaticism to prevail in his soul. On the contrary, he always strove to calm spirits. Once a visitor asked him, "Elder, do you follow the Old?"

"Yes."

"Who are you with?" She meant, with which faction.

"With all."

"But they have quarrels with one another."

"I am not with quarrels."

He was very discerning and refined in his ways. Even when he went so far as to censure, he did it with the utmost love, and not only did he not cause adverse reactions, but on the contrary he elicited confession and repentance, which was his intended purpose.

CHAPTER EIGHTEEN
In Mine Affliction Thou Hast Enlarged Me[1]

THE LIVES OF THE SAINTS are full of trials and temptations. No one ever ascended to Heaven with ease. All struggled and were tried "as gold in the furnace." In a certain way, these temptations serve as a kind of examination, by which the faith and devotion of those tempted is distinguished. "Take away temptations, and no one will be saved," says the distilled patristic wisdom. And wise Sirach informs us "My son, if thou come to serve the Lord, prepare thy soul for temptation" (Ecclus. 2:1). When a man is unprepared and does not take this warning into account, he will quickly be discouraged and succumb under the weight of the trials and adversities that unavoidably accompany him.

Many times in his life Father Ieronymos received the visitation of divine Providence in the midst of temptations and sorrows. And what suffering hadn't assailed this "afflicted and hapless bird" of Anatolia, as he often referred to himself: persecutions, slanders, dangers, expulsions, etc.; all of which he endured with great and exemplary fortitude, with absolute trust in divine Providence and continual doxology to God. In his greatest trials, not only did he not buckle, but on the contrary at such times he gave himself even more up to prayer, with thanksgiving and doxology.

But behold how, when he had already passed sixty, and was

---

1. Psalm 4:1.—TRANS.

found at the threshold of old age, a new and serious trial awaited him.

Father Ieronymos, as we said above, knew a goodly number of home remedies, by which he used to heal many sick folk. This was known to almost all the people of Aegina and they had recourse to him to be healed of various sicknesses and especially from wounds. Thus, during the occupation of Greece, a certain German soldier who was serving on Aegina had a sore on his leg, which, even though he had gone to many physicians, did not close up. A certain woman informed him that there was a priest there who healed every kind of such sores with home medicines.

Losing no time, he visited Father Ieronymos, asking him to heal him. Father Ieronymos initially refused, because he feared possible consequences. But at the German's insistence he yielded, and with a certain salve that he had, he was able to heal the wound. When the German left his cell for the last time, now healed, he left a hand-grenade on Father Ieronymos's table, whether out of carelessness or on purpose, no one is able to say with certainty. Father Ieronymos himself was cautious on this score and did not wish to impute to him any treachery.

"It could be he forgot it, it could be he was not a good man and left it on purpose," he would say.

A considerable amount of time passed after that. In 1945—August 18, to be specific—he had gone down to the port city for his usual spiritual industry. There he saw someone holding a similar grenade, which he had converted into a lighter. So as soon as he got back to his cell, he threw himself into copying the lighter he had seen. He took the grenade and began to saw off its top with a metal hack-saw.

Suddenly there was heard a terrifying noise and Father Ieronymos was found on the ground covered with blood. The grenade was full of explosive matter and as soon as the saw came in contact with it there was an explosion. Father Ieronymos was seriously wounded throughout his whole body and especially in his left hand, while on account of the deafening noise he lost his hearing. They immediately took him to the hospital of Aegina where he received first-aid (bandaging of the wounds, and so forth) and forthwith, on account of the seriousness of his condition, he was conveyed to the Tzanion Hospital in Piraeus.

For the entire duration of the trip, until he reached the hospital, his mind was turned to God and his lips continuously whispered "Glory be to Thee, O God" and "Lord Jesus Christ, have mercy on me."

The doctors at the Tzanion Hospital verified that his condition was grave. His eardrums were broken and his hearing was irrevocably lost. His left hand had to be cut off without fail, to avoid infection and adverse effects throughout his whole body.

Father Ieronymos accepted the doctors' conclusion and decision with exemplary patience and a martyric mind. "His will be done," he whispered. He saw everywhere the finger of divine Providence and believed that behind every trial is hidden the will of God. The only thing that grieved him was when the doctors informed him that he would have to remain in the hospital for at least two and a half months for medical care. This period of time appeared to him to be quite excessive. Two and a half months away from his cell, from his beloved stillness, was a very heavy and unbearable burden. He did not say anything to the doctors, but he spoke about this matter to God. He prayed much and fervently and implored God and the holy Unmercenaries to cut short his stay in the hospital as much as possible. And God, Who always hearkens to His faithful servants and together with the "temptation" provides the "way of escape" (I Cor. 10:13), comforted him through the holy Unmercenaries, who appeared to him in a dream and revealed to him that in one month he would be out of the hospital.

Indeed, although the doctors amputated his forearm a little

above the elbow, and its healing, like that of the other wounds, required long convalescence in the hospital, with the help of God he was healed quickly.

One month after his entrance in the hospital, even as the holy Unmercenaries had revealed to him, the doctors permitted him to leave. But his hearing had not come back. He could not hear anything whatsoever.

Yet he ceased not to glorify God continually. He did not permit himself even for a moment to grow fainthearted and lose his patience.

"Lord," he said, "I had nothing when I came into the world. Thou broughtest me into being, Thou hast given me all. May Thy Name be glorified. May it be done unto me however it is pleasing to Thy Grace. If it is to the profit of my soul, take my other hand too."

Surely his patience could be compared with that of the much-suffering Job, and these words of his strongly remind one of the words of that ancient namesake of patience: "The Lord gave, the Lord hath taken away: as it seemed good to the Lord, so hath it come to pass: blessed be the Name of the Lord" (Job 1:21).

As the venerable Eldress Eupraxia relates, from August 18 until the middle of the Great Fast of the following year, no one could communicate with him at all; he couldn't hear a word. On the Tuesday of the fifth week of the Fast he felt a certain restlessness, a certain anxiety, throughout his whole body.

Late at night he asked her to take him to the hospital of Aegina. On the morrow when she visited him in the morning she found him much better and well disposed. As he related to her, he had seen in his sleep the holy Unmercenaries dressed in the monastic Schema and wearing *skoufas,* and they injected him with something. From the pain, he awoke, and felt completely well. And the most astonishing thing of it was that his hearing had come back, which the doctors he had visited in Athens assured him there was no hope of ever regaining.

Father Ieronymos fervently thanked God and His Saints for this miraculous intervention and returned to his hermitage. A short time later, as a token of gratitude for these two miracles—the quick healing of his wounds at the Tzanion Hospital and the restoration of his hearing—he built a little church in honor of the holy Unmercenaries Cosmas and Damian, about 200 meters distant from his hermitage.[2]

2. This is presently the parish church of the followers of the Church Calendar on Aegina.—TRANS.

Church of the Holy Unmercenaries on Aegina built by the Elder Ieronymos as it looks today.

CHAPTER NINETEEN
The Hermitage

HENCEFORWARD, advanced in years and disabled, he settled permanently in the hermitage of the Annunciation. This became the place of secret struggles and prayer for him, and a spiritual oasis, a true pool of Siloam, for his suffering fellow men.

For the Elder Ieronymos, a new page had turned in his life. From his youth it was his wont to entrust everything to the Providence of God. Thus it was now also; after his accident, he ascertained that it was the will of God to remain on Aegina. The dream of the Holy Mountain was abandoned. Things on their own led him to perpetuate in Aegina the tradition of Cappadocia, where the monks known as *troglodytes*—that is, cave-dwellers—side by side with their struggles of *hesychia* which they never forsook, ministered to the poor, the sick, the strangers, and invalids. Father Ieronymos believed, with the cave-dwelling monks of Cappadocia, that the spirit "bloweth where it listeth," it does not recognize absolute fixed boundaries of the expressions of the spiritual life. The ascetic who prays day and night in his cell does not differ, in the offering he makes to God, from him who ministers to the least of his brothers, when the loving disposition and the self-offering of both are for God's sake. And the Elder Ieronymos combined both these aspects of the spiritual life—that of the secluded hesychast, and that of the merciful minister to men in society—to a miraculous and perfect degree.

The partial curtailment of his services to the community, after his resignation from the hospital church and more especially after his accident, gave him the opportunity to devote himself even more to prayer. And prayer led him to the height of divine vision, where his mind was illumined by the uncreated light. And this illumination of the Holy Spirit he in turn transmitted to the people of God, who as time went by visited him more often.

We believe that from the moment he left the hospital of Aegina and took up permanent residency at his hermitage, it defined what was to be the most significant passage in the course of his life. He was forced to cut back his other activities, such as the continuous upkeep of the hospital church and various kinds of manual labor, and to give himself up more to prayer. He himself, besides, had from the beginning had the conviction that man's primary pursuit should be his union with God and for that reason he should avoid any occupation that could hinder him from this goal.

His activities accordingly were limited chiefly to three realms: a) prayer; b) benefaction; c) confession and guidance. Saint Abba Isaac the Syrian writes somewhere that for him who struggles in stillness, and has no money or other material goods to give out as alms, it suffices to have contrition of heart and prayer. The Elder Ieronymos—besides prayer, to which he literally gave himself up, and contrition of heart, which was always a given—also found a thousand and one ways to provide those in need with material goods and, in most cases, in a marvellous way, without their even asking him.

But surely the fact that he spent himself in teaching and guiding the multitude of his visitors, despite his physical weakness, cannot but be imputed to him as almsgiving. The venerable Eldress Eupraxia, who was his true disciple all her life and closely served him after his disability, related to us that on many occasions, perhaps to anticipate any possible murmuring on her part because of the fatigue she felt from serving so many visitors, he told her with humility, "Nun, as for us, we don't have any money to give as alms; for this reason even these few words which we say, they are reckoned as alms."

THE ELDER IERONYMOS had a monastic conscience. He believed that prayer, the union of the mind with God, was his primary work. And for him prayer, even the daily services, was not just some formal proceeding, but rather a total giving. He insisted that the church services are indispensable. He never omitted them himself, even if, rarely, he found himself far from his cell. But he maintained that it was equally necessary that during the time of prayer a person let himself free, that he might make confession before God.

He was wont to say to us, "When your mother or some relative dies, do you take up a book to mourn them with? Of course not. The words will come by themselves to your mind, from sorrow. It's the same way with prayer. We have to let ourselves confess to God whatever is on our mind."

This immediacy and freedom of speech was the main trait of his prayer. He had the feeling of the omnipresence of God to such a degree that whenever he prayed, he wept, this being also a sign of the grace of God. As soon as he intoned "Through the prayers..." to begin any service, a sigh was heard and his eyes would run with tears. He had become so accustomed to this condition that he considered it inconceivable to have prayer without tears.

That is why he often counselled us, "Do not rise up from prayer, if there does not come at least one teardrop."

The daily services he read completely and in their entirety. He usually got up at 3 o'clock at night and read the Midnight Service, Matins, along with the Kathismata of the *Psalter* and the Hours. As soon as he finished the service he withdrew for a little to his cell whispering, "Cast me not away from Thy presence and take not

Thy Holy Spirit from me" (Ps. 50:11). His mind was always on prayer. Most nights he didn't go to bed at all. He would recline on a folding beach-chair he had in his cell, where sleep would overtake him for a little, and thereupon he got up again to pray.

In the afternoon, about 4:00, he had Vespers. This service would be attended by three or four pious women who also chanted. It was also attended by any who were then there to visit him and go to confession or to ask his counsel, usually from his immediate spiritual circle.

Before any service began, he himself saw to it or commanded somebody else that all the books be prepared, so that at the time of prayer there be no interruption or confusion. "In the presence of the King, there is order," he was wont to say; and he endeavored during the time of prayer (in the presence of God our King) that there be no disorder and distraction, but that order and attention should reign. He was totally opposed to the reading of the services in an improvised and rushed manner, because prayer in this manner remains fruitless.

"If you yourself do not hear or understand what you are saying, how is it you want God to hear it?" he used to counsel us.

His absolute attention in prayer and his continuous and unceasing exercise of it bountifully brought the illumination of the Holy Spirit, which was often visible to his little flock. Many times his face was seen shining with a world-transcending Tabor-like light, whereas not rarely his whole cell would emit a divine fragrance. These were the moments that his spiritual children felt shivers of emotion, which afterwards culminated with his divine teaching.

Prayer for the Elder Ieronymos was his real nourishment; it was not only spiritual, but that which supplemented even his bodily food, to which he was totally indifferent.

He was very frugal. He never bought fruit. If his spiritual children brought him some, then only did he taste any.

The Chapel of the Annunciation built by the Elder Ieronymos.

In the same manner he was indifferent to all material things. He avoided wearing new *rassa* or shoes and when he had to, he was assiduous to get them dusty quickly. Once he said to us that many years had passed since he had worn new shoes.

"And the old shoes, where do you find them, Elder?"

"The priest from the convent up there (he meant Saint Nectarius) gives them to me."

Prayer was not only food for the Elder Ieronymos, it filled all his other needs also. Through prayer he dealt with the cold of winter and the heat of summer. He never complained about anything. One winter, some of us, his spiritual children, brought him a stove, so that he might not catch cold. After he asked us how it worked, and we lit it, within five minutes he said to us, "Enough, now put it out, because my head hurts from the heat."

It is to be understood that we were still shivering from the cold in his frozen cell.

But he had another source of warmth, which at an unexpected moment he revealed to one of his spiritual children, "I, when I am cold, I pray, and the grace of God warms me."

This reminds us of Saint Seraphim of Sarov, who while he sat outdoors with his disciple in the middle of winter and thick snow was falling upon them, they felt such warmth within as if they were in a hot bath-house. It was the same Holy Spirit that dwelt in them and warmed them.

But the temptations God permitted him to undergo from Satan at the hour of prayer were not few. From the scanty incidents that have reached us, since he himself never spoke to us about his secret spiritual struggles, we mention the following, as it was related to us by the venerable Eldress Eupraxia.

"One night I heard a great commotion, and when I entered with fear into his cell and asked him what happened, he answered me seriously: 'Nothing.'" (The Elder had received Holy Communion that day.) But later Father Ieronymos himself related to Father

Nicholas's[1] mother that there had appeared to him a priest with a holy chalice who told him that he came to give him communion. When the Elder asked him who he was, who sent him, and how he had entered his cell, he answered that he had entered through the keyhole. The Elder then began to pray and to rebuke him to get out, but not by the keyhole but through the slit under the door. And indeed, he rushed to the slit, and when his whole body had gone out his tail appeared, which was over nine feet long. And when it had gone out there was also heard a great commotion and the air was filled with a ghastly stench.

Many were they—both many years before, when he served the Liturgy, and also in later years, when he was walking to his cell—who saw that he was about a forearm above the ground, and they marvelled at his sanctity.

The cycle of services ended at night, about eight o'clock, when he read Compline along with the Akathist to the Theotokos. Afterwards he withdrew to his cell to pass his night between sleep and prayer till three in the morning, when there would commence the new cycle of his twenty-four hour glorification of God.

I F ANY WERE TO COLLECT the Elder's teachings and accomplishments, they would assuredly fill whole volumes. He was an inexhaustible well-spring. And the astonishing thing was that he had the capability (was it only capability?) to unfold to each one exactly those matters which most preoccupied him and simultaneously to give fitting solutions, before he who was speaking to him could even ask him. From this standpoint, the Elder had no rival. Of all his gifts, that of clairvoyance was possibly not his greatest, but assuredly it was the most impressive. He who spoke

---

1. Father Nicholas was the parish priest of the church of the holy Unmercenaries which the Elder had built. He was a married man, and quite pious. He reposed many years after the Elder.—TRANS.

with him would be nailed to his chair when the Elder, simply and calmly, as if he were relating some ordinary thing, began to unfold to him every aspect of his inner world, even his inmost and secret thoughts. Many times he would reveal things that even the person himself who was speaking to him was not aware of, or which he had never spoken about to anyone. People who saw him for the first time would be astonished at all he revealed to them and they departed with the impression that they had met a Saint. His revelations were so impressive, that you would think he was able to observe everything from some other world, as if he had an open window on eternity through which he was able to see things present and future.

The prophetic flame of his preaching, leavened with the fire of love for God and for his fellow man, wrought miracles. Many were the souls that, from the first time they saw and heard him, felt certain stirrings within and were guided to the Church. And numberless also were those who arrived at his cell shipwrecked and left it literally saved.

People who met him even once felt such spiritual profit that they continually spoke of him and were astonished by his holiness. The following letter which was sent by one of his spiritual children, Archimandrite Nectarios Marmarinos, chancellor of the Sacred Metropolis of Corinth, is indicative of all that is written above.

SACRED METROPOLIS OF CORINTH

My reverend Elder,

Rejoice always with the most sweet joy of the Lord!

With the deepest reverence I kiss your right hand, beseeching your paternal prayers and blessings.

If the Lord permits, I will try to hop over to Aegina for a couple of days. And if it is blessed, I would like to visit you to obtain new spiritual strength. The Lord only knows how much profit your holy words procure. You cannot imagine how much the young girl with me the last time I visited you was profited; she speaks of your holiness everywhere. Souls that feel stirrings within them towards virginity greatly desire to hear you. What can I do? I will bring one again, just so she can see you. Please do not misunderstand me on account of my audacity. You will benefit souls.

Forgive me for my verbosity.
Convey my humble prayers to the sister.
With deep reverence I kiss your right hand,
Your spiritual son,
Archimandrite Nectarios Marmarinos

The Elder's speech was simple, practical, concise, and had the aphoristic quality of proverbs. You did not encounter in his words complicated dogmatic theories. He always spoke "about our Christ," "about our Panagia" and "about our Saints." And if on occasion he was asked about "lofty" dogmatic matters, he would answer that one had to be a Saint to talk on such subjects. Of course, he adapted the content of his teaching to his audience. But his goal was always to evoke compunction in the hearer and to increase his zeal for repentance and prayer.

He had deep humility, which made his words even warmer, more full of love—we might say alluring, like a fisherman with his bait. Judging and censuring a third party had no place in his speech. If anyone provoked him to make criticisms of this or that person, he would answer, "Even if I come out with a judgment, it will not be as I say. I did not see, I did not hear, I do not judge. God will judge. As for us, let us keep silence."

He spoke with boldness but with discretion also. Once he was visited by a certain clergyman who was wont to criticize others very sharply. The ever-smiling and tactful Elder was reserved and taciturn. For the hour or so that the clergyman stayed in his cell, the Elder spoke very little. The Eldress Eupraxia who went in and out to serve them refreshments was surprised at his deportment, and when that clergyman left, she asked him, "But, Elder, why didn't you speak to that priest?"

"He did not come to receive benefit, but to try me. For this reason I also did not wish to speak."

While he had a freely flowing spontaneity, his words were always "seasoned with salt." He never said an unnecessary word or anything that would grieve his guest. His speech was always circumspect and, above all, full of discretion. Following the exhortation of Basil the Great, "when needful, see; when needful, hear; when needful, speak; when needful, answer," he avoided not only speaking idly, but even listening idly. Whenever he heard his interlocutor judge someone, he would stop him with discretion. He stigmatized the sin many times over, but he never judged the sinner.

Once the Elder was visited by two of his spiritual children and he was speaking to them about the Orthodox Faith and the reverence that we ought to have towards the traditions of the Church.

"We have to take great care to preserve our Faith even as it was delivered to us by the holy Fathers. Today, alas, I behold many disquieting signs. The clergy cut their beards and hair, they take off their *rassa*. Monks mill around Omonia Square like laymen. What business has the fox at the fair? I heard that at one convent the archimandrite compelled the nuns to take off the Orthodox *rassa* and to wear ones similar to those of the Latins. Where is all this leading to?"

"Ah, I know, Elder," someone interrupted him. "He is so-and-so from such-and-such convent."

"Did I ask who he is? Why are you quick to judge? I simply mentioned something I heard. The persons do not matter; it's the actions that I judge, in accordance with what I hear."

Many times he censured to his face the one speaking with him —always with love, discretion, and humility: but he never said a bad word behind his back. And together with the censure, he consoled. He did not wish, nor did he ever permit a man to leave his cell uncomforted. And he always advised his spiritual children to conduct themselves with discretion in all their dealings.

All that he spoke was based on Holy Scripture, the Fathers, and the liturgical life of the Church, and frequently made reference to the liturgical texts themselves. As a rule he ended his talk with the exhortation, "Let's chant something now: 'Let us worship the Word...,' or 'It is truly meet...'" (He usually chanted "It is truly meet..." in Second Tone, as the Archangel Gabriel first chanted it in his appearance to an Athonite monk.)

Often, when he spoke, he used parables or examples from everyday life, in order by these means to transport his hearer to things spiritual. The ease with which he made this transition, using very apt symbolic images or allegories, was marvellous:

"I marvel at this box here [*it was a radio*]. The other person speaks from the other end of the earth, and I hear him here. So it is with prayer also. We pray here, and God hears us from Heaven."

All, without exception, he received with love. Nor was his help limited to spiritual guidance and teaching alone, but when there was need, this spiritual help was accompanied with material help also. He did this without being asked, when he determined that he ought to do it. The money that he gave in these instances was, as a rule, exactly the sum needed by him to whom it was given. There are very many examples of such instances.

His cell had become a spiritual infirmary, a true pool of Siloam. When a person came out of it, no matter how distressed or despairing he had been, he felt spiritually regenerated, consoled, and full of strength.

The Elder Ieronymos, c. 1960.

CHAPTER TWENTY
Daily Ministry

AFTER THE MORNING SERVICE of Matins, the Elder rested a little. Then he had a cup of coffee, slung a knapsack over his shoulder, his "bag of love," and went down to Aegina. In the beginning this took place daily; later, towards the end of his life, three times a week.

His mission was great. There were souls that hungered and thirsted, some physically, some figuratively; the Elder felt responsible for them all. It was necessary to say a word to each, in order to console and build up, or to give food, so that the hungry would be filled.

Let us accompany him on one of these blessed excursions of his, and from the few incidents that have reached our ears, try to fathom the greatness of his so rich and unobtrusive offering of service.

With prayer on his lips and mind, he began his descent to Aegina at about eight in the morning. As many as met him in the way ran to kiss his hand and receive his blessing. And he, with his blessing, would say a good and timely word to them. In one of the first narrow alleys of Aegina, he stopped at the wall of a certain house and cried out to the lady of the house, whose son was scourged by an illness, "How are you, E.? How is your son doing?"

"How *can* he be doing, Elder? He's in a pitiful state and I'm very distressed, because the doctor said that he absolutely has to have an operation."

"Have patience and God will help. God loves us greatly, and

whatever He gives is for our benefit, provided we ourselves accept it with patience and do not grumble.

"God permitted in my case that my hand be cut off. I didn't need it. God knows what He's doing. Better with one hand in Paradise, than with two in hell. I never said to God even once: 'My God, why?' Yea, not even one time have I ever said it. God loves me and He knows what is profitable for me. I thank Him for all things and I glorify Him. And you also should thank Him. Suffering is a gift of God. Many have come to know God after an intense and heavy trial of suffering. One monk on the Holy Mountain wept and lamented because God had forgotten him and did not send him afflictions. And should we protest and grumble whenever there comes to us a slight affliction? We ought to be patient and beseech God not to abandon us.

"Let us entrust our life to God, and may it be done as He wishes. Whatever the outcome may be for us, that's the one that is for our good. For God does not want the perdition of man, but his salvation. There is no need for despair, rather we should have courage and hope in God. Despair is disbelief. He who sincerely believes in God never despairs. You despair because you don't believe in the power of God, Who governs all things. Without God we cannot do anything. Excessive sorrow and despair are of the tempter. When I was in Constantinople, and they would tell me to leave, I did not even want to hear of it, I preferred that they should kill me. But the thought comforted me that maybe God wished it. And when I was practically compelled to leave, I learned some time later that many of those who remained were killed by the Turks. Always say, 'May Thy will be done.' Have joy and sorrow as guests, but not despair. No matter how much sorrow the evil one brings, do not despair. Say, 'I have my Christ, He was crucified for me and loves me.' When you have a difficult case, you hand it over to a lawyer, and you don't speak, he speaks for you. And so it is now. Entrust what bothers you to God and He will take it over. Run to our Christ, implore Him to give you strength, do not despair. You are the work of His hands, He will help you."

"Thank you very much, Elder. You also say a prayer, please, that my son get well."

"I will pray, but you pray also. In any event, my thought says that you should avoid the operation. Have patience for a few days and God will show His will. Don't worry, your son will get well."

"I thank you very much, Elder, may we have your blessing."

It should be noted here that E.'s son in fact recovered in a few days without the need of an operation.

As soon as he departed, he met a woman and called her to himself. "How are you, my child, Barbara, why are you so sad? Listen: your husband John is not a bad man but rather is led astray by the devil. Go to Saint Nectarius and pray—make much supplication and he will help you. Your husband will get well."

The woman lost her color. The revelations came to her one after the other. This little father called her by name, without knowing her; told her her husband's name; understood furthermore that she was going to Saint Nectarius to pray, because her husband was an alcoholic and was abusing his family. She couldn't collect herself enough to say a thing. She only sought his blessing, as she beheld him already departing.

A little while later, she visited him in his cell to thank him. Her husband had stopped drinking and tranquillity had returned to the house.

The Elder went further on and entered a machine-shop. He greeted all who worked there—there were seventeen of them. Immediately all approached him, kissed his hand, and asked his blessing.

"May God bless you," he said. "I envy you all and I congratulate you. A man should have zeal and should work, not be idle. Idleness brings many evils upon a man. The indolent man is a thief, he steals from the labor of others. He who works, benefits both the soul and the body. All kinds of work are good, provided that a man wants to work. Iron, if you leave it, rusts; when you use it, it shines. Likewise with man, when he does not work the commandments of God, he rusts. He who is lazy in physical labors will be slothful in spiritual ones also. I admire you, because you make such good things. I often marvel at the works of man, the radio for example. You turn it on and you hear a voice from America, from the other side of the world. And I think that so it is in the spiritual realm also. We pray—in other words we speak to God from here where we are—and He hears us in Heaven. This is a great thing. So long as we do not become proud in what we do. We see a beautiful garment. Who gets the praise, the needle or the seamstress? The seamstress, of course. We too are a needle in the hands of God. All things are made by God through us. For this reason we should not be proud.

"Take care as much as you can to work at bettering the spiritual part. Every man, whatever he wills, he accomplishes. Volition and diligence advance him spiritually. If a man wills it, he is even able to become a Saint. God is not a respecter of persons and does not sanctify only certain people because that is what pleases Him, but because they themselves desired it and struggled exceedingly. Holiness came from God as the reward of their volition. My elder, Misael, would go up into the mountain before sunrise, would lift his hands up high and bring them down with the setting of the sun. When he returned home at night, his clothes dripped from the tears and sweat—and he was a family man and lived in the world. But he had a strong will and much zeal in spiritual things, and for this reason he was able to accomplish what was impossible for others."

Then he turned to the owner of the machine-shop and said, "I have a thought. Maybe it is better that you do not work any more today? It would be preferable to close the shop and have all of you leave, that nobody work."

"Why, Elder? Is it some feast-day? Why should we not work?"

"No, it's not a feast-day, but I fear that something bad will happen. Do as God enlightens you. Farewell, and may God bless you."

The owner was somewhat upset at these words of the Elder's and said, "What kind of a jinx is this, first thing in the morning? Don't get me wrong—we love Father Ieronymos, we respect him, he's a holy man. But to stop working because he feels uneasy about it? Forward, men, on with the work and God be our help."

Yet not even an hour passed before a deafening noise shook the machine-shop. Everybody fell to the floor. The steam-boiler of the machine-shop exploded and all the workers were wounded or burned, fortunately not seriously. They took them all to the hospital, where the good Elder later visited them to console them and care for them, without mentioning what had taken place in the morning. And they all marvelled both at his love and tactfulness, and at his clairvoyance.

After the machine-shop, the Elder proceeded to the other end of the harbor, on the road leading to the prisons of Aegina. He stopped at the house of an acquaintance of his and rang the bell. The lady of the house immediately came out and welcomed him with joy.

"Good morning, Elder, how are you? Please come in and have a cup of coffee."

"No, thank you, I can't stay. I only passed by to say Good Morning. How are you, how is your husband and the children?"

"We're well, Elder, glory be to God! Everything is going well, the only thing is that, well, my husband, on account of his work, is dictatorial. He's used to giving orders in the army and he behaves likewise towards us, his family. I'm tired of being around him, I can't endure him anymore, and I'm thinking of separating from him."

"Listen, my sister, there is no such thing as separation, only death separates. You should not get angry; speak with kindness.

Bring before you the image of a man who is laden with many heavy burdens. What would you do? Wouldn't you run to free him from his weight, to give him rest? That's what you should do, my sister, your love should pick up the burden.

"Make it your care to love our Christ greatly, and this love will move you to love people also and to acquire patience. Bring to mind our Christ. His sacrifice on the Cross was not because we loved Him, but because He loves us and poured out His blood in order to free us from sin. Pray, and God will help you. Kneel before your icon corner and say to Him, 'Having been far from Thee for so many years, I have grieved Thee, living in darkness. But grant me now a little of Thy light and forsake me not, O my Christ. Thee alone do I have. People love today and abandon tomorrow. I am a sheep of Thy rational flock. Seek me out who am gone astray, O God, and have mercy on me…' 'Thy fatherly arms do Thou open to me quickly…'[1] Chant when you can, and implore God to bring you close to Him and to give you patience. He is compassionate and will hearken to you, provided that you seek it from Him."

At that moment he was approached by the woman who lived in the house across the street. She was from the Peloponnesus and a few years ago had gotten married in Aegina. Since her arrival, her soul thirsted to find a good spiritual father. She had heard many things concerning Father Ieronymos and his holy life, but had hesitated to approach him. She would see him when he visited her neighbor from time to time and her soul longed to speak to him. But she didn't dare; she had heard that he followed the Old Calendar and this made her even more hesitant. That morning, however, she had a very serious problem. Her son Paul was suffering in bed with a fever of 104°. Her great love for her son enabled her to overcome her hesitation, and with great trepidation she approached him.

---

1. Compunctionate hymns from the tonsure service.—TRANS.

"Good morning to you, Father, how are you?"

"Glory be to God. And who might you be?"

"My name is such-and-such and I live right across the street. I earnestly implore you, my Father, my son has a fever of a hundred and four degrees, and is suffering terribly. Would you come to read a prayer over him so that he might get well?"

"The problem isn't with your son, but with you [*he meant her pathological love for her son*]. But I'll come to see him."

They proceeded together and entered the house. The woman was so overjoyed that he had agreed to come to her house that she didn't know how to attend on him.

"What can I make for you, Father, shall I prepare you something to eat?"

"No, just make a cup of coffee."

"How do you like it?"

"Sweet. Let it be sweet, so that we can speak sweetly."

The woman ran to the kitchen and shortly returned with two coffees.

"You love your son very much. But don't worry, he'll get well."

"I'm very distressed, Father, for three days now he's been broiling with a fever and I don't know what to do."

"Listen! This wall neither grieves nor rejoices. We humans both grieve and rejoice. But grief should not overpower us, because great sorrow brings despair, which is the greatest sin, it's a lack of trust in the power of God. You have many thoughts, and they tire your mind. Say the Creed and the Supplicatory Canon to our Panagia. Learn it by heart. Begin to chant it, so that your mind adheres to it, and our Panagia will help you. Our Panagia and our Lord's Precious Cross guard man from the snares of the devil. Without fail, kneel half an hour a day and pray to God. When you have a great affliction, pray without ceasing, do not stop until you're aware of some relief in your soul. God beholds our persistence and faith and sends His help. If you do not receive, do not depart from prayer. He is compassionate and will give it, but He wants us to seek it from Him.

"And one more thing. Do not finish your prayer if there does not come the drop of a tear. When compunction comes, do not speak of it anywhere, so that you will not lose it. Compunction is a divine gift. Say the Creed continuously, many times a day. Don't wait for Compline to say it. I say it five or six times a day. Whenever I have thoughts, I say the Creed and the thoughts vanish. Gather yourself in prayer and do not slacken nor let your mind roam about. The greatest sin is for the mind to wander away from God at the hour of prayer. We have said enough for today. Let's go now to see your son."

He approached the bed of the sick boy, took his hand, and then recited the prayer for the sick.

"Don't worry, he'll get well. Only, I beseech you, do not tell anyone that I read him a prayer."

"Thank you very much, my Father. I've greatly profited from the things you've told me. May I come some time to your cell to see you?"

"What do I, a naughty sinful priest, have to offer you? Instead of wasting your time coming to me, you'd be better off praying. But at any rate I do not refuse, as often as you have a need and you wish to come, come. Well then, may our Panagia always help you and Divine Providence cover you."

And he left her house.

The poor woman watched him in confusion as he went away. Waves of inexpressible joy flooded her breast from this unhoped-for meeting. "My God, what kind of man is this, and all this time I never went to see him and get acquainted," she thought and ran inside to see her son. But here awaited her an even greater surprise. The little thing was already up and playing with his toys. She put in the thermometer and discovered that his temperature was absolutely normal. She was overcome and broke down in tears. She then went before the icons, knelt down, and thanked God for this great benefaction of which she was deemed worthy this day. From then on she became his devoted disciple.

The Elder now proceeded to the market-place. As he was passing the fish market, the first fisherman who saw him called out with eagerness, "Elder, good morning, may we have your blessing. Come let me give you a few fish."

Straightway he put a package of fish in his bag.

"Take a few from me also, Elder," said the next one, also putting a few in his bag.

Likewise two or three others gave him some fish. As he went on, he stopped before a fisherman who was bent over and sorting out the fishes. He pretended not to see the Elder and continued to remain bent over the fish. At a certain point he lifted up his head and saw the Elder observing him with a smile.

"I know what you're thinking now. *What's he going to do with the fish? Why does he want so much fish?* Hearken, beloved, I did not ask for fish, neither from you nor from the others. If you want to, you give, if you don't want to, you don't give. As for me, from those which you give me, some I eat, and some I give away. At any rate, farewell, and may God bless you." And thus he departed.

The fisherman stood with his mouth open. He had heard a lot about this priest, but to be able even to read his thoughts as he had just done was unbelievable. Certainly he was a real Saint. From then on, every time the Elder passed by, he was assiduous with exceeding zeal to put his share in his bag.

Coming out of the fish market, the road brought him outside the grocery stores. In the same manner each of the grocers put some fruit in his bag. To all he said a good word and gave them his blessing.

He proceeded now to walk along the pier. At one point he stopped and called out to the owner of a coffee-house, who was sitting outside his door and was evidently worried.

"Come here, I know what is happening to you so that you're in despair. Don't be troubled, everything will straighten out. Just be patient and you'll see, it was a cloud and it passed. Your wife is good but, look, at one time or another the devil draws all of us down. When you see that you are not able to come to an understanding, do not persist. But you should not hate her, rather you should pray for her. Prayer will bring you relief and will give you strength. Only pray with fervor. I, when I pray for my brother, my heart bleeds. I cannot pray without offering part of myself as a sacrifice. I melt after praying, I don't have strength to speak to anybody. I am of the opinion that the prayer a man offers without his heart bleeding from love and pain does not reach God. Flee to prayer for refuge just as a little child runs to its mother with love. Can it be called love when one forces the child to go to its mother? So should it be with you also—love God to such a degree, that this love will push you into the bosom of God during prayer. And prayer will both give you rest and help her. I'm going now; give her my regards and my blessing."

As soon as the Elder left, the man was unable to hold back his tears. Even if he had seen an angel, he would not have rejoiced as greatly as he had from all that the Elder said to him. The prelude to this had been a marital fight, and black thoughts were tormenting him. He felt a heavy slab on his heart and his soul was overcome by despair. But now that he had seen his spiritual father and had revealed everything to him, his heart was softened and serenity and tranquillity spread through his soul.

Going further down the pier, the Elder suddenly heard someone uttering a fearsome blasphemy. It was an electrician, who from his youth had the bad habit of swearing thus, without reason, at the drop of a hat. He immediately called him to come and said to him, "Forgive me, my brother. I know that from your youth you have sworn without reason; but down deep you're a good man. I'm going to ask a favor of you. I'll stand opposite you, and I want you to begin reviling me with loud insults, until you are exhausted, until you empty out whatever you have within, so that nothing will remain, so that you won't have anything left to revile with again. What do you gain, my brother, by reviling the things of God? God has given us everything. Someone gives you a glass of water and you tell him Thank you. He has given us so many good things, eyes that we may see the world, ears to hear, and all our senses. Should we not thank Him? Do we pay rent for all these gifts? Of course not. Instead then of glorifying Him and thanking Him for all these benefactions that He gives us for free, shall we even revile Him on top of that?"

"You're right, Father. Forgive me, I won't do it again," answered the man and left with his head hanging down.

He went a little further down along the pier. At a little table sat two fishermen talking. They did not have the money even to drink a cup of coffee, and they appeared to be in despair. The Elder drew near them, greeted them, and began a conversation with them. At a certain point, without their observing him, he discreetly left a little money on the table, and departed quietly. They, who had not said a word to him on account of their depression, when they saw the money, marvelled as much at his love as at his discretion and clairvoyance.

The Elder presently left the quay and went up an alley. He proceeded a little, then stopped at a certain door. He knocked and entered. A young widow was trying to restore order among her children who were hungry and were asking for food. She was poor, could not work since she had three little children, and didn't know how she was going to provide for them. She welcomed the Elder and asked him to sit down.

"How are you faring, my sister, how are you managing with your children?"

"How can I be faring, Elder, can't you see? A great misfortune has come upon me and I don't know how I'm going to make it through."

"I know it, but be patient and God will help you. Whatever preoccupies us we should entrust to God and He will not abandon us—provided only that we have steadfast faith in Him. We are all temporary in this life. We are nothing. Where is your husband? He died. He departed, he went to where the true life is. There is where we should set our gaze; all things here below are perishable, we shall leave them all here behind us. Only our soul is immortal. Do not be envious for anything. Avoid the world as much as you can, that you may be saved. The causes are what throw us down—protect yourself from the causes, guard your eyes, your ears, your tongue, your hands. Do not like pretty and showy clothes. A certain woman in my homeland was widowed when she was young, and she was beautiful. So that they would not take notice of her, she wore old clothes and smudged her face with coals. Care and prayer are needed. God will not abandon you.

"Oh, and one more thing. If someone gives you something of his own pleasure, do not refuse it. Because you both deny him his reward, and you yourself are not humbled. For my part, when they give me something, I never refuse it. If I need it, I keep it for myself, but if not, I give it to others. When I give something, even one drachma or a little blade of grass, my ego goes before. But when I am constrained to stretch out my hand and beg, then I am humbled."

He got up, discreetly left on the table a bag of fish, some fruit, and a little money, and left.

The woman thanked him and entreated him to come by from time to time to strengthen her.

He proceeded a little further up the same narrow street. He stopped at a certain door, set down some fish and fruit, rang the bell, and departed quickly before the needy woman who opened the door could see him. She then saw on her doorstep the goods which God had sent her.

He continued distributing things this way at two or three more doors, until he had given out everything he had in his bag. Now unburdened of the weight he had been lugging about, he took the road leading to his cell.

A little before he reached it, he stopped at a door on the right side of the road. He knocked and there immediately appeared an elderly woman, with a countenance obviously distressed. The Elder put some money in her hand and said to her, "Somebody gave me this money and I have no need of it. I ask you to take it, because today you'll have need of it."

The woman took the money and thanked him. The remarkable thing is that on that very evening her daughter, who was with child, suddenly needed to go to Athens and enter a lying-in hospital. And the money the Elder gave her was all that she had.

He went a little further on. A certain youth was coming down the opposite side of the road singing. As soon as he approached, he called out to him and said, "You chant well, bravo!"

"I don't chant, Father, I sing. I don't know letters to be able to chant."

"And the songs, how did you learn them? Listen: if you were zealous in spiritual things you would have learned to chant. Increase this zeal. You have a good voice and you will chant beautifully."

He finally reached his hermitage. But before he was even able to cross the threshold, a woman approached him and begged him to give her some money.

"Help me, Father, I'm a widow, and poor, and I have five orphans to feed. I don't have anything whatsoever to give them to eat."

"I know it; you're both a widow and poor. But you have five gold sovereigns hidden away. Why don't you cash them in and feed your children?"

The rear door to the Elder Ieronymos's Hermitage.

The woman turned pale. Why, no one knew her secret of the gold coins. How was this priest able to reveal this to her with such precision?

"Forgive me, Father, you're right," she whispered and departed with drooping head, to tell her acquaintances that this priest knows everything, he has God's illumination.

H E FINALLY ENTERED HIS HERMITAGE. There some of his spiritual children were awaiting him, having come for confession with him and to seek advice. He greeted them all and then said to the Eldress, "Nun, did you treat them to loukoumi and coffee?"

"Yes, Elder. But come now, I've set the table. I'll keep them company until you've eaten and after that you can receive them and talk with them."

"No, nun, I'll receive them before I eat."

He loved his fellow men and had so much solicitude for their souls' cultivation and their spiritual edification that he preferred even to remain hungry if only he might profit them.

He went straight to his cell. He remained alone for a few moments and then immediately invited in those who had come first. It was a couple who came regularly to see him, who had him as their spiritual father.

They had made a secret agreement between them never to hide absolutely anything from each other without confessing it to the Elder. But the wife once contemplated putting aside some money to give as alms to a certain family in great need. Since, at the time, they themselves lacked money, she feared that her husband might refuse. As soon then as the two of them entered his cell and went to bow and kiss his hand, the Elder received them with the following words, "Welcome to B.," he said to the husband. And then, turning to his wife, "Welcome to the thief! Didn't you make an

Eastern side of the Church of the Annunciation,
the origin of the Elder's Hermitage.

agreement between you not to hide anything from each other? It was a good thing. Why did you hide the money? If you had asked him for it, wouldn't he have given it to you?"

"Forgive me, Elder, I won't do it again," answered the "thief."

Her husband hadn't the foggiest idea what was going on. His wife explained the matter to him and they both marvelled yet again at his clairvoyance.

"In my homeland," continued the Elder, "there lived a priest-monk Seraphim. He was very meek, humble, and a struggler. One month before he died, he was informed of his death; he called us to him and said, 'I implore you and I give you commandment, whatever man you see, implant in his heart compunctionate prayer (that is, the prayer of the heart). And whoever knocks on your door for alms, if you have nothing, though it be but one drachma or an onion, give it to him, that he might not leave empty-handed.' Today such people do not exist. In Anatolia there were many such. People there greatly loved prayer. I know people who, if a little time passes and they don't pray, they cannot endure it, they suffer. They consider the moments that they want to pray, and are unable, as a martyrdom. Others again raise their hands in prayer at night and they don't bring them down till it dawns. Sometimes they pass whole days and nights in prayer. When I was young, for many years I never slept at home but under the Holy Table, in order to pray. Prayer has great sweetness, but one has to struggle in order to understand it. I pray every night for myself and for the whole world. I even remember all the inhabitants of my village. I begin and I commemorate the names from one end of the village to the other, and after that, all my acquaintances. I do not omit the name of anyone. The Lord says that we should shut ourselves up in our closets and pray. You also should endeavor to steal time from your various engagements in order to pray. In the spiritual realm, you ought to become a thief. Make use of the time. The violent seize the Kingdom of God by force. And the greatest profit, you shall find in prayer. Let not a day go by without prayer. And prayer should not end without at least one teardrop."

"How can we acquire tears, Elder? Our hearts are hard as rocks."

"We have to love our Christ very much. Not so much for the future blessings, or for the many benefactions with which He has gifted us now, but because He is Love. Those who have progressed far in the spiritual realm, when they fall, they don't give a thought to the punishment, but they are distressed and their soul is pained because they have grieved God. We should love all and do good to them as much as we can. But our mind should be bound to the love of God alone. Do not be excessively bound to the love of men, because they can accompany you only as far as the grave. Today men love, and tomorrow they forget. To God only should we surrender ourselves. If we bind ourselves with men, what shall we give to God? If you love God much and pray with fervor, then the tears will come. Give special attention to the words, 'Have mercy on me, O God...' (Psalm 50) in Compline, strive to concentrate your mind on the prayer. Say, 'Give our soul love, O our God, forsake us not. We are the creation of Thy hands, we want to struggle but we are unable. Strengthen us; Thou alone art able to strengthen us, to help us. Thou, if Thou wilt, art able to save us. Have mercy on us, O our God, we are alone, we have no protector. Do Thou protect us...'

"Many say the prayer [*that is, the Jesus Prayer*], but do not reap any fruit. The prayer should be said with the fear of God and not out of habit. The prayer has much sweetness, it is union with God. But it is necessary that you feel it, in order to experience compunction. And to experience compunction in prayer is not your doing only, it is God's. When He wishes, He grants, provided only that we persist in prayer. And one more thing. If you want the Lord to hear you, never offend anyone. Your words should be peaceful, sweet, leavened with honey."

"What else should we do, Elder, to be profited and to progress spiritually?"

"Read the Holy Scriptures and patristic books. I especially recommend that you read Abba Isaac the Syrian, even if it is one page a day. Abba Isaac is a mirror. Therein you will find yourselves. And whatever you read, reflect: Do I put this into practice? Strive with zeal to lay a beginning. This is the purpose of these books, to teach us virtue. I love the blessed Abba Isaac very much. I have him as my elder. Many times the nun says to me, 'Elder, let me read to you, since you can't on your own and you don't see well.' And I tell her, 'Let me make an attempt to read by myself, because that way I feel things more deeply. He who reads is like one who harvests, whereas he who hears is like one who gathers the ears of wheat that are left behind.'"

"Elder, so-and-so said something nasty to me and I'm distressed —I feel a disturbance within me. What should I do?"

"Listen! The grocer, whatever he has in his basket, that's what he shouts. You, on your part, see to it that you have good thoughts, so that what comes out of you [*your words*] may be good. Never speak a bad word, because it doesn't go away. Pepper is not eaten like sugar. A monk once spit out blood and they asked him, 'What has happened to you, why are you spitting out blood?' And he answered, 'Because they said a bitter word to me and within me it became blood.' The work of a Christian is great. He will either be burnt or he will be saved. Pray for the other man also, that God might enlighten him. If he understood, he would not speak badly. 'We then that are strong ought to bear the infirmities of the weak' (Rom. 15:1). Prayer will soften your heart and you will quiet down. Well then, you be going now, because others are waiting also. May Divine Providence cover you."

"We thank you very much, Elder. And do pray for us."

"I will pray for you, but know, that if you are not found on the other end of the line [*that is, if you do not pray also*], God will not hear my prayer. If I telephone and you don't pick up the receiver, will you hear my voice? No. You ought to pray also, so that God may also hear my prayer."

"Farewell, Elder, may we have your blessing."

"May you have the blessing of Christ and the Panagia."

As soon as the couple left his cell, three young men entered. They immediately made a bow and kissed his hand.

"Bless, Elder."

"The Lord bless. Have a seat. How is the spiritual life going? Are you struggling? Care is needed, and prayer. Be careful with your senses. Wherever you find yourselves, whether at home or on the way somewhere, pray. Do not look with curiosity here and there. As often as I come from Aegina to my cell, I don't look either at windows or at doors. It's possible even without wanting it to see something and be scandalized. Many times, until I reach my cell, I say the Creed continuously. You do likewise. When you walk in the street, say the Creed or whatever other prayer you wish, and

God will protect you from temptations. Do not take notice, do not look at, and do not listen to what does not concern you. Take heed to all things concerning yourselves, even your movements or the way you dress. If someone is scandalized by your conduct, you will give account on the day of judgment. Have it as a rule in your life, that whatever man you meet, you are careful either to be benefited or to give benefit; otherwise flee.

"Avoid idle talk. For the forty-some years that I have been a clergyman in Aegina, not once have I sat at table with anyone. When they are insistent, at the most I will have a coffee. Nothing more. Too much boldness, freedom of speech, and familiarity weakens a man's resistance and little by little temptation enters and gives rise to grave situations. For this reason it is better to refrain as much as possible. And when you perceive that there is a possibility that a danger and scandal could come about, don't take anything into account, just flee far away. Never permit the physical to overpower the spiritual part. Be careful of your mind. Do not permit anything to captivate it and separate it from God. If you pray, and in the course of the prayer you remember me or any other person, endeavor to distance yourself from him immediately. Otherwise that person will be your greatest enemy."

"Elder, what should we do to protect ourselves from sin?"

"Be heedful of your thoughts. Oppose them. They do not easily leave a person. They come over and over again and war against him. But you, strive to chase them away. There comes an evil thought and it tells you to do something. You counter saying, 'No, I will not do it.' The thought insists: you insist, too. See to it that you have strength to chase it away. If you don't do what the thought tells you, it's not a sin. Sin is the act, not the assault of the thought. But there is need of care, because many times the thoughts are elicited by us ourselves, by our passions. On most occasions, if you do not give cause, the thought does not come by itself. For example, if you look at something with evil intent or just with curiosity, that which you saw will come at night, and especially at the time of prayer, to torment you. The fault lies in our passions, which we allow and do not war against them. Since we do not endeavor to avoid the causes, then it can't be otherwise, the war will come. But even then we should not be negligent, but we should fight. In such instances, of course, the warfare will be harder; there will be need of a more intense struggle to overcome our thoughts. For this reason it is better to avoid the causes of the passions. There is need of great care. If you are not thus careful, or if you allow the thoughts to take root, the tempter will leave you in tatters. Take refuge immediately in prayer. Prayer is the greatest weapon. Make the sign of the Cross and say, 'Most Holy Theotokos, save us,' or 'O Cross of Christ, save us by thy might.' If you call upon God and the Panagia and pray with humility, you will quickly be delivered from the evil thoughts. But you should not relax your vigilance. Take heed continuously, secure yourselves, in order to escape this war of thoughts. If your mind is found continuously in spiritual things, if you give a spiritual significance to whatever you see and hear, then the enemy will not be able to find any way in by which to enter, and will depart.

"Likewise be careful of something else. After any good deed, or after some spiritual joy which you might possibly experience, take heed lest you be tempted by a thought of pride. Because not only will you lose what you have gained, but the war that shall follow will be greater. The enemy is full of envy, and if he is unable to hinder the good work, he tries to blacken it with thoughts of pride. If you do not drive away these thoughts, God will allow a fall so that you might come to yourselves. Lucifer was not driven out of Paradise because of evil deeds, but because of his pride."

He stopped for a little and then, addressing himself to all three, he asked, "Tell me, which has greater strength, water or fire?"

"Uh... water, Elder," answered one.

"If we have a great fire and you pour out a glass of water, will it be put out?"

"No, Elder. The fire has greater strength," said the second.

"If you have a little fire and you pour out a big can of water, will it be put out?"

"Yes, Elder."

"It is neither the water nor the fire that has the greater strength, but the quantity. So it is also in spiritual things. If the worldly way of thinking prevails within you, that will overcome the spiritual. But if your mind is turned to the spiritual, it will overcome the carnal.

"In Anatolia I knew a certain priest who had a very beautiful voice. He also played the violin. Once he was invited to a wedding together with the Bishop. At table they asked him to sing a little, but he was embarrassed and would not sing. The others understood this and entreated the Bishop to permit him to sing some song. He gave him leave, and the priest began to sing. But with the song, he got warmed up and then wouldn't stop for anything. So at a certain point, the Bishop said to him, 'That's enough, now—stop.' Then the priest took off his *kalimavki*, set it on the table, and answered, 'My Bishop, over this alone do you have authority. As for me, no one can stop me now.' Thus also is it with the man who comes to experience the sweetness of prayer. No power is able to hinder him from praying.

"You have to struggle, to increase your zeal for God. It should become for you a daily way of life. Struggle for perfection. If you can't gain a drachma, gain at least a tenth of a drachma. Virtues are not acquired easily. There is need of struggling. And know, that if we acquire virtue quickly, we shall also lose it quickly. Whereas if we acquire it with labor, it doesn't go away.

"Have zeal. Obstinacy is one thing and zeal is another. Obstinacy is a fault. But if it is transformed to zeal for spiritual things, then it becomes virtue. Try to gain this divine zeal. If you do not have persistence and zeal in the spiritual realm, you will quickly be brought to your knees, and at the first difficulties you encounter you will give up. Do not expect in your life to encounter joy all the time. The path of man has more thorns than flowers. You have to be very strong so that nothing will be able to shake you. Even if all are shaken and all oppose you, if you have zeal for God, if you are strong and have our Christ in you, fear not. It is only from ourselves that we are in danger, not from anyone else.

"Everything depends on our will. My hand is not able to steal if I do not wish to. What you do apart from your own will and volition has no value. A small child, if it takes Communion, and afterwards you tell it to spit, it will do it. It doesn't know and consequently has no responsibility. But it also has no virtue. It has to know and not to do it, in order to have virtue. If you want it, the grace of God will visit you. If you leave the window open, light will enter. But if it is shut, no matter how much light there is outside, from what quarter can it get in? All things are dependent on us, on our will. I teach you; but if you are indifferent and do not listen, you sustain the loss. I throw you an apple: if you don't catch it, I am not at fault."

"Elder, how often should we receive Communion?"

"Receive Communion often. I won't say how often, even as there is no need for me to tell you how often to eat. When you're hungry, you eat. So also with Holy Communion. See to it that you hunger for Christ. And be careful; before you take Communion, read without fail the service of Holy Communion. Delve deeply into the words of the prayers. They will help you come to compunction and will bring you tears. Without tears, do not receive Communion."

One of the three young men had a special calling to the priesthood. Addressing himself to him, the Elder said, "Struggle in humility and entreat God to enlighten you whether it is His will to serve Him at the altar. You are still young and are not able to understand the depth of the priesthood. The Saints avoided the priesthood out of great piety and reverence, not because they did not love it. Some even went so far as to cut off some member of their body (such as their ear or nose), lest they be compelled to become a priest. The office of priest is fearful. He who is to be ordained a priest should be blameless. Theophylact of Bulgaria says that if someone has killed even a bird, he cannot become a priest.

"The priest should be an example in all things, because whatever he does, he is observed by all. Even his gait and the movement of his hands should not be disorderly, but restrained and modest. When you are in friendly company and find that the others know more than you, don't talk, just listen. But when the others are weaker than you, then you are obliged to speak, but only as much as will benefit. Wherever you go, profit should ensue. Whatever harms or scandalizes, leave it alone, give it no attention at all. Never be ungrateful; show gratitude to all. But also find a way to avoid all. And when you are amid the world and you wish to pray, do it inwardly. In spiritual things you have to be a 'thief' and exploit if possible every moment. Love the whole world, but not to excess. And in your prayer chase everybody away from your mind and think only of the Lord. Watch your senses. Just as in a house, we close the doors and windows in order to be safe, thus also in the spiritual realm, we secure the senses to protect the health of the soul. But we should take care for the health of the body also, so we have the strength to work for the soul. Well now, let's go see what the nun has prepared for us to eat. You shall stay so that we might all eat together, since it's past mealtime and you are probably hungry."

"It doesn't matter, Elder, we should be going."

"No, be obedient, we'll eat together. It's nothing. Whatever God has sent."

They went into the kitchen, where the Eldress Eupraxia had set the table. The Elder told her to set another three places, he blessed the table, and they all sat to eat. Having eaten a little, he began to counsel the young men again.

"Elder, eat a little more," said the Eldress. "You've eaten very little."

"Nun, we'll eat again tomorrow."

He ate very frugally and greatly loved fasting. He never broke the fast, even if he was sick. He never ate meat. Nor was he interested in the kind of food set before him. Whatever was offered him, that he partook of. And as with all the Saints, while he was austere with himself, he condescended to others. He did not like extremes in fasting; he insisted more on spiritual virtues.

He continued his admonitions to the young men.

"Fast as you are able, commensurately with your health. Can you lift two hundred pounds? Of course not. You lift what you can. Eat oil every day, except Wednesday and Friday. In all things have measure. Only have humility without measure. Do not leave off prayer. No matter how tired you are, you can pray for half an hour. Feed your body as if you were going to live a hundred years, but care for your soul as if she were going to die tomorrow."

"But you, Elder, eat very little, and we see that you are very enfeebled," said one of the youths.

"Let me tell you: I attend both to my nourishment, and to that which is immortal."

In the meanwhile there was a knock at the door and the Eldress Eupraxia ran to open it. She returned in a little and announced that two girls had come.

"Tell them to wait a little," said the Elder. "Treat them to loukoumi and coffee. At any rate, you should go now also," he said, addressing the young men. "And be careful in the street. And be careful about your companions. It is good to have friends, but avoid frequent meetings. No matter how much you speak spiritually and of things profitable to the soul, you will fall into idle chatter and will also lose your quiet. Love others, but with discretion, not to excess. When the faucet runs too much and won't stop, it needs fixing. Have discretion. Salt is what makes food tasty. But if you add too much, it becomes excessively salty and can't be eaten. If you don't add any, it will be tasteless and again is uneatable. Have measure in all things. May God and the Panagia be with you. May Divine Providence protect you."

The three youths made a bow, kissed his hand, and left. The Elder came out, greeted the girls and said, "Sit with the nun so that I can rest a little, and afterwards I'll call you."

He entered his cell. According to the assurances of the Eldress Eupraxia—but also from what he himself told us many times under the form of parables—after each conversation he wanted to withdraw a little to pray. That which he used to relate, that "there are people who, if a little time passes and they are not able to pray, they can't bare it, they suffer…," certainly referred to himself, and it was only out of humility that he ascribed it to others. These intermissions were the hours of the gathering-in of thoughts and of prayer, of union with God.

After some twenty minutes he called them. He began his admonitions, which he addressed to one of them, who was a widow.

"How are you doing? You seem to me to be better than last time. Endeavor to increase your zeal for spiritual things. And be careful, because you are going to have warfare. Do not wear luxurious clothes, in order to protect yourself. When a person wants to practise virtue, he finds many ways. Avoid the causes of temptation. The devil is going to war against you, because all these years in the world you did his will. He is going to war against you, but it depends on you whether he will prevail. Without your own will, he can't do anything. The holy Martyrs, Saint Catherine, Saint Barbara, and the others, held the Cross in their hand and said, 'Thy Cross do we worship, we do not desire sin.' He who loves our Christ, has to take up His Cross and follow Him. In this manner will he mortify his passions. Do not be afraid; the beginning is difficult, because you have to change your way of life, to leave the world and become Christ's in order to be a partaker of His Kingdom. Where there is a will, 'The things which are impossible with men are possible with God.'" (Luke 18:27)

"In what manner will I be saved, Elder?"

"The Apostle Paul says 'at sundry times and in divers manners' (Heb. 1:1). In other words, every man will be saved in proportion to his volition and the struggle he wages. Observe the commandments of God. Dig deeply in yourself. A certain youth went to study, to become wise, but was unable. Returning he saw by the roadside, close to a village, a woman drawing water from a well. He approached and saw that the rope, with time, had carved into the stone lip. He thought, 'Why can I not become wise?' And he made the decision to return and continue his efforts. So you likewise, have a strong will, be patient and be persistent in your struggle, and you will be saved. Never despair. For God there is no unforgivable sin. His compassion and mercy are an abyss. Pride and despair are from the devil. Why despair, since there is a God Who is longsuffering? Even if you kill somebody, do not despair. Say, now it has happened, it cannot be undone. But Thou, O my God, forgive me. Despair is a great sin, it is unbelief. Have your mind in Hades, but let not despair prevail over your soul. A certain monk, in whom the devil sowed thoughts of despair, answered him, 'Why do you push me to despair? Even if I go to hell, I'll be above you.'"

"How can I avoid despair, Elder? I'm very weak and the truth of it is that many times I despair, and think that I won't be able to be saved."

"When there is true repentance, despair has no place in the soul of man. Even Judas the traitor, if he had repented, would have been saved. But he did not repent. He simply regretted his action. When there is awareness of our sinfulness, repentance follows. But repentance has to be sincere, and has to be accompanied by contrition of heart. Real repentance and contrition of heart bring immediate results. Now I look to the west; I am a sinner. I turn to the east; I am righteous. But repentance has to be continuous in man, it must never end. If the Apostle Paul said not only that he was a sinner, but the most sinful of men—he who reached the third heaven—what shall we say? This is why I say that we must always repent. David sinned, but afterwards his whole life long he would say, 'Have mercy on me, O God,' (Ps. 50) and he was saved. There is no sin able to overcome the mercy of God. As often as you fall, arise. God forgives immediately, if only we repent sincerely."

"Elder, many times despondency seizes me and I have no desire to do anything. How do I handle that?" asked the other girl.

"When the devil fights us, we ought to fight him back. Our greatest weapon is prayer. Do not be negligent; kneel immediately and pray fervently to God, and quickly you will feel strong. Prayer is conversation with God. When we experience the joy of prayer, then we will feel great exultation. It is a foretaste of the life of Paradise. But you have to struggle, in order to experience that joy. And if you struggle mightily, God will give it to you. Prayer leads up to the heights of divine vision. Misael, my elder, when he prayed, the whole of him glowed with light. And when he reached this state, he no longer prayed with words, but noetically. Words are like the kindling wood, until the fire is lit. When the fire is kindled, in other words when contrition and compunction come, a person is no longer able to speak. He senses and hears God within himself. Then come tears. This is a great gift. Then the man abandons the senses and nothing speaks but the heart, the longing, the sighs that cannot be uttered."

"You have raised us very high, Elder. We, who are inexperienced and indolent, how can we acquire compunction and tears?"

"For tears to come during prayer, the heart has to be pure, without thoughts. Prayer chases away thoughts. When you abandon prayer, thoughts will make war on you. Some say to me, 'I don't feel compunction in my prayers, what can I do?' I answer, 'You aren't praying right. Come before Him with humility and implore Him, weep and beseech His mercy. Then contrition will come to the heart and you will feel compunction.' Do not leave from prayer without tears; and you should feel the things that you say. Do not go to sleep without prayer. No matter how exhausted you are, pray, even if it's in bed, for at least half an hour. When you have your mind in God, then wherever you find yourself, on the road, at home, in bed, you are able to pray. Whereas when your mind runs elsewhere, then even if you are in church, compunction will not come and your prayer will be formal and dry."

"I try to pray somehow, Elder, but I can't gather my mind. It runs here and there."

"Listen! Be careful of your eyes and your ears. Let them not see and hear unseemly things, because all that you see and hear will come at the time of prayer and will scatter your mind, and will hinder you from being united to God. Likewise in church: we go there to pray. If we are found in church and our mind runs elsewhere, there is no gain. It's like going to the doctor and not listening to his advice. Therefore before we set out for church, we should think for what reason we're going and should endeavor to gather our mind."

At that moment there was a knock at the door and the Eldress appeared.

"Elder, Mr. So-and-so is here with a priest."

"Good, let them wait a little and I'll call them afterward."

And turning to the two young women, he continued, "I am very tired, but what can I do? I feel like a debtor to all. I have done no good to any man. May God account these few words which I say as almsgiving. Well now, you should be going. When you can, come again. And do not neglect prayer. No matter how many cares you have, find a little time, at least half an hour a day, to pray. Take care that the spiritual part is not harmed; everything else is temporal, it will not accompany us into eternity. May God and our Panagia be with you."

The girls left and the Elder called his two new visitors.

The door to the Elder's cell, where countless souls were unburdened and consoled.

As soon as they entered his cell, the Elder attempted to bow and kiss the hand of the priest. But he restrained him, and bowing himself they kissed each other's hand.

"Your blessing, Elder, we should make a deep bow to you, not you to us."

"Listen! I honor the priesthood. As for who is virtuous, God only knows. But the priesthood is the highest office, and it is also the greatest responsibility, that a man can undertake on earth."

"Are you well? I had some time and came to see you."

"Glory be to God for all things. I pray to God not to take my soul until I have time to repent sincerely. Because God desires sincere repentance, not that which is hypocritical and just humble talk. Two elders once quarrelled and one went to the other to ask forgiveness. But he was not sincere and humble, and did not ask forgiveness from his heart. The other was discerning; he perceived it and didn't forgive him. The first went to a spiritual father and said to him, 'I quarrelled with so-and-so and whereas I asked his forgiveness, he won't forgive me. What should I do?' The father answered him, 'You didn't ask from your heart, that's why he didn't forgive you.' After a little while he went back with sincere repentance and said to him, 'I am the one at fault, forgive me.' And then he forgave him. So it is with God. He doesn't listen to the words, He looks at the heart. As long as we have time, therefore, let us see to it that we repent.

"Before death, the voice of God comes and numbers a man either in salvation or perdition. With the last breath, the seal is set. For this reason a man should always be found in repentance and prayer. And God, right beside the sorrow for our sinfulness, gives us joy. This is the joyous sorrow of which the Fathers speak. There is no life sweeter than the spiritual life. Love our Christ greatly. Today we're alive. Tomorrow or the day after we might not be. No one knows the hour of death. And then, where shall we find ourselves? We shall desire with longing to return to this life and struggle more, repent more, love our Christ more, and we will not be able to. From now, therefore, let us be careful not to give sorrow to our Christ. 'Now is the acceptable time, now is the day of salvation.' Say continuously, 'I am a sheep of Thy rational flock, and I flee unto Thee, the Good Shepherd. Seek me out who am gone astray, O God, and have mercy on me... Thy fatherly arms do Thou open to me quickly, for like the prodigal have I wasted my whole life...'[2] Ah, how beautiful the spiritual life is! If people understood what they are losing by not repenting, they would leave the cities and run to the mountains to pray.

"Every night, before lying in bed to go to sleep, reflect on how your whole day passed. Think if you pleased or grieved God. Your conscience will inform you. If you are not pleased, say, 'Since I am not pleased with myself, how shall God be?' And try continuously to correct yourself, so that you will not grieve God. A conscience without censure is either pure, or callous and hardened. Since we aren't able to have a pure conscience, it would be good to have at least a certain censure."

Then the Elder turned to the other visitor, "How are you? How goes the spiritual life?"

"Glory be to God, Elder, I try. Lately I've been charged to preach, and I don't know what to do. How do you advise me?"

"I'll tell you. If your life is such as to agree with what you teach, and you are an example, undertake it. The Saints lived what they wrote and taught. And all who write or speak concerning the holy Fathers, ought to have a corresponding way of life. To preach is good. The rabbit does not fear the thunder of heaven as much as the devil fears the preaching of the Apostles. But teach only what you yourself practise. If you don't taste sugar, are you able to say how sweet it is? Surely not. Take care to study thoroughly. And whatever spiritual book you read, think, 'Do I put this into prac-

---

2. Hymns from the monastic tonsure service.—TRANS.

tice?' If you don't practise it, then the knowledge of it will not benefit you. Theology is not studied, it is lived. Are you a theologian? Then you know letters. You don't have the fear of God? Then you've only learned a trade. There are theo-logians [3] who have words but don't have God.

"Read, without fail, even if it's one page a day, the homilies of Abba Isaac the Syrian. After the Gospels they will be a guide for you. And when you finish the book completely, begin it again from the beginning."

"What other spiritual book should I read, Elder?"

"Abba Isaac."

"Fine, you told me about Abba Isaac. Do you have another book to recommend?"

"Abba Isaac. I cannot have enough of the blessed one. If I were able to apply even one tenth of what he writes, I would be very pleased. The other day there came to me a sacred preacher from Athens, and when he saw the book that I have (the Elder had the homilies of Abba Isaac in translation, done by the monk Callinicus of the Monastery of Pantocrator), he said to me, 'This is no good—it's a translation into spoken Greek, and doesn't render the original well.' And I answered him, 'Let me understand well and apply those things that it does render, and I don't need anything more.'

"Attend now to make profitable use of the years of your earthly life, to manage them well, because they have their consequences in eternity. Do not judge and do not tell lies at all, even for a joke. It is better to avoid speaking, than to tell lies."

"He is good, Elder, and he struggles," interrupted the priest.

"Listen. Do not call blessed and do not praise anyone until death, for there is always the fear lest he fall. And do not despair over any sinner, for there is always hope that he can be saved. Love humility. Imitate the Master Christ. Even as He, being incorrupt-

---

3. Θεο-λογοι (*theologians* in English). A play on the Greek word, *God-words*.—TRANS.

On the desk is the Elder's copy of Saint Isaac the Syrian, the Elder's Elder.

ible, was clothed with corruption, so you also, being corruptible, be clothed with the worm. Are you able to do it? To become a humble worm, to be trodden under by all and not to protest? Do this, and you will be saved.

"God is pleased with humility and blesses the humble man twice as much as other men. Every day He blesses all men with one hand, but the humble with both hands. Oh, how I could wish to be a worm, that all might trample upon me! If our Christ, the incorruptible and incomprehensible, was clothed in human flesh, that is, corruption, what is it if we humble ourselves?"

"How can we acquire humility, Elder?"

"With the consciousness of our sinfulness. If we believe that we are truly sinners, we will humble ourselves. But be careful. Humble-mindedness is one thing, and humble talk is something else. Someone came and told me that he was humble and I said to him, 'You always put the "I" in front, how then are you humble?' He didn't have a humble mind.

"When they accuse you, do not answer. The man who is patient when accused, God will number with the Martyrs. In all things give way, that you might always profit. Even as the iron door has need of the wooden one, so the strong man has need of the humble. For one to come to know God, it is not necessary to be a learned man or a scientist, but to be humble. Do not trust yourself. When you don't know the way and do not ask, you can get lost. When you don't know and you ask, you don't get lost. It is necessary for you without fail to have a guide.

"Do not desire that they love you or praise you. He who praises you is your enemy, he is not your friend. He sends you to hell. Do not pursue praise, because this will bring you sorrow. If you acquire pride, then God will allow temptations so that you'll be humbled. It is good that we be humbled before our Christ allows the temptations.

"Above all, do not forget prayer. Kneel at night before the icons to say your prayers. Feel that you are condemned by your sins before the feet of Christ and implore Him, 'My Lord, Thou Who becamest man for me, Thou wast reviled, Thou wast mocked, Thou wast spit upon, Thou wast scourged, Thou didst wear a crown of thorns, Thou wast crucified, Thou didst pour out Thy precious Blood: whereas I have defiled Thine image by my sins. I implore Thee and entreat Thee, condemn me not, give me time for repentance and confession that I may weep for my sins. Help me, O my God, because by myself, without Thy grace, I can do nothing.' With these and other such words speak and implore God to give you compunction. And when compunction comes, do not open up a book to pray. Say those things that you feel, even as a little child speaks to his mother. Bring to mind the sacrifice of our Christ, His martyrdom, His pain, and all that He endured for us. He sacrificed Himself for us out of love. And you, implore Him not to abandon you. He is compassionate and if you ask of Him, He will help you.

"Also take refuge often in our Panagia. I love our Panagia very

The Elder speaking to visitors outside his cell.

much. You love her also. She is the mediatress for our salvation. Every object shines under the light of the sun, according to its form. But the mirror reflects the entire sun. Our Panagia is a mirror, she reflects all the glory of our Christ. She has become the Mother of all Christians. For this reason all men, because we fear to face Christ on account of our many iniquities, take refuge in our Panagia, that she might intercede for our sins, even as we run to our mother with much boldness. Now let's all chant something together."

"It is truly meet..."

"I like this very much. You chant also when you can. 'If any be merry, let him chant.' Oh, and one thing more (addressing himself to the priest). Do not serve the Liturgy ever, before you pray at least half an hour with tears. You ought to come to compunction before you serve. And never take heed of money, because it is worse than the devil. The worst sickness of the clergy is greed. I have been a clergyman fifty-four years, and how a baptism or wedding is performed I know not, precisely so that I might not be entangled with money. May God and our Panagia be with you. May Divine Providence cover you."

And the Elder arose and accompanied them to the door.

IN THE MEANTIME, a certain gentleman much beloved of the Elder had come into the courtyard together with three young men.[4] They also were awaiting to see him. The Elder rejoiced to see them, greeted them one by one, and invited them into his cell. It was four in the afternoon. Time for Vespers. He called the Eldress and two other women who had come to attend Vespers, and they all went into his cell. They brought in the analogion and the books and when everything was ready, the Elder said the "Through the prayers..." and the Eldress read the Ninth Hour. The Elder also chanted at Vespers. Despite his fatigue, he chanted with ardor. His voice was melodious and stentorian and throbbed with emotion. It was impossible for anyone to observe him without himself feeling emotion and hot tears rolling down his face. He had the power to transmit his own spiritual state, at least in part, to those present. As many as had the good fortune to attend these blessed gatherings will never forget the Tabor-like spiritual exaltation that prevailed. And for all, the one dominant thought at such

---

4. This was Mr. Eleutherios Koumbis. One of the three youths was the author of the present book, Peter Botsis. The other two later became monks.—TRANS.

moments was, "It is good for us to be here." The Elder chanted the Doxasticon, with tears noticeable in his eyes. At the end, when he had said the Dismissal, everyone took his blessing, the women left, and the Elder remained with the three youths and the gentleman accompanying them.

"Nun, make each of us a coffee to drink now. And bring some sweets for the boys."

"How are you, Elder?"

"Glory be to God. Today, the whole night long I was in Bethlehem. I tried to comprehend the great mystery that took place there. The mind cannot contain it. The Great God, Whom 'nothing can contain,' how was He contained in the womb of the Virgin, our Panagia? Can this be contained by the mind of man? I marvelled and my mind was thinking of the beautiful hymns of the Nativity: 'Why, O Mary, marvellest thou, amazed at that which is in thee? Because I have given birth in time unto the timeless Son...' My mind stays there and I don't want to leave. Without fail, before you die, you must go to worship in Jerusalem."

The Elder's countenance appeared altered. His gaze looked somewhere on high; it seemed that he had no fellowship with this world as he said these things. Surely during these moments he was living in those Holy Places and his mind was striving to enter more deeply into the supernatural mystery of the Incarnation, into "the greatest event known to mankind," as he himself would say. He remained silent for a few moments and his visitors did not dare interrupt this divine preoccupation of his. Afterwards he continued the conversation.

"The spiritual life is the art of arts and science of sciences. The only thing is that for one to come to know it, he has to struggle greatly, to dig deeply in himself. Shut yourselves up one hour daily in your room and think of Christ and what is your foreordained purpose. Quietude is indispensable for the spiritual cultivation of man. You can't stop the wind blowing outside; but you can close the door. Secure the door of your soul and remain in quietude, lest you be swept away by the current.

"Hate no man, love all, but also avoid all. Do not pursue frequent visits. They come, they're welcome; they didn't come, it's well they didn't come. Don't get into arguments; avoid talkativeness. Have your mind continuously in God and think of the day of judgment, the hour of death. 'What manner of ordeal doth the soul endure when it is parted from the body!... Behold the Bridegroom cometh in the middle of the night.'[5] The hour of death is uncertain. We know not when it will find us. Our bed is a grave; we do not know if we will arise in the morning. We should always be prepared.

"Increase your zeal for God. A day should not pass without praying for at least half an hour. When two young people fall in love and get engaged, once a week they see each other and discuss all their dreams and desires. Afterwards they separate and all week long they continually think about the things they discussed. The mind of one is glued to the other. The same thing happens with compunctionate prayer. When you finish, you think continuously on those things which you prayed, and thus your mind is attached to God. Go to church and receive the divine Mysteries often. And reverence your spiritual father. He tries to bring you close to God. During confession, three are present: God, the confessor, and he who confesses. The work of the spiritual father is to reconcile the repentant with God. All these things—quietude, prayer, confession, and the like, will help you, they will increase your zeal for God. When the tile is fired well in the kiln, even if rain falls on it, it is not quenched. Thus also with the soul. When it is fired up with the love of God, no matter how many temptations arise, it is not shaken.

"This one," he continued, indicating one of the three young men, "you have not brought to me before. Where are you from?"

---

5. The first is from the funeral service, the second from the services of Holy Week.—TRANS.

"From Kozani, Elder."

"What is your name?"

"Demetrios."

"Your last name?"

"I go by Geronikos."

"No, that's not your last name. It's something else."

"Geronikos is my last name, Elder. That's my father's last name also. But one of my uncles, my father's brother, has another last name, even though they're both from the same father and mother. I don't know why, but he is named Sgiaras. Is that what you mean?"

"No, it's not that either. Your real last name is something else. You will learn it later."

The young man became confused. This was the first time he met the Elder personally, even though he had heard much about him and his gift of clairvoyance from his friends who had brought him here. He was unable to understand the Elder's words. He thought that maybe he meant something else or that in this instance he had made a mistake.

A few years later Demetrios became a monk in one of the monasteries of Meteora. When after the passage of many years he visited his village, he met his abovementioned uncle, who greeted him with the following words: "So you became a monk? Well, bravo, you did well. It was evident that one day you would end up in a monastery. Besides, we have a tradition for priestly things. Your grandfather was a priest and was named Papadopoulos. That's our real last name. But they changed it and now we're called by our nicknames. When your father was little, he was very prudent and wise, like an old man [*geros*, in Greek], and everybody called him *gero-Niko*. And that's the name that stuck. As for me, I don't know why, they called me Sgiaras and in the end they changed my name too. These things took place a long time ago."

The monk was now left with his mouth agape. He immediately remembered the words the Elder had told him some ten years ago and could not hide his astonishment. He verified then to an even greater degree how illumined that blessed man was whom he had been deemed worthy to meet, who had revealed to him something that he not only did not know, but didn't even have an inkling of. He immediately related the incident to his relatives.

After his conversation with Demetrios, the Elder began to admonish one of the other young men.

"Be careful who you keep company with. Speak well to all, but at the same time do not become close. Keep your distance, protect yourself. Do not keep company with people who have a worldly mind, and tell your secrets to no one. The holy Fathers say, 'Out of a thousand, let one be your friend.'

"When you see that you are angry, don't answer. Go away and when you come to yourself, think again about what you're going to say, with love and peace. When you're trying to do something good for someone, beware that you don't harm somebody else.

"Edifying conversation never does harm. The more you wipe a glass, the clearer it gets. But care is needed, because with much conversation we can fall into prattling and judging. I see that you have an inclination for spiritual things, for this reason I tell you these things. There is nothing higher than the choir of virgins. It resembles the choir of Angels. If ever you enter a monastery, practise three things: obedience, patience, and humblemindedness. If you observe these things, you will succeed and be saved.

"Many go to monasteries but do not succeed. Whosoever wishes to become a good monk should not a) be educated, b) know a trade, and c) have money. In other words, he has to renounce knowledge, self-confidence, and greed. All three of these things lead to pride, which is man's greatest enemy."

"How can I protect myself from pride, Elder?"

"Listen, it takes struggle. When they provoke you, do not react. Even if they should spit in your face, do not talk back or get angry. When others disdain you or criticize you, do not be distressed.

God will permit some to disdain you, but He will enlighten others to love you. As for you, never return evil for evil. Always offer what is good. If someone gives you pepper, you give him honey. Say, this I have, this I give you. Pepper I have not. Never admit anger into yourself. Whatever another may do to you, you are obliged to forgive him immediately. Reading will help you much in the beginning. Regularly read the Holy Scriptures and patristic books. But strive to apply the things you read. Otherwise, the knowledge will not only not profit you, but it will fill you with pride. Someone mentioned to me that he had memorized the Gospels and the Old Testament. I answered him, 'If you don't experience the things you learned, then you have filled the air with words.'

"The spiritual life has need of great care. It is very sweet. But for anyone to experience its sweetness, he has to struggle a great deal. For a man to be saved, he has to wash himself either in his blood or in his tears. The holy Martyrs were washed in their blood. We at least should shed a few tears."

"Elder, an acquaintance of mine does not behave well towards me and oftentimes he grieves me," said the first of the company. "What do you say, is it right for me to reproach him?"

"Hit, but do not kill. Everything should be done with discretion. See this stick? If I hold it from one end, it falls. If I hold it from the other, again it falls. But if I hold it from the middle, it stands. Have measure in all things. Someone came some time ago and roundly criticized the clergy. Fine, I said to him, in an olive grove some trees have rotted or gone bad. What shall we do? Should we uproot all the olive trees, because some went bad? The best reproach is that we take pains to show ourselves as an example of virtue. If we are virtuous and perfect, the other person will be embarrassed and will cease from sinning. If you throw oil on the sea, it doesn't sink; it remains on the surface. So with virtue. No matter what others do, it doesn't disappear and cannot be destroyed; it remains and is a praise to the virtuous and reproach to the sinner. At any rate, if we are careful, we will be able to avoid becoming a scandal.

"When you see that you are unable to come to an understanding with someone, do not persist. But do not hate him. Pray for him, only avoid his company. And if he visits you, do not speak without his asking you. And be careful to say what he is able to bear, so that the result is benefit and not harm. As for myself, when I go somewhere, or when someone comes to see me, I implore God that when he leaves I might not feel any censure."

"What is your opinion about dreams, Elder?"

"It is better for us not to believe in dreams at all, because many have gone astray on their account. There are three kinds of dreams: those from God, those from our thoughts, and those from the enemy. If they are from God and we don't believe them, God does not take offense, because we don't believe them out of fear, lest we be led into deception. If I should come in the night and knock on your door, and you don't open to me because you do not recognize my voice, I am not offended. So it is with God, He is not angry when out of fear of God we don't believe dreams. Wine and vinegar have the same appearance. From the taste you understand the difference. If the dreams are from God, they bring calm; if they are from the enemy, they bring turmoil. Beware of deceptions. Better to protect ourselves and not believe anything outside of what our Church teaches."

The Elder paused a little. He leaned back on his folding chair and gazed on high. For a few minutes absolute silence reigned. No one wished to break it. Then he sat up somewhat and continued, "Action precedes divine vision. God first created the body and afterwards breathed in the soul. Jacob first worked seven years for Rachel, but he received Leah, who symbolizes the practical virtues—many children. After that he worked another seven years and received Rachel, who symbolizes divine vision. You are now at the beginning of the spiritual life. You have to struggle to acquire the practical virtues. Struggle with prayer, fasting according to your ability, confession, divine Communion, and the rest. Likewise read spiritual books, mainly the Holy Scriptures, the *Psalter*, and Abba Isaac. Have a care to take away time from conversations and devote it to reading. If there is good preaching somewhere, it is good to attend. A sermon is like the rain; it rains and irrigates everywhere. Speech, edifying conversations, are like a small brook, which irrigates to a limited degree.

"If you want your prayer to reach God, be careful not to wrong anyone. Once a stranger visited me and said, 'A certain acquaintance of mine didn't trust his wife and asked me to keep two thousand gold crowns for him. Now he's died and his wife doesn't know anything. Can I keep them?'

"'How are you going to keep them, are they yours?' I said.

"'But his wife knows nothing.'

"'That has no bearing. They belong to her.'

"'I'll give you a hundred crowns, too.'

"'But from what are you going to give them to me—do you have crowns? Those which you have are not yours.'

"'I understand: you don't know—I'll ask somebody else.'

"He obviously wanted to keep the gold crowns, but he sought for a blessing also, so that he would feel at peace about it. If he found someone weak, he may have succeeded in his purpose. The only thing that he didn't think about is God. It is easy to deceive people, but God is not mocked. Whatever you do, think that before you is God. This will help you not to sin. Well now, maybe you should be going, since I'm a little tired. I've been talking almost the whole day. May God and the Panagia protect you and Divine Providence cover you."

"Elder," said one of the young men. "This book is sent to you by so-and-so."

It was a book by a well-known theologian and author, who at the time was also making religious broadcasts on the radio.

"Thank you very much. And please tell him, that if all that he says and writes he also puts into practice, he shall be blessed. May God and the Panagia be with you."

The visitors left and the Elder remained alone in his cell for a little. But it was not meant for him to rest, for the day's ministrations had not yet finished. Ten minutes later the bell rang again. The new visitor was an elderly and very virtuous priestmonk, accompanied by two nuns. The Eldress Eupraxia announced him and immediately brought them in. The Elder arose and made a deep bow to him and each kissed the other's hand.

They exchanged the usual greetings and all spoke together for about ten minutes. Then the nuns went out and only the priestmonk remained in the cell. After twenty minutes he went out also, and the two nuns entered the Elder's cell, each one separately. When the first nun came out, she approached the priestmonk and said to him, "What a holy man this is, Elder! He revealed to me something that only I know. I haven't even told it to you."

"Yes, I completely agree with you. He is worthy of his reputation for virtue and holiness," he answered.

After the second nun came out, all three entered his cell again to bid him farewell. The priestmonk then asked him, "Elder, I would like to go to confession. Will you receive me?"

"No! I am not able to confess you. It would be better if you found some other virtuous spiritual father to hear your confession."

After this, all three of them left. But the nun who had made the favorable critique of the Elder's holiness was grieved. Her elder was very virtuous, and also had the reputation of being a holy spiritual father. Why then did Father Ieronymos not accept to confess him? "For him not to have accepted my elder for confession," she thought, "it seems that he might not be that holy, and maybe the revelation that he made to me was just a coincidence."

But what astonishment she experienced, and how much her awe and reverence for the ascetic of Aegina increased, when on the next

The Elder's cell, with his bed, and the chair he sat in when receiving visitors.

day, through an acquaintance, the Elder sent her word saying, "Tell T. not to be angry that I didn't confess her elder. As soon as he entered my cell his whole face shone. How then could I confess him?"

As the priestmonk with his synodia were leaving, a couple with their daughter entered the hermitage. They were ship-owners and well known to the Elder. They visited him regularly, especially the wife, and made their confession to him. Their other daughter was seriously ill and at that time was staying in one of the convents of Aegina for rest, quiet, and spiritual reading. They were on their way to see her and passed by first at the Elder's to get his blessing.[6]

6. This was the Pateras family of Oinoussai, Chios: Panagos, Katingo, and their daughter Calliope. The parents and the ill daughter, Irene, later became monastics.—TRANS.

"Forgive us, Elder, we're a little late."

"It doesn't matter, come in."

They all entered his cell.

"How are you doing, are you well?"

"Glory be to God, Elder, for all things; you know our woes. May His Name be glorified. Just pray that our faith does not fail us."

"Listen, God along with the temptations also gives patience. He never gives more than we are able to endure. For people who love God, 'all things work for good.' I will pray for you, but it is necessary that you pray also. Pray and beseech God to give you faith and patience, to be freed from thoughts of despair. The Saints had the power to rebuke the enemy. We, when we have temptations, ought to take refuge in our Christ and Panagia, just as a little child runs to his mother."

He then turned to their daughter, who was married with children, but was confronted with many great personal and family problems.

"And how is it with you, are you better now?"

"No, not so well, Elder."

"Tell me, do you have a house?"

"Yes, Elder."

"Do you have a car?"

"Yes, of course."

"Do you have servants, to help you in the house?"

"I do."

"Did you ever work in a factory, in order to live?"

"No."

"And then you also want not to have woes? It can't be. God loves us, but often we do not understand it. If we enjoy everything here on earth, then we will forget God. God gives us opportunities to come to know Him, if only we take hold of the messages. He finds a thousand ways to make us come close to Him. Saint Basil says somewhere, 'Make weakness material for virtue.' No matter what evil comes upon us, if we have patience, it is possible that that which we see as evil, will guide us to virtue. The greatest evil is to become estranged from God. I know it's difficult, because you were accustomed to a worldly life and it will be difficult for you to put away its memories. Effort and struggle are needed. But if we make even a little effort of will, God will strengthen and support us. Do not worry and do not despair. God is great and loves us greatly. He saved the thief on the same day, and shall He abandon us?"

"I, Elder, used to play cards, but now I've stopped," said the father, with a fair dose of satisfaction.

"Well, the illness left the hand and went to the foot."

This seemed to trouble him somewhat, and he went out into the courtyard and started pacing about. The Elder addressed his wife and said, "I grieved him a little, but what can we do? When we are freed from one passion it's necessary that we take care not to acquire another one. And pride is the worst of the passions."

After a little while he approached him and said some comforting words to him, and he calmed down and left benefited.

After these last visitors had also left, the Elder withdrew to his cell. The time was approaching eight o'clock. He rested for about ten minutes and afterwards got up and read Compline and the Laudations of the Theotokos (that is, the Akathist).

When the service ended, he closed the door of his cell and remained isolated in this secret treasury of his spiritual struggles until three in the morning, dividing the time between sleep and his beloved prayer. As the Eldress Eupraxia would relate to us, many nights it happened that she passed by outside his cell and heard him praying with sighs, sobs, and contrition of heart, so continuing the tradition of compunctionate prayer that he had been taught by Misael, his elder. In this way he recovered that necessary spiritual strength which one is able to draw only from God, in order to continue on the morrow the same laborious work, with new experiences, new visitors, and always with the same kindness and love.

CHAPTER TWENTY-ONE

My Strength is Made Perfect in Weakness

His fame as an excellent father-confessor and clairvoyant Saint passed beyond the boundaries not only of Aegina and Athens, but even of Greece. The faithful who visited him, even from abroad, continually increased. And the Elder spent himself in hearing confessions and giving guidance, in doing works of kindness, and in prayer.

The years were passing, his age was advancing, and his much-afflicted body began to be weighed down from asceticism and privations. But he persisted, "as much as he had strength,"[1] in fulfilling the work of God. His love for God and his fellow man was so great that he disregarded the labors and hardships, for the sake of benefiting his neighbor while not being deprived himself of the joy of asceticism and prayer.

He would not stop receiving the continually increasing visitors, even when, having just passed the age of eighty, his health showed signs that it was beginning to break down quite seriously. His body seemed unable to continue its exhausting service; but his spirit was willing. He was so aflame with love and zeal for God that he did not take his bodily weakness into account and gave himself over with unmitigated intensity to his beloved occupations.

In the summer of 1964 we observed the first disquieting indications. Somewhat protracted colds and a certain persistent little hoarseness of his voice indicated that his health had suffered a se-

---

1. From a hymn of the Church.—trans.

rious breakdown. He seemed no longer to have the previous ease in his motions. Certain traces of fatigue marked his face. But everyone attributed it to normal physiological wear, after so many visitors that he received daily and the continuous admonitions that he was obliged to give.

About two years passed like this with the same annoyances, and the same fatigue, and the same spiritual intensity. It seems that he had decided to continue his spiritual ministry until his last breath, sacrificing himself, rather than to withdraw and rest in order to protect his health. He did not wish under any circumstances to abandon "the least of his brethren" who ran to him to find consolation and refuge in their sorrows. He became in the end a living candle which consumed itself in the service of God and neighbor.

In the summer of 1966 things began to worsen. The cough had become very persistent and prolonged. Many times he coughed so intensely that he could stop only with difficulty and had no strength either to move or to talk. Some of his spiritual children of his immediate circle, when they saw him in such a condition, implored him to enter a hospital in Athens for examination. There, they would be able to ascertain the cause of these annoyances and some sort of therapy would likely follow. But he persistently refused to leave and be away from his cell. His only concession was to have a chest x-ray taken at the hospital of Aegina. But this was without results, since it did not come out clear at all.

In the meantime the cough grew continuously worse, while a sharp pain in the left side of his stomach began to bother him. Seeing his unyielding opposition to being taken to Athens, we thought of visiting him with a doctor friend, as much to examine him as also to try to convince him to go to a hospital in Athens, if he judged it necessary. And in fact, we visited him with the doctor J. Moustakis,[2] who verified that his condition was bad. But he

2. Dr. John Moustakis, since deceased, was the doctor of the Pateras family, who were spiritual children of the Elder's.—TRANS.

couldn't diagnose the illness before seeing the results of certain special examinations he judged necessary. Yet before he was able to recommend that he be admitted to a hospital, the Elder surmised his intention and said to him, "I am not going to Athens."

In vain did the doctor and all of us try to make him change his mind. He would not be persuaded. In the end the attempt was abandoned lest we grieve him further.

The Elder, in spite of his terrible condition, was well disposed and discussed spiritual subjects with the doctor, whom he met for the first time. He rejoiced to make his acquaintance, because he was truly a most honorable and conscientious man. Even jesting with him, at one moment he asked him, "Tell me, if you were born again, would you marry again?" (The doctor was married and the father of two daughters.)

"Hmm! I probably would marry again."

"Apparently the first time didn't correct you," answered the Elder, moving us all to laughter with his humor.

The Elder deeply loved monasticism as the most perfect expression of the Christian life, and he desired if possible that all men might become monks. But he was always careful and discreet in his recommendations.

The doctor finally left, having first recommended with love that he enter some hospital in Athens for examination.

A few days later, since the symptoms worsened, the Eldress Eupraxia was compelled to invite Dr. Xydeas from Aegina. He examined him and also recommended that he go to a hospital in Athens for examination. When the Elder repeated to him also that he did not want to leave his cell, and for this reason did not want to go to the hospital, the doctor knelt before him and implored him with tears, "Elder, Aegina needs you, we all have need of you. I implore and beseech you to go to a hospital—it could be that you'll get well there. Do not refuse, I beg you, do it for us, if you won't do it for yourself."

The Elder was moved by these love-filled words of the doctor's. He embraced him, kissed him, and declared to him that he would give way before his love. He himself had never believed that he functioned as a spiritual leader and instructor for the inhabitants of Aegina, even though he had spent his life in the service of all. In spite of his enormous offering, he had the consciousness that he was an "unprofitable servant," who is a debtor to all. But he was exceptionally sensitive and he yielded to Dr. Xydeas's humility and love. The doctor at that moment evidently represented all the inhabitants of Aegina, who understood his beneficent presence on the island.

Thus, after his spiritual children undertook to find the appropriate hospital and to arrange what was needed for his admission, the Elder left on the morning of September 13 for Athens. He was very feeble by now, and could barely walk. They put him in a car and drove from his cell to the harbor. As the car was boarding the ferryboat, the mailman who was passing by there noticed him and approached him to give him a registered letter. The Elder immediately handed it over to the Eldress Eupraxia with the injunction to open it and give him "what it has inside." The Eldress Eupraxia obeyed and discovered that in the envelope, besides the letter, was also a handkerchief, which she handed to the Elder. He made the sign of the Cross over it with his hand and told her to return it to the address of the sender.

Later, when the Eldress Eupraxia read the letter, despite the fact that she was accustomed to such "signs," she was unable to hide her emotion and her wonderment at the Elder's gift of clairvoyance. The letter had been sent from America. A sick man who had heard many things of Father Ieronymos's holiness had acquired very great faith in him. So he decided to send a letter with a handkerchief, that the Elder might only make the sign of the Cross over it and return it. It would be enough for him to touch it himself and he would be healed, since he was unable himself to make the long journey to Greece. The Elder, even before he opened the letter, knew everything.

The faith of these simple Christians towards the Elder Ieronymos was so great that it reminds us of the fiery faith of the first Christians of the apostolic era.

The car finally conveyed him to Piraeus and from there to Athens, to the hospital "Alexandra."

I had as probably the greatest blessing of my life not only to know him and to have him as my spiritual guide and instructor, but also to be at his side nearly all night and day, from the first moment that he set foot in the hospital, until the moment he let out his last breath. I was able in this way to follow at very close range a Saint's last struggles and the preparation for his "exodus"—his deep faith, his great love for God and man, his Job-like patience, his indomitable spiritual strength. His whole life was characterized by an insatiable thirst for the Kingdom of the Heavens, a seeking for the Kingdom of God, and communion with the Persons of the Holy Trinity. And he encountered God within himself, digging deep within, in his heart. For this reason he was able to face all his trials, even the last one, with heroic perseverance, having absolute trust in the love of God. These days that I lived close to the Elder Ieronymos are the most moving and most significant of my life.

The Elder's admission into the hospital had been previously arranged and it was unnecessary to go through many formalities. He was quickly transferred to a private room and the examinations began almost immediately. Notwithstanding his illness and the hardship of the trip, he was pleasant to all the hospital staff, doctors and nurses, and even had a good word to say. He even had the disposition to jest with the male nurse who rendered him the first services, a simple man, named John, "John, don't scrub too much. Take a look at this arm (he raised the stump of his left arm)—scrub, scrub away at whatever's left."

The Elder's first days in the hospital passed without anything special. The examinations followed one after another—blood tests, x-rays, and so on—but without indicating anything in particular. The doctors' attention was turned mainly to the lungs, because there was an intense cough and his breathing was not normal, but was done with difficulty. In the end they drew fluid from his lungs for a cytological analysis, the results of which would come out in about a week.

The days that followed were nightmarish. The Elder suffered exceedingly. On the one hand, the shortness of breath and the coughing tormented him and he was unable to breathe easily; on the other, he had various other symptoms (pains in the chest, in his legs and feet, and other points of the body) and above all an interior heat, which he felt was burning his entrails, whereas exteriorly his temperature was normal. His singular relief was to refresh his hand a little in cold water. The more that the days passed, the more his condition worsened. To the abovementioned symptoms were added sleeplessness, dizzy spells, giddiness, and a tendency to vomiting, which made him suffer even more.

His answer to all these physical sufferings was prayer. There was never heard the slightest murmuring nor any complaint. He continuously glorified God. On the occasions that we understood from the contortions of his face that he was suffering more severely, the only thing that he was wont to say was, "Lord, do not take me, if I don't become all Thine!"

His anxiety was not over the outcome of his health. That was in the hands of God. If God willed that he get well, it would be so. If not, may His will be done. That which concerned him was finishing the course, his salvation. After a whole life of struggles, prayer, and communion with God, he still desired repentance. As for the rest, it appeared that Paul's "for me to live is Christ and to die is gain" had become for him a fact and experience of life.

All these days of his cruel trials he not only showed a martyric patience and submission to the will of God, but he even set himself aside and endeavored to benefit all that came to him. Even before he left Aegina, all necessary measures had been taken so that it would not be known which hospital he had entered. We were afraid that if the contrary happened, his spiritual children would inundate the hospital and the Elder's love for them would certainly be stronger than the doctors' orders for complete rest. But it was not long before he became known in the hospital.

In the clinic in which he was hospitalized, all the nurses were religious. They belonged to religious organizations and truly performed their work with a great deal of love—with singular dedication, one might say. Those among them who first visited the Elder for medical reasons quickly discovered, and communicated to the other nurses also, that this was a holy man. Slowly but surely they began to visit him more frequently with the excuse that they had come to bring him medicine or to tidy up the room. They lingered as long as they could, speaking on spiritual subjects with him.

The secret did not remain confined to the nurses and doctors of the hospital, but spread to their relatives, and the visitors of the other patients in that wing, and the circle progressively enlarged.

His room was transformed into a spiritual infirmary. Often outside the door of his room awaited a great multitude of people. They begged the Eldress Eupraxia to permit them to enter, if only to kiss his hand. And he, who often perceived what was happening outside the door, yielded to their love and told the Eldress to open to them. To some of those who came by and kissed his hand, he didn't say a word. But to others he said a few words or asked them questions, which often brought them to perplexity or embarrassment. We convey some of these conversations, of which we were witnesses.

"What is your name?"

"Demetrios."

"How many [*girlfriends*] do you have?"

"... None."

"Listen! I've been a spiritual father for fifty-three years. Tell me the truth."

"Right now, I don't have any."

"Ah, you had, and you left them? You have not left them. Leave them, if you want to get well."

The young man left with drooping head. When he was gone the Elder told us, "The girls he has had relations with were circling around his face."

To a young woman who was sick, approaching him with dishevelled hair and supported by others, he said, "As your hair is all dishevelled, so are your brains! Take care to gather your mind and cease from sinning and you'll get well."

"Yes, Father, I'll try," answered the young woman and left crying.

A certain elderly woman, as soon as she entered the room, knelt, and in this position she reached his bed and kissed his feet. The Elder was conscious of her but did not protest, remaining motionless. When she came closer, he stretched out his hand and said to her, "This has the blessing, and not the feet. Humility is good, but empty humble forms is pride. Humility requires contrition of heart and not display. Take care to become humble and you will be saved."

The woman departed pale and pensive.

Such incidents are without number. Everyone was left astonished by this priest's holiness and gift of clairvoyance. When, during the doctors' visits, we came out to the visitors' lounge of the hospital, we heard nothing else save the conversations of the patients and their relatives about their impressions of Father Ieronymos.

"My good one, that man is a Saint! He revealed everything to me. He even told me that I have to fulfill a vow that I made when I was young and myself had forgotten about. What a shame that I never met him earlier! That such a Saint should be around and we didn't know it!"

"He told me astonishing things, too. He even told me a great deal about my husband, whom he has never seen, and described his character exactly. He told me that he is a very good man and generous, but that he swears and doesn't go to church. And that really is the case. He's very good and I have no complaint, except for the things this holy man told me."

"To me, he revealed something with so many details and such accuracy, that if I weren't sure that no one else knew of it, I'd say that somebody revealed it to him. It's astonishing. This man has made me believe that there really are Saints and that everything that's written about them is true. What a blessing this is, my God, that I should get to know a Saint!"

"I think that what happened to me hasn't occurred to anyone else. Without my telling him what I had, he told me that I would get well and would not need to have an operation, though I was scheduled to have it the following day. And as he said it, so it happened. The operation was postponed, and today the doctors told me to leave, because I'm well. This man has God in him, he's a Saint. Otherwise these things cannot be explained."

The longer one was around him, the more one learned of further "signs" and "prophecies" done by "this holy man." Everybody waited for the door to open so they could go in, to see him and hear him or even just kiss his hand. As the report spread quickly that in such-and-such a room they had a Saint for a patient, the line of those waiting outside his door continually increased.

One of the spiritual children of the Elder's intimate circle was Mrs. S. Her mother suffered from Parkinson's, and since she had no one to take care of her, she didn't come to the hospital very often. But one evening she left her young niece to watch over her and rushed to the hospital to offer her services to the Elder even if it were only for a few hours.

Five minutes had not passed since she entered the Elder's room when he asked her, "Did you leave anyone with your mother?"

"Yes, I did, Elder."

"Whom did you leave?"

"My niece."

"Depart quickly. Your mother is alone."

"But, Elder, I left her with my niece and only then departed. She's not by herself."

"Go quickly. Now she's by herself."

The woman was confused. She wondered what she should do and finally decided that the two of us should go down to the pastry shop next door and phone. She called home, but no one answered the telephone. She was surprised. What could be wrong? She phoned again and persisted. After some time her mother picked up the receiver.

"What do you want? S. is not here." (Evidently because of age and illness she did not recognize her daughter's voice.)

"Mama, it's me. Do you hear me?"

"Yes, I hear you."

"Are you alone?"

"Yes, I'm alone."

"Where is Popie? Did she leave?"

"Yes, she left. I'm by myself now."

One can easily understand our surprise, our wonder, our emotion. As soon as we returned to the hospital and entered the Elder's room, we found him smiling enigmatically and stretching his hand to S.

"Come on, daughter, go to your mother," he told her gently.

His behavior was such that it was obvious that he knew everything. Not only that Mrs. S.'s mother was alone, but it was even as if he had overheard the telephone conversation. But our reverence for the Elder, besides our familiarity with such "signs," did not permit us to ask him how he knew all this. We accepted them as signs of the Grace that had clearly come to dwell in him, and we glorified God, Who had shown mercy to us and deemed us worthy to know a true Saint.

T̲w̲o̲ ̲w̲e̲e̲k̲s̲ ̲h̲a̲d̲ ̲p̲a̲s̲s̲e̲d̲ since the Elder entered the hospital. One morning, when I was alone in his room, the doctor tending to him called me and reported to me that the cytological analysis showed that the Elder was suffering from lung cancer. It seems that the much-afflicted Elder had to pass through this trial also before leaving this temporal life and departing for the eternal, to Christ, Whom he had loved with his whole soul from his childhood. The doctor also said that it would be good to keep him in the hospital for a certain period to undergo therapy.

Even though we had suspected that there was something quite bad going on, the report struck all of us like lightning. We then understood that the Elder would not long be with us. And this for us his spiritual children, who had him as guide and support in our every problem, was a very heavy thing. But there was nothing we could do to reverse the matter. We contented ourselves with praying that God would extend his life as long as possible.

We didn't mention anything to him. We only told him that there was some problem with his lungs and that the doctors advised that he stay a few more days in the hospital to undergo therapy. He himself did not initially reveal anything to us. This seemed curious to us. Whereas he could read the hearts of men and even reveal the most innermost thoughts, how was it possible that he didn't know what he himself was suffering from? Did he know it and not reveal it, or did God, in His inscrutable judgments, not reveal it to him? God only knows.

In this manner another five martyric days passed in the hospital. His pains had intensified; he completely lost his appetite. But he was tormented most of all by an intense difficulty in breathing and an interior fire which he felt was burning his whole being. Yet he did not complain even for a moment. He prayed continuously, praising God, and his attention became even more concentrated.

On one of the last nights of his stay in the hospital, he said to the

Eldress Eupraxia who stayed with him continually, "Nun, I think we shall not return to Aegina alive."

We tried to encourage him, telling him that it was nothing serious and that he would get well, and so forth, but he did not speak. It seems that he understood everything by now and was not saying anything to us in order not to grieve us.

On the morning of the twentieth day since his entrance in the hospital, he said to us suddenly and unequivocally, "Today we leave for Aegina." In vain did we try to convince him to remain hospitalized a little longer to continue his therapy. He was not to be persuaded.

"Twenty days have I been in the hospital and have seen no good," he answered. "What more can I do? At least I'll go to my cell and have some quiet."

Seeing his irrevocable decision, we notified the head nurse and the doctors to issue the release, and we began to prepare for the trip to Aegina. As the preparations were being made, two spiritual children of the Elder's came from Aegina to visit him. Having spoken with them a little, he suddenly asked them, "How was the trip from Aegina, is the weather good?"

"Yes, Elder, the weather is quite good."

I intended to accompany him to Aegina and for this purpose went to my house at Ampelokipos where I was living at the time with Mr. Eleutherios K. About 10:30 a.m., as I was returning to the hospital, a nun of my acquaintance greeted me from afar, saying, "Run, because the Elder isn't going to Aegina, he's coming to your house."

I was caught by surprise. I returned to the Elder and he told me, "The weather is not good, there's a sea storm. For this reason we're not leaving for Aegina, we'll go to Leutheri's."

I was confused. I myself had just heard the two people from Aegina affirming the opposite. How is it the Elder now says that the weather has changed? But I rejoiced that he was coming to our house and so I didn't ask him how he knew about the change in the weather.

A few hours passed until the proceedings for the Elder's exodus from the hospital were finished, and at about three in the afternoon we put him in a taxi and headed for Ampelokipos. The Elder had worsened a lot. He wasn't even able to walk. When we reached home we were faced with the problem of getting him from the taxi into the house. We brought an armchair and put him in it, but now who would carry the chair? Besides myself there was no other man to help and the Elder was relatively heavy. I was forced to stop a passerby and ask him to help us. The man offered readily and suddenly asked, "Who is the Elder, does he happen to be Father Ieronymos of Aegina?"

"Yes," I answered him in astonishment. "Do you know him?"

"*Po! po!*—can you imagine that!" the man cried out. "I was seeking you in heaven and I found you here. I am so-and-so and for some time now I've wanted to come to Aegina to meet you but was not deemed worthy of it by God."

"Now you were needed, so now you've come," replied the Elder.

With his help we were able to carry the Elder into the house.

Not even half an hour passed after we entered the house before one of his spiritual children from Aegina, Panagiotes T., telephoned to ask how the Elder was faring. We related to him the particulars and the Elder's decision to come to our house, and he answered, "You did well not to embark for Aegina, because the weather has changed and you would have risked your lives at sea."

Once again we marvelled at the Elder's clairvoyance. There was not an event in his life or even in the life of others that he did not foresee. In his every word and action, it was evident that the grace of God dwelt in him and operated wondrously. He was a living vessel of the Holy Spirit. Enclosed in the four walls of the hospital, he knew all that took place outside in the world, even the change in the weather conditions.

CHAPTER TWENTY-TWO

Last Struggles

THE STATE OF HIS HEALTH steadily deteriorated. With the exception of some short intervals when the pain left him a little, the greater part of the twenty-four hour period, day and night, he suffered greatly. He was especially tormented even here by a fire which he felt was burning him from within, and a frightful shortness of breath accompanied by coughing. Virtually his only relief was to put his hand in a plate with ice cubes, which he even found rather amusing.

But out of his mouth was never heard the least murmuring, not a single complaint. Most of the time we saw him praying with attention and fervor. A few times we heard him loudly calling upon the Lord, the Panagia, and various Saints. On the last days we often heard him crying, "My Mommy." Once the Eldress Eupraxia ventured to ask him, "Elder, are you calling out for your mother?"

"It's our Panagia I am calling upon, nun, our Panagia."

Not a few times we saw him in ecstasy and whispering certain words we found incomprehensible, among which we were able to distinguish a few phrases, such as, "All around my head they're putting on the crown," or, "Aegina, Aegina! You're going to be very sad, but then you'll rejoice again and will compose verses."

One week passed in this climate of strain, agony, and perseverance. Night and day, someone stayed beside him either to keep him company or to watch him or to offer some service. But his condition continually worsened.

On Monday, October 10 (September 27 o.s.), in the evening, I intended to go down to Piraeus to pick up some of the Elder's clothes, which S., whom we mentioned above, had taken to wash. A little before I left, the Elder called me and said, "Tell S. to come today without fail so that I can see her. Both of you come together."

I didn't understand at all; but I transmitted the Elder's message to S. as soon as I saw her at the port of Piraeus, where we had agreed to meet. She herself also asked what it meant and we departed together for the house. As soon as we entered, we found the Elder very moved. He called us all: the Eldress Eupraxia, Styliani, Eleutherios, Helen, John, and me, and said to us with tears, "I see myself that I am not well. Until Sunday, if God wills, I will remain in this life. For this reason I called you, to give you my last counsels. Styliani, I implore you kindly to have the nun as your mother and your sister. Go to Aegina and live together as sisters, but know that she is older."

The Elder said other things also. He counselled all the others and then fell silent. We on our part were not able to restrain ourselves, and being moved, we wept, some quietly and others out loud. It was the first time that the Elder revealed to us his innermost thoughts and specified the exact time his end would come.

The atmosphere weighed down heavily, because we then began to realize much more clearly that the hour was at hand when we would lose forever that heavenly man, who was for all of us a tender loving father, a dear friend, and a sanctified spiritual father. We could no longer do anything to keep him in this life. Everything indicated that the Elder was hurrying with "joyful step" to depart, to go to the true life, to the Lord, Whom he had loved "with all his heart and with all his soul and with all his strength" from his childhood. He had struggled hard his whole life long, with consistency and full awareness, for this moment. And now when he felt—or was informed—that this moment had arrived, he wanted to be prepared in all things.

Beside his spiritual preparations, he felt, as it would seem, the necessity not to leave anything unresolved behind him. He had arranged everything pertaining to the transfer of the hermitage and the church of the holy Unmercenaries, which were in his name. Now he wished to attend both to the succession of his hermitage, and to providing for the Eldress Eupraxia, who had remained his faithful disciple for forty-seven years. Many souls, during the latter years, had expressed their fervent desire to remain and become monastics close to him. But the Elder remained reserved and cautious, and would not express himself. On this day he chose to settle this matter also, choosing for this ministry her who later became a nun, being renamed Eupraxia also, and who today continues his tradition in his hermitage.

On the morrow his condition gave perceptible signs of having worsened. He ate very little all day and spoke even less. In the evening, in order to please him, we played some tapes on the recorder so that he could hear some rare performances of Byzantine chant. Despite his weakened state, he listened attentively and with evident emotion. When the tapes finished he said to us, "What beautiful things! They remind me of Constantinople, of the Patriarchate. How beautifully they chanted. In my days, the precentor of the Great Church of Christ was Iakovos Naupliotes. What a voice that was! But how much piety and devoutness he had also! Whenever he chanted, he wept. Where can you find such chanters today? My soul within me skips for joy and longing. As long as that [*the tape recorder*] chanted I was saying within me, let it stop and I'll start to chant. But the flesh is weak."

He even tried to chant a little; he said, "The impassable and boisterous sea...,"[1] but his voice failed him. It could just barely be heard.

---

1. The First Ode Heirmos in Second Tone, used in the Triodion canon of Holy Monday, and the prefestal canons for Nativity (on December 20) and Theophany (on January 2).—TRANS.

Late that evening he was visited by an archimandrite of his acquaintance. He had also seen him in the hospital two or three times, where he had gone to give him Holy Communion.

"You will become a bishop one day," the Elder said to him.

"I, become a bishop, Elder? I neither want it, nor will they ordain me."

"You might not want it, but someone who wants it will ordain you."

Some years after the Elder's repose, this archimandrite became a bishop.[2]

Three days more passed, during which his condition was for the most part the same. He was totally without appetite; the only thing he had was a little milk and a few spoonfuls of soup. He had also stopped speaking. He said only what was strictly necessary. But his attention was ever sharp. He prayed continuously and made the sign of the Cross quite often, saying, "Glory be to Thee, O God," or "Lord, Jesus Christ, have mercy on me." Evidently he was preparing for his end and prayed unceasingly. He wished his mind to be united to God at every moment. He spoke to us rarely, to give us his last counsels and admonitions or to thank us:

"I am a sinful man. I have not done any good to anyone. Yet even so, there were found people to serve me in my illness. May the Lord repay you bountifully both in this life and in the one to come."

From Friday morning on, his condition showed signs of worsening. He almost totally stopped taking food and he limited his speech even more. His movements also began to be made with greater difficulty. Seeing this condition, in the evening we all conferred with the Eldress and decided to inform his closest relatives and his most beloved spiritual children to come by and receive his blessing for the last time. Thus, late that night we informed a few people.

---

2. This was Father Gerasimos Brakas who was later ordained Bishop of Boetia by Archbishop Auxentius. Both have since reposed.—TRANS.

From morning of the next day on (it was a Saturday), the house began to overflow with relatives and acquaintances who came to bid the Elder farewell. We were astonished that although only a few, and that late at night, had been informed, yet early the next day they were coming to see him in groups. The report had obviously travelled like lightning.

One could discern pain and sorrow depicted on the faces of all, like a group of companions losing someone exceedingly close to them. You might even think you were seeing people passing in procession before the Epitaphios on Holy and Great Friday. All were weeping and sorrowing. And all were relating how they had met the Elder, how beneficially he had influenced their life and the divine gifts, both of prophecy and of healing, that adorned him. In the consciousness of all he was a real Saint. And now all these people, his "little flock," were mourning that they were losing this angel-imitating hesychast, in whose cell they had laid aside all the burdens of their soul and in whose person they had found consolation and deliverance.

One related the decisive and singular solution that the Elder gave to some terrible impasse he had been in. Another, the surgery he had avoided by his blessing alone. A third, the domestic tragedy from which he was delivered by having recourse to his counsel. Everyone had some impressively astonishing event to relate and did not want to part from him. But the hours were passing and the time was growing shorter that separated him from his departure to the heavenly tabernacles.

On the evening of the same day we asked him if he wished to have Holy Communion and he said he did. We called Father Niphon, an archimandrite well known and loved by him, and he performed the unction service. The Elder followed the whole unction service sitting, and afterwards he communicated.

When all those present left, the Elder lay down and did not speak anymore. He passed a relatively peaceful night, during which he was evidently praying continually, because his lips often moved, and with his hand he made the sign of the Cross.

On the morning of the next day, Sunday, the number of those who came to bid him farewell and receive his blessing increased continually. An impenetrable press of people filled the house. And the more they saw that the Elder was living out his last hours, the more their pain increased and they all dissolved in tears, some even with loud crying and sobs. The pilgrims came and went and the narrations concerning the Elder followed one upon another. A person could compose whole volumes if he gathered them all. Through it all, the Elder remained speechless, devoted to his prayers, and awaiting the Bridegroom, Whom he had worshipped his whole life long.

Around 12:00 noon, he was visited by a certain hierarch,[3] who read him a prayer of absolution. Afterwards he asked him, "How are you, Father Ieronymos?"

The Elder was no longer able to speak, but he was possessed of all his senses. He shook his hand from right to left, as if saying, "So-so," and then was peaceful.

But he continued here and there to make the sign of the Cross and his lips trembled. It was evident that he was praying. We who were near him observed the last moments of a Saint, as well as his undiminished combativeness. His whole life was an unceasing prayer and an offering unto his brethren. And he did not abandon prayer until his last breath. He lived with prayer and ended with prayer. A little before he gave up his last breath, his face acquired a certain unworldly tranquillity and brightness reminiscent of the Transfiguration or Resurrection. It was evidently the "gladness of

---

3. This was Archbishop Auxentius of blessed memory. He had also visited him in the hospital, which was the first time they met. After the Archbishop left the hospital, the Elder told those present two things: "His countenance is as the countenance of Daniel the Prophet," and "He ascended (the archiepiscopal throne) worthily."—TRANS.

salvation," the foretaste that God-loving souls experience in these critical hours, when they are found between corruption and incorruption, between temporal and true life, when they behold their expectations and struggles vindicated.

In this state we beheld him make the sign of the Cross many times. After that, a smile formed on his lips, and he said, "Glory to Thee, O God," he seemed to give a kiss, and he closed his eyes. The time was exactly 12:33 in the afternoon, Sunday, October 3, (October 16 n.s.), the feast of Saint Dionysius the Aeropagite, 1966.

CHAPTER TWENTY-THREE
Departure

THE MOMENTS THAT FOLLOWED were heart-rending. It was distressing yet deeply moving to see adults crying like little children and publicly declaring that the Elder had been quick to rescue them from desperation and despair, that he had saved their life, and the like. Two priests revealed that as long ago as spring he had already notified them that he would need them in October. Another said that the first time that he saw him, the Elder revealed to him that when he had gone to Jerusalem he had committed a great sin, and that he needed to go back again to correct it; it was something that not even he had been conscious of. And the narrations came and went. Each one had something wondrous to relate of the Elder.

In the meanwhile two priests[1] with the help of two young men did all that is proper for the dead—the washing and preparation of the body, and so forth. By 5:00 p.m. the coffin which conveyed him set off with a multitude of people for Aegina, where the Elder, having a continual remembrance of death, had already prepared the grave where they would place his body.

As soon as the boat drew near to the pier of Aegina harbor, we beheld to our surprise a large multitude waiting to receive the "holy spiritual father," the guardian and benefactor of the island. Various people, of every age and class, awaited him with tears in

---

1. They were those mentioned above—Niphon and Gerasimos—who have both since reposed.—TRANS.

their eyes and accompanied him on foot to his hermitage. There the body was placed in the little church of the Annunciation of the Theotokos for the veneration of the faithful.

All night long, and especially from the morning of the following day, thousands of people, both from Aegina and from elsewhere, began to come by to venerate the body. There came nuns from Saint Nectarius, Saint Menas, Saint Catherine, and other convents of Aegina and Attica. Bishops, priests, and monks also stopped in.

Especially moving was the weeping and lamentation of many orphans and widows who had lost their provider. It was the first time that we ascertained with our own eyes how many had been given relief by that "little bag of love," which he always bore on his shoulders. As long as he lived, it is evident that he had prohibited those who were benefited to mention anything about this activity of his. But now they felt released from this prohibition, and they began to relate with tears in their eyes the manifold benefactions they had received from his holy hands.

Nor was it only the widows and orphans who acknowledged his work and wept. All the local authorities, with the mayor of Aegina at the head, came and venerated the body and attended the funeral. The entire board of directors of the hospital of Aegina—which also published a proclamation that, among other things, mentioned that "it proclaims him as a great benefactor of the Institution... because he offered the highest services for the duration of the construction of the chapel of the Institution"—attended and resolved "to be present as a body at his funeral... to display his photograph in a conspicuous place in the hospital..." and so forth.

At about 3:30 p.m., after a great multitude had flooded not only the church and courtyard but also the whole area around the hermitage, the funeral service began. During the service, eulogies were given by the officiating bishop, who emphasized the holiness of his life; the mayor, who proclaimed the gratitude of the entire island of Aegina towards the great deceased; a representative of the hospital, who expressed the grief of the entire board of trustees and its gratitude to the great benefactor; and Panagiotes Togias, on behalf of his spiritual children, who sketched out with broad strokes his personality and the void left by his demise that no one would ever be able to fill.

At about 5:30 p.m., after the whole multitude present had given the last kiss, the sacred body of Father Ieronymos was lowered into the grave which he himself, many years ago, had prepared on the south side of the church.

This was the last act which sealed a whole life of struggles and sacrifices, prayer and vigilance, of a man who passed through this world, but lived in it only to benefit and profit others. As for everything else, his mind was continually found "outside this world," in Heaven, given over entirely to God. And now his soul flew to his desired fatherland, leaving behind "on the seashore," as the poet said, "the moving graves."[2]

---

2. From the poem *The Elder Ieronymos* (in Greek) by P. Paschos, in his book Αιχμαλωσία Ὕψους [*Capture the Heights*].—TRANS.

*The Tomb of the blessed Elder Ieronymos,
by the southern wall of his Chapel of the Annunciation.*

Epilogue

TWENTY-FIVE YEARS have passed since Father Ieronymos reposed. Twenty-five years that have proved insufficient not only to erase him from our memory, but even to diminish in the least the perception of his presence in our midst. Quite the contrary: the more time passes, and the more we are impoverished spiritually, this perception, and our nostalgia for him, continuously grows more intense. His admonitions and his teachings, moreover, have such a timeliness that we continually see events coming to pass, at a totally unsuspected time, that he himself had foreseen.

Very many who either met him personally, or heard or read of him and his wondrous and holy life, wonder if and when he will be recognized as a Saint by the Church—all the more because to those who call upon him, he supernaturally appears and performs many and wondrous miracles.

It is not our intention to circumvent the Church or to hasten to a proclamation of his sanctity, which is the work of God. If God wishes to console us with the appearance and presence of a new Saint in these evil and dark days of ours, He knows the time and the way He will do it. This is also the reason that, in the present edition at least, we avoid giving an account of the very many miracles he has performed to known and unknown persons who call upon him: miracles—mainly healings of serious illnesses—which might presage the existence of a second wonderworking Saint on Aegina.

For the present I will limit myself to only one observation. On one of my recent trips to Aegina, I had the opportunity to meet and speak with people who either were bound spiritually to the Elder or were ordinary secular people, whose relations with the Church range from non-existent to bare formalities. And the testimony of the first perhaps does not concern the matter at hand, because one could argue that it is influenced by subjectivity, on account of their acquaintance with and reverence for the Elder. But the opinion of the second is of very great interest: those who came to know Father Ieronymos without any kind of personal bias toward him. The opinion, we mean, of the fishermen, the merchants and small vendors, of the shop owners and the workers, all that anonymous multitude which had known him.

I was impressed by the fact that all were talking about him with great wonderment and particular reverence. And nearly the identical expression, which like some conclusion issued from the lips of all, was that "Father Ieronymos was a Saint." All of them narrate marvellous things about his clairvoyance and his great love for the poor. Without my even seeking it from them, they all spontaneously made haste to inform me of others also who knew him and had something to add to the information which I sought about him.

The universal recognition of his sanctity by people who could under no circumstances be accused of subjectivity or emotionalism, is surely a piece of evidence that cannot escape notice. This consciousness, acceptance, and admission of sanctity by the people, along with the miraculous interventions, are the main criterion for the recognition and proclamation of Saints.

It is a known fact that the Church permits a considerable period of time to pass after the repose of a Saint before proceeding to the recognition of his sanctity. This is so that even the last survivors may die out, who could possibly have been displeased by some human imperfections or even personal misunderstandings with him. This precaution, we can maintain with certainty, has no validity in the case of Father Ieronymos, since no one at any time was heard to express the least complaint against him or to doubt the all-encompassing sanctity of his life. Even the proclamation of the Master that "a man's foes shall be they of his own household" (Matt. 10:36) and "a prophet is not without honor, but in his own country, and among his own kin, and in his own house" (Mk. 6:4) is not applicable to the person of Father Ieronymos; for with his angelic life, his love, and his discreetness, he succeeded in never offending anyone, but rather in impressing himself upon the consciousness of all as a veritable Saint.[1]

1. In his introduction to a book of hymns composed by Haralampos Bousias in honor of the Elder Ieronymos, printed in Greek by the "Friends of the Elder Ieronymos," Peter Botsis states that "At the time of the uncovering of his bones, they were found to be free of any stain whatsoever, like amber, and they gave off a delicate fragrance."—TRANS.

Reliquaries containing the Elder's skull (left) and bones (right);
the former is a gift of our monastic communities.

Mother Eupraxia at the tomb of the Elder Ieronymos with Father Nicholas (see pages 174–75).

Appendix
Eupraxia Galanopoulos, Nun of the Hermitage "Annunciation of the Theotokos," Aegina

IT IS NOT EASY FOR ME to speak about the Elder. Even from the few things written in the book about him, anyone can comprehend who and what kind of man he was.

Without my knowing it or seeking it, God permitted it—the circumstances came about in such a way—that through my brother, Arsenios, monk, I was found at the feet of the Elder and was deemed worthy to minister to him till the end. From that time on, I understood that this was a holy elder; but even as it was with our Lord's disciples on the road to Emmaus, so with me also, my eyes were holden, so that I did not perceive precisely who he was in all reality. Had I known it, I fear that I would not have been able to serve him.

There are so many things that even if I could relate them about the Elder in a very simple account, another book would need to be written. For this reason I shall limit myself to a very few.

His whole concern was how to please God. All his love was directed to our Christ and His teaching. The tears of his joy-making sorrow were unending. As for his lovingkindness towards the afflicted and helpless, it was more than fatherly.

He was inexhaustible in his counsels to everyone, which he provided in proportion to the thirst, the faith, and the receptiveness of those who came to him.

His chief aim was that the faithful come to know and love our Christ. He often said, "To please both God and the world is not possible. As much as you can, avoid the things of the world, which are in opposition to the spirit of our Christ. It is difficult to please God, but not unachievable. God has given the key into the hands of man; the key of freedom and good volition. Only the key of perdition does He hold, because He does not want man to be sent to hell. But the key of Paradise He has given into the hands of man."

He never spoke to us about his gift of clairvoyance. But very many times he would foretell everything to us exactly. Once I asked him, "But how do you know these things, Elder?" "Thus it came to me," was all he said. He would not explain further, nor did he leave any room for further superfluous questions. He would not permit anyone to praise him. "Praise," he would say, "is not permissible. Virtue of course is laudable. It is praiseworthy, but not in the person's presence. For, what sin did the Angels commit, so that they were punished? They were Angels, but they fell into pride." "Do not praise anyone," he would say, "because in one moment a man can be damned, as also in one moment he can be saved. But neither surrender anyone to despair, because till the end there is hope."

Concerning his food—since I was asked—he was indifferent, and very frugal. A little macaroni, stewed potatoes, coarse ground wheat (bulgur), octopus or fish was what we prepared for him and what he usually ate; never meat. It was always very little; and when we implored him to eat a little more, he would say, "Eh, we're going to eat again tomorrow, it doesn't matter!"

Prayer was everything, his all! This was his food and his joy. The Church and participation in the Holy Mysteries was his strength and his renewal, his rejuvenation.

The exact keeping of the evangelical commandments and ecclesiastical canons was his vigilant endeavor. As regards the Orthodox Church Calendar, which from the year 1940 he followed unwaveringly and remained faithful to it to the end, often, especially after an awesome vision he had seen, he exhorted the faithful to follow it. But he did this in a fatherly manner, without obstinacy and fanaticism. He was wont to say, "The Church of Greece, by the change of the festal calendar, has become 'diseased,' and the change became the beginning and cause of many evils. Many bad things will come to our Church through this 'door,' i.e. the change of the festal calendar, which has 'been opened.' Things which we already see, which in the name of 'love' and 'economia' are already being brought to pass. May God take pity on us..."

He lived the last days of his earthly life with continuous unceasing prayer. Three days before his repose he communicated the Immaculate Mysteries, and also on that very day (October 3), it being a Sunday, he partook again with the rejoicing of one that is ready in all things, having first made the sign of the Cross many times, and rising up a little, he gave a kiss to an Icon that was invisible to us, and with a strong voice, that of a healthy man, he said, "Glory be to Thee, O God!" and forthwith "he bowed his head, and gave up his spirit."

Three days before his repose, he called us, the few persons nearest him who served him, and filling us all with great compunction he gave us his last instructions and commandments.

And to me, unworthy as I am, he showed his tender kindness, entrusting the care and protection of me to a known and tried sister of ours, but simultaneously having it in mind to prepare for the continuation and succession of our sacred hermitage, he said, "You will live together, everything will be done with understanding and agreement, all that we know and follow will be observed, and you will be obedient to the nun. And as for me, do not forget to do all that is due me," that is, Liturgies, memorial services, mer-

The Eldress Eupraxia in her later years, after the Elder's repose. Behind her is Archimandrite Panteleimon of the Holy Transfiguration Monastery in Boston; on the left is Mother Seraphima, present Abbess of the Holy Nativity Convent in Boston, and on the right is Mother Myrophora of the same convent.

cy meals, alms, and the rest. Afterwards, turning to me, he said three times, perhaps to lessen the pain of being deprived of him, "Nun, love God!

"Nun, come to love God!

"Nun, come to love God!

"Do not leave your cell. No matter what happens."

He told me others things besides, which I continuously have in my mind, but which I am not able now to write.

I abide according to his command, but then I would not be able to do otherwise, in the hermitage, in my "cell," at Aegina, and I try unworthily to live as when he lived, to observe my monastic rules and order, and to derive strength from our Christ and our Panagia, from the Saints, but also from the extremely alive presence of the Elder, who already unto many, as also to me the unworthy, shows a miraculous audience and succor. By two or three, as they related it to me, he was seen openly, as if he had never left.

May we be deemed worthy, as many as lived with him and knew him, to please him with our life and our works.

Through the prayers of all my brethren,
The unworthy, Eupraxia, nun
Aegina, January, 1986.

NOTE

The venerable Eldress Eupraxia reposed on July 29 / August 11, 1990. This appendix is translated from *The Elder Ieronymos of Aegina, 1883-1966*, by Soteria Nouse, pp. 356–58. Although both her life of the Elder Ieronymos and the present one have a certain inevitable overlap, each contains much of importance that the other does not, and it is fervently to be hoped that a complete translation of Mrs. Nouse's book will also appear in English. We mention as an example the following incident from her book not included in this one:

Once an elderly couple visited the Elder. They had no children of their own, but had an adopted daughter who tormented them, treating them very harshly. As soon as they heard of the Elder Ieronymos, they went to visit him to express their pain to him. He said to them reproachfully, "She has done very little to you. She ought to have broken your head." As they sat in shocked disbelief at his answer, after a moment's silence he explained to them that when God had given them their own child, they didn't want it and they killed it, and that it wasn't the fault of this girl, but it was their own sin that was tormenting them. At this revelation they melted in tears and with contrition confessed to him what they had done. Then, with paternal love and saintly discretion, he comforted and counselled them, promising to pray that God would change their daughter for the better. They left relieved and full of joy. Upon their return home, they expected to be met by the usual grim looks, shouts, and so forth, but were astonished to find their daughter transformed, kind and meek, and telling them she regretted that they were unable to live in peace, and that she was going to try to change her ways. They understood that this was a miracle worked by the Elder's prayer (pp. 137–38).

Memoirs of the Elder Ieronymos of Aegina

TWENTY-FIVE YEARS HAVE PASSED since the time I came to know the blessed Elder Ieronymos, and the first meeting made such an impression on me that I remember it as if it were yesterday.

It was the summer of 1960. I visited Greece with a group of pilgrims from the United States. We went first to Jerusalem and the God-trodden Mountain of Sinai, and afterwards to Greece in order to go (as many as were men) to visit the Holy Mountain. I was then twenty-five years old, newly ordained a deacon, and since I had lived for some time both on the Holy Mountain and in Jerusalem, the group of Christians I was with chose me as the guide for the pilgrimage.

When we came to Athens I telephoned the family of Mr. Panagos Diamantis Pateras (who later in the schema was renamed Xenophon, monk), unknown to me at the time, to convey greetings from a clergyman in the United States who knew them.[1] The then lady of the house, Mrs. Katingo Pateras (presently Maria Myrtidiotissa, nun), told me that one does not convey greetings by telephone, and that it would be right for me to visit their home. After

1. This was the late Father John Romanides.

Opposite page: Above, the Elder Ieronymos speaking to visitors outside his cell; below, saying a prayer of forgiveness. Behind him is Archimandrite Panteleimon of the Holy Transfiguration Monastery in Boston. The photographs were taken by Father Neketas Palassis of Seattle in July, 1966, three months before the Elder's repose.

a good deal of trouble I found their mansion at Palaio Psychico when it was already dark. Once there, I learned that they had an ailing daughter on the island of Aegina at the Sacred Convent of Saint Menas the Great Martyr. The family therefore implored me to visit their daughter (later the blessed nun Irene Myrtidiotissa), and although in the beginning I did not consent since my time in Athens was quite short, in the end I gave in to their pleas and agreed to visit Aegina on the morrow with Mrs. Pateras. As usual, the lady was late in coming down to Piraeus and we missed the ferryboat. We were thus obliged to wait for another boat to take us to the island. The lady came with a maidservant (presently a nun at the Sacred Convent of the Annunciation on Oinoussai) and countless baskets full of nuts, figs, and other foodstuffs.

When we finally arrived at Aegina, Mrs. Pateras told me, "First we'll stop by at an elder's place to leave a few things and then we'll go on to Saint Menas." I didn't say anything, but I saw that the day was already far spent and that it would be impossible to return to Athens the same day. We finally got a taxi and after we had loaded it with all the baskets and packages we set out, first for the Elder's and then for Saint Menas.

Here I should point out that I had never heard anything about the Elder Ieronymos. I had first visited Aegina in the fall of 1956 on my first trip to Greece. My purpose at the time was to visit the Convent of Saint Nectarius where I had a relative on my mother's side, the nun Eugenia (Gennematas), who has already reposed. I was then twenty-one and was on my way to the Holy Mountain. But I had not heard anything concerning the Elder Ieronymos, neither at the time nor afterwards. Wherefore as I now went with Mrs. Pateras, I did not expect to meet anyone exceptional. Greece is full of monasteries and hermitages, and so I thought I was about to see a simple little old man on the way to the Convent of Saint Menas. But what a great surprise awaited me.

After we had come a little way from the port city of Aegina, we took a narrow dirt road and after a short while arrived at a humble hermitage. We unloaded some of the provisions and knocked. Soon we heard footsteps and the door opened. I saw a short, thin nun welcoming us. From her appearance and her speech I understood that she was from Anatolia of Asia Minor, for I had grown up in the United States with people from those parts, refugees from the destruction of 1922. Entering into a narrow corridor I immediately felt compunction. It was as if the walls and the ceiling and the floor were speaking and welcoming me with love and tenderness, and telling me concerning the man that lived there, that he was a man of God. The corridor ended at an inner court—to the left was the Elder's cell and straight ahead, the little Chapel of the Annunciation.

The Elder was outside of his cell at the moment working at something in the courtyard. The whole courtyard was full of boxes, small tables and counters, tools, clocks, and the like. It was already getting dark and the light was dim. The first thing I saw was the Elder's face—as it had been the face of an Angel. It was as if a ray came forth from his face and entered into my heart, and I was completely filled with compunction. I immediately began to weep, even before I approached and kissed his hand. When I finally made a bow and kissed his hand, I observed that his left arm up to the elbow was missing. Later I learned how this had happened.

Such compunction I had felt before that only on two other occasions in my life. One was on the Holy Mountain when I first met the Elder Joseph the Cave-dweller, in 1957; and later, in 1958, when I met Abba John the Romanian in the caves of Hozeva (Wadi Kelt) in the Holy Land. Since then, only on two other occasions did I again experience such compunction on meeting a person—when I met the Elder Theodoulos of Koroni in the Peloponnesus, and Archbishop Andrew of Novo-Diveyevo in Spring Valley, New York.

Just from the compunction alone I understood that I was not dealing with simply a man, but with a God-bearing Elder—with a

The Elder Ieronymos and Mother Eupraxia in the courtyard of the Elder's Hermitage. Note repaired clocks in the background.

man in whom God dwelt. What awe then overcame me! It was as if a great flash of light had dazed me. Fear and trembling took hold of me, but at the same time joy and gladness. Fear, because of sin—I thought where I might hide—"the rock is refuge for the hares" (Psalm 103:20). Joy, that I found a man of God—love, tenderness, hope, comfort. I withdrew to a corner of the courtyard, into a shadow, and wept quietly. Fortunately the Elder did not speak to me—I would have dissolved.

The Elder knew Mrs. Pateras well and began straightway to speak with her. From his pronunciation I understood that he was a Cappadocian. A knot formed in my throat, so that even if I wanted to I would not have been able to speak. I just stood in the half darkness of that corner and listened and wept.

The lady informed the Elder that she was just passing through and was only stopping to get his blessing and to leave a few things. She also informed him that I was a hierodeacon from America. The Elder told her that her daughter Irene had come twice from Saint Menas to see him and they had spoken of spiritual things.

At one moment he said to the lady, "God loves you. We owe it to Him to love Him too."

"I have no doubt of that, but the problems and sorrows are many, both in the family, and from illnesses."

"I call you blessed; God shows you abundant love. I wish I had known you before your husband and daughter became ill."

"Why, Elder?"

"Tell me, before the illnesses and the sorrows, did you do this?" And with his hand he made as if painting his lips.

"Why, yes, I used makeup."

"And did you wear this?" And he showed his ear and his neck.

"Yes! I wore both earrings and necklaces."

"And you made up your hair, and you played cards?"

"Yes, Elder. I went to the hairdresser, and sometimes I played cards with my lady friends when we got together, and on occasion I even went to the casino."

"And now, how is it that you do not paint yourself, but wear a covering on your head, and do not go to the casino, but rather run all the time to churches and monasteries?"

"After so many illnesses and sorrows, am I crazy enough to

make myself up and go to evening socials—with a sick husband, a sick daughter, and another daughter with family problems?"

"God loves—yes, He loves! It is because of this that I call you blessed. As for myself, I have never even once said to God, 'My Christ, why?'" At the same time he lifted up the stump of his left arm which had been amputated at the elbow. "God took my hand. I didn't need it. Better with one hand in Paradise, than with two in hell. As our good God wishes! He loves me. He knows what is to my profit. Yes, not once have I complained. I have never said, 'Why did God take away my hand?' I thank Him. I thank Him always and for all things. You also should be thankful and give glory to God for all things."

"I thank Him, Elder, and I glorify Him. But I'm human. Please pray for me."

"Everyone tells me to pray for them. I, the pauper, the sinner, that I should pray. Right now I will pray for Katina." This is what he called Mrs. Pateras.

While standing, he lifted up his right hand and his eyes to Heaven and prayed with tears. "My Jesus, my most sweet Christ. I, the worm, the sinner, entreat Thee on behalf of Thy handmaiden Katina. Send forth Thine All-holy Spirit into her heart, into her mind, into her soul. Enlighten her, give her understanding, comfort her, heal her, strengthen her. Yea, hearken unto me, O Lord of Mercy, and disdain not my entreaty."

As the Elder was saying these things, you understood that in truth he was praying noetically—face to face. Afterwards he turns to Mrs. Katingo and says, "God hears my humble, my impoverished prayer. Well, now He will get in touch with Katina. He picks up the receiver. *Tring, tring, tring*. He dials the number. The telephone rings—*tring, tring*." Saying these things, the Elder went through the motions of picking up the telephone and dialing. All this most demonstratively, without of course a telephone being present.

"The telephone rings—*tring, tring*. No answer. Katina is away—Katina is sleeping. The phone rings, God speaks, saying, 'Katina, My daughter Katina!' Katina does not lift the receiver. She's absent. She has gone out for a stroll. Well, I ask you. What is the profit of all this effort and labor? I the sinner to make entreaty. God to be dialing. The telephone to be ringing. And Katina not to be answering."

We that were present hearing all these things continually sighed, understanding well what the Elder meant.

Now I had not yet even uttered a word, nor had the Elder said a word to me. I had withdrawn into a corner, and only observed and listened. In the meanwhile the nun went and prepared treats. She brought me the customary loukoumi and water. But on account of compunction I couldn't take anything. I just lifted the glass of water and put it to my mouth as a formality, whispering, "Bless." While the Elder was speaking with the lady, the Eldress took the opportunity to speak with my sinfulness. She began by asking me where I came from. I told her from America, but that I became a monk on the Holy Mountain. She told me that she surmised this from the *skoufo* that I was wearing, and went on to ask me what synodia I belonged to.

"The synodia of the Elder Joseph of New Skete."

"Which Elder Joseph—the Cave-dweller?"

"Yes, the Cave-dweller. It's now one year since he reposed."

"Do you know Father Arsenios?"

"Why, of course. He's our Elder now. He succeeded the Elder Joseph after the latter reposed."

"Father Arsenios is my brother. He made me a nun."

"He also sponsored me in the schema."

"We're spiritual brother and sister!"

Whereupon the Eldress began to shout, "Do you hear, Elder? This young man is from the synodia of the Elder Joseph the Cave-dweller. He knows my brother Father Arsenios—he's his Elder."

The Elder Arsenios, holding the skull of the blessed Elder Joseph.

A rare photograph of the Elder Joseph (center, with cane) and Synodia. Seated to the left of the Elder Joseph is the Elder Arsenios.

Saying these things with emotion, the Eldress wept, because, as she explained, it was now over twenty years that she had not seen her brother. Before the war, Father Joseph and Father Arsenios would come out of the Holy Mountain and occasionally met with Father Ieronymos.

The Elder, hearing the nun shouting, stopped his conversation with Mrs. Pateras and said to the Eldress with austerity, "Nun, be quiet! You hear 'brother' and you shout and weep. You hear 'Jesus,' and you neither shout nor weep. You hear the name of your brother and immediately you get excited. I want you to hear the Name of Jesus and weep. Love Jesus, and hearing His Name, be moved."

"Come now, Elder, don't I love our Christ? We all love our Christ. But your brother is still your brother. And what a brother! He isn't a man of the world. He's a monk, an ascetic, a struggler. Should I not then love my brother?"

"Nun, we should love Jesus, and Him alone we should have in our heart and mind. We should hear the Name of Jesus and weep with tears. Neither parents, nor brethren, nor relatives, nor friends avail anything. All these do not profit. Thou shalt love the Lord thy God, and Him alone shalt thou worship."

Then he turns to me and says, "You are young. You are in the middle of the river. As you wish, you may turn, either to one side or to the other. Either you become fervent or you cool off—it's in your hand. If your Elder smokes, you will smoke too."

"What kind of words are these?" interrupted the Eldress. "Do the fathers on the Holy Mountain smoke? Does the synodia of the Elder Joseph smoke?"

"Nun, I have spoken!" answered the Elder sternly, and all the while observed me closely.

And verily, during the summer of 1960 I was in the middle of the river. For when I returned to the United States in the fall of the same year, the bishop who was offering me hospitality had already been transferred to Canada and was imploring me to follow him, even though during the two years I had stayed with him after my return to the United States from the Holy Mountain, I had not consented to cut my beard or my hair, neither to take off the *rasso*, as the clergy in the United States are wont to do, nor even to follow the New Calendar. Since at the time there was no Greek church in Boston that followed the Ecclesiastical Calendar, I attended the major feasts—Nativity, Theophany, Annunciation, Transfiguration, Dormition, and so forth—in Russian churches. Fortunately, on returning to Boston, I did not follow the bishop, and I remained a monk, and today we have a monastery, and I glorify and thank God.

Many times the Elder Ieronymos said things that those present found difficult to understand or even comical, but for the person to whom they were directed they had great meaning. And the marvellous thing was that the Elder had the gift to give a person to understand the meaning of his words without the others' perceiving what he meant. So it was with that which he said to me, "If your Elder smokes, you will smoke too." He did not mean the Elders on the Holy Mountain, but rather the bishop with whom I stayed in the United States. And it was not a matter of smoking, because the bishop, who is no longer living, didn't smoke. But the moment he said it to me, I immediately understood what he wished to tell me. I observed this in other meetings with the Elder also.

He didn't say anything else to me. He only looked at me closely. On leaving I kissed his hand (the taxi was waiting) and I whispered, "Pray for me, my Father."

Immediately he said to me, "I can't hear."

Startled, I said for a second time with as much voice—not much, I must confess—as I had, "Pray for me, holy Elder."

"I can't hear," he said to me a second time with more emphasis.

I almost keeled over. My knees gave way. I said to myself, you're so sinful that the Elder doesn't even want to hear to pray for you.

"What has happened to you, my Christian man? All of a sudden you can't hear?" said Mrs. Pateras to the Elder. "The man asked you to pray for him."

"Hearken, he is a monk. Let him pray himself. Two sit at table. One eats and the other observes. Who is filled? Surely he who eats. If I pray, I will be filled, but he remains hungry. I want him also to be filled and not to remain hungry."

Then, turning to me, he said with a smile and meekness, "Forgive me. I do not wish to grieve you. I don't want you to leave with sorrow. I will pray for you, but you also do likewise for me. In this way both of us shall be filled. Go now with the blessing of Christ and the Panagia."

THIS WAS MY FIRST MEETING with the Elder, in the summer of 1960. Until his demise, in October of 1966, I visited him many times when I came from the States to Greece, which was every year except 1961.

From the first time I met him I understood what a treasure he was, and had great respect and love for him. As Philip bid Nathanael, I also urged many to go to meet the Elder. When I could, I accompanied some of them in person, as in the case of Mr. and Mrs. Alexander Papademetriou of the "Astir" Publishing House. I had found a precious treasure, and wanted all whom I loved to profit thereby. As for Mr. Alexander Papademetriou—*Kyr Aleko* to his dear ones—and his modest spouse Maria, I loved and continue to love them like my own parents. Thus, after many exhortations, we went together to Aegina once and they met the Elder. Both the couple and the Elder rejoiced over this meeting. The Elder was overjoyed like a little child. He spoke with overflowing love and tenderness to Kyr Aleko, concerning his spiritual publications, on the spiritual life, about love for God and one's neighbor, and so on. As for Kyr Aleko, he liked it all very much—even his moustache was smiling, as the Greeks say. He beamed like a little child when one caresses it and praises it. But to Kyria Maria he gave little attention. Even the little that he spoke with her was somewhat austere and cold. This made an impression on me and I didn't know how to interpret it. Kyria Maria was a very loving and delicate person with overflowing love; Kyr Aleko was a good man, a Christian—but a businessman. The man had many business transactions, obligations, concerns. Yet the Elder acted with them in the opposite way, giving the honor to Kyr Aleko. This was because the Elder saw the depth of a man and not that which is without. This behavior of the Elder towards the Papademetriou couple made an impression on me, and from then on I paid more attention to Kyr Alexander, and I observed how he reacted on many occasions, to family circumstances and others, and I esteemed the guilelessness of the man and how innocent and harmless he was, like a little child. All this—and much more surely—the Elder perceived immediately, and for this reason rejoiced and received Kyr Alexander the way he did.

As for Kyria Maria, she was not offended that the Elder did not pay her much attention; rather she rejoiced that he gave his attention to Kyr Aleko. But at a certain moment the Elder turned and said somewhat sternly to her, "If today, this evening, your husband died, what would you do?"

Just at the sound of such a thing, Kyria Maria literally shuddered and was greatly affrighted. She changed color and began to make the sign of the Cross over and over.

"You, from early youth, have feared death greatly," continued the Elder. "Yet we shall all die. But we Christians believe in the Resurrection, and consequently death no longer holds sway over us. You, being a Christian, how is it that you fear death so greatly?"

Indeed Kyria Maria had an uncommon fear of death, so much so that she was unable to go to funerals. Thus, whenever there was a funeral, even of a relative, Kyr Alexander usually attended, and Kyria Maria would stay at home and light candles and offer incense and prayers. But the Elder had no way of knowing all this. Nor had anyone ever said anything about the Papademetriou couple to him. This was the first time they met.

After a few words about death and what it means to be a Christian and to believe in the Resurrection, our visit ended. It had lasted a little over an hour. We kissed the Elder's hand with reverence; we received his blessing and departed.

On the ferryboat returning to Athens we discussed our visit. All three of us were filled with compunction and joy—full of spiritual delight, peace, and exultation. It was not possible to visit the Elder and not leave peaceful, with consolation and hope leaping within oneself. The Elder had so much grace that without exception all who visited him received of it bountifully.

Kyr Aleko said to me, "No matter how many things you could have told me, my Pantelaki—and you told me a lot about the Elder—they would not suffice to describe the man we just met. We're indebted to you for urging us and bringing us to meet him. Today I went to the Thebaïd, I went to Nitria and met one of those great Abbas who are mentioned in the *Gerontikon* and the Lives of the Saints. Had any man told me such a thing, even as you did, I would not have believed it. But now, not because of what you told me that he told you do I believe, but with my own eyes I have seen and heard and have come to know that he is an Abba, as one of those who shone forth of old."

After I had left for the United States, Mr. Papademetriou took Dr. Alexander Kalomiros, who was visiting from Thessalonica, to meet the Elder. In this way one would tell another, and by word of mouth many would come, both from Greece and even from abroad, to see the Elder.

ONCE WHEN I WAS A YOUNG MONK and was struggling alone some forty miles from Boston, I was visited by a seminarian. He was from Greece but was attending seminary in the United States. He related to me many marvellous things from his life when he was younger—visions, miracles, experiences. I didn't know what to say. He either had to be a Saint (that is, to have reached a very high spiritual state) or to be in delusion. Being from the Holy Mountain, I had been taught to beware of dreams and visions as being delusions, and not to give any attention and trust to such phenomena. But what to say to the man—that all his experiences were from the enemy? He had related all these things to priests, bishops, and professors, and they all made fun of him. Whereupon he would not speak to anyone anymore. Then he heard about a certain monk of the Holy Mountain in the area, and with labor and expense he came and found me. The man appeared pious and balanced. None of the things he related to me gave any evidence of delusion, but then again, the devil has many devices. Should I tell him that everything was of God? How could I know for a certainty? Should I tell him that it was all of the devil? Neither could I say this with confidence.

So I told him, "Listen, brother. I'm a young monk and have no experience of these things. I have neither seen dreams nor visions, nor do I wish to see such things, since the devil often appears as an angel of light in order to deceive men. You need an experienced spiritual man to help you."

"Do you know of any such person?" he asked me.

"Here in the United States, no. In Greece I came to know a holy Elder, with gifts of the All-holy Spirit—clairvoyance, foreknowledge, prophecy."

"What is his name? Where does he live?"

"His name is Elder Ieronymos, and he lives on the island of Aegina."

This was in the spring of 1961. That summer he went to Greece and found the Elder at his hermitage. He related to him all the things that he had told me. The Elder listened in silence without speaking. When the student had finished, then the Elder opened his mouth and said to him, "I feel sorry for you. So weak are you in faith, that God, lest you drown, has given you His hand. Blessed are they that have not seen, yet believe. Yes, you are very weak, and that is the reason for all these things. Pray and be careful."

When I heard all this later—for the student himself informed me—and when I saw the Elder again a year later and he told me about this incident, I marvelled at the discretion that the Elder used. With one word he protected the student from pride.

Another time, when we were already a small brotherhood here in Boston, we received communications from a grieved mother from the depths of the United States, over two thousand miles away. She had a little three-year-old who suffered from cancer.

Sometimes she phoned and sometimes she wrote. Someone had told her about our monastery, and she was asking for help—that we might pray that her little one be healed. From time to time she would send us some of the child's clothing or handkerchiefs to place on the holy relics and read prayers over them and then return them in hope that a miracle would take place. We sent her oil from Saint Nectarius and Saint John the Russian and tried to console her as much as we could. The woman was of Greek descent, born in the United States, but didn't know Greek very well. Many times she asked us over the telephone why the little child was born with cancer, and in what it was at fault that it should suffer so. Why would God permit an innocent creature to be tormented? We would answer her that these things are the judgments of God, and we are not God, that we should know His wisdom in ordering all things. She would always ask, "Isn't there any man of God who can give me an answer?" We would answer her that we were sinful people and didn't know of such a man. But she continued to ask, whereupon I said to her once, "Don't waste your money in vain continually phoning us from so far away. We pray continually, but God does not hear us. Here in the U.S. we don't know of anyone who can give you an answer. In Greece there's an Elder, on the same island where Saint Nectarius is, but that's very far from where you live—over 7,000 miles away—and besides, he doesn't speak English."

That was it. She lost no time. Her pain was so great that she took a plane and went with her child to Greece. She reached Aegina. She found a taxi cab driver who knew a few words of broken English—she also knew a few of broken Greek—and she went to the Elder's hermitage. She didn't find him there. He had gone down to the port city, to the marketplace. She returned to the city and found the Elder on the road. She began through the cab driver to relate to him her grief, and what she had been told by us.

The Elder said to her, "You are the cause of the little one's illness, because you left your lawful husband and took another. It was not your husband who dissolved the marriage, rather it was you who fell in love with someone else. Why complain now? Your little boy is innocent. He will be saved without a doubt. He shall be with the Angels. But if you wish you can be saved also. God loves all and wishes all to be saved. He is giving you an opportunity to repent and be saved. Before your little one became ill, did you think about God? Did you go to church? Did you make the sign of the Cross? Now you are praying all the time. You even took the airplane and came such a great distance in order to worship Saint Nectarius, to ask for help and to speak of your great grief. If you were not grieved, you would not remember God. Yes, if you wish it now, you can be corrected, you can become a good Christian. Your little one goes to God, he is not going to remain any longer in this false world. But you, do not grieve. Thank God for all things. Glorify Him."

When she returned, she telephoned me herself and related to me her meeting with the Elder and what he told her. After a little her child reposed, even as the Elder had told her. How could I, the sinner, have known the life of the woman? In my life I have known six holy men with clairvoyance, but in the Elder Ieronymos, the gifts of clairvoyance and foreknowledge were the most intense of them all.

WHEN I WENT TO THE ELDER, without fail I would hear something about his Elder Misael and other holy people that he knew in his life. Misael was a layman, married, with a family. He had nevertheless reached such a height of prayer that every Thursday he left his village by night just before it dawned and climbed the nearby mountains that surrounded the area, which were honeycombed with churches and ancient monasteries all carved out of the rock. When the sun rose, he would already be on some summit, and there, in one of the numerous chapels, he stood with hands upraised until the setting of the sun, without moving from his place and without bringing down his outstretched arms. In this way he fulfilled the Psalmic verses, "From the morning watch until night, from the morning watch let Israel hope in the Lord." (Psalm 129:5) We who visited the Elder would hear these things and we would all be ecstatic, that such men of love for God and prayer reached even into this century. There came to mind Saint Arsenius the Great, who stood with hands lifted to Heaven in prayer from sunset until the rising sun shone on his face, and our righteous Mother Irene of Chrysovalantou, who stood in prayer like a statue with upraised hands for ten and fifteen hours on end, so that the demons would cry out of envy, "Woody Irene! Woody Irene!"

The Elder Misael had such prayerful compunction and tears that many times blood came forth with his tears when he had mourning and lamentation in prayer. Often, when he was recounting to us about the Elder Misael, the Elder Ieronymos said to us, "I ask you, how did an illiterate man in the depths of Anatolia, without knowing the Greek language, without books, attain to such heights of compunctionate prayer? (For thus was noetic prayer called in my country—we did not even know the term 'noetic prayer' or 'prayer of the heart'—we would say 'compunctionate prayer' or 'prayer with tears.')"

We didn't know what to answer, and he gave us the answer himself, "DILIGENCE! He was diligent. He would hear one word in church, one verse from the Psalms, and immediately he applied himself to fulfilling it. He was not indolent. He would not leave for the morrow what he was able to do today. Thus with the help of God (for, without God we can do nothing) he attained to whither he attained, to the heights. God gives His grace to whoever seeks it persistently."

The Elder Ieronymos told us that Misael had a daughter who,

from a tender age, when she was but a tot, would imitate her father, and would whimper in prayer. Misael did prostrations—she did prostrations also. Misael fell prostrate for hours—she fell prostrate too. By the time she was a girl of ten or twelve, she had progressed so far in prayer that she had both divine vision and the word of God to instruct others. The more she grew, the more women would gather to speak with her on spiritual things. The men went to Misael, the women to his daughter. There they heard words of compunction, and were moved with mourning, with tears and sighs that cannot be uttered.

Much benefit and spiritual profit came from this to the Christian villages round about. When Misael's daughter grew up, and at the age of eighteen or twenty had already reached the measure of being a God-bearer, she fell seriously ill, even unto death. The women were exceedingly grieved at the prospect of losing such a treasure. They went to Misael and told him to offer intense prayer that his daughter get well, not so much because she was his daughter, but more because she was an Angel of consolation in the depths of Turkey, and if she died, the well-spring whence they were refreshed with water springing up unto life everlasting would dry up. And that man so blessed and ever ready for obedience, when Thursday came and he went up into the mountains before dawn to pray, prayed for his daughter, not so much because she was his daughter and he was pained as her father, but rather as it had been told to him so that she might be a consolation for the Christians. He then heard a gentle voice within himself, "Do you give surety?" "I didn't even pause to think," Misael said later, "but immediately said *'Yiok!'* (Turkish for 'no') I do not give surety. I cannot give surety even for myself, for I know not what the morrow brings. How then shall I give surety for my daughter? Thou, Lord, as Thou wishest, do. May Thy holy will be ever done in all things." These things he said, and towards evening there came a messenger running from Kelveri, with the announcement that his daughter had fallen asleep and to be quick to return for her burial.

On another occasion he told us about a certain priest of Kelveri named John, married and with a family. He was very compunctionate and when he served the Liturgy he wept and sighed and cried like a little child. He would often tarry at the time of the *epiclesis* when the Precious Gifts are sanctified—five minutes, ten minutes, fifteen minutes, and more. The chanters didn't know what to do in their bewilderment. They would slowly chant "We hymn Thee, we bless Thee,…" once, twice, thrice—after that they didn't know what to chant. Begin to chant the *Polyeleos*? But that would be out of place. Chant the Communion Hymn? That wouldn't do either. So one day they said to some of Father John's disciples, "The Teacher [*that is, the priest*] takes a long time at the *epiclesis,* and we fall into despair about what to do. We chant "We hymn Thee" over and over, but the blessed one doesn't finish, we don't hear the "Especially our all-holy, immaculate…," and everything's in confusion out here."

They in turn said to Father John, "Venerable Father, you often take a long time at the *epiclesis,* and the chanters and the people are waiting outside.[2] The chanters fall into despair and perplexity about what to say. Forgive us, is it not possible for you to finish the prayer, that confusion might be avoided?"

And that blessed one answered them, saying, "How can this be?"

"Easily," they said. "As you are prostrate, get up, seal the Precious Gifts with your right hand with the sign of the Cross, and say 'And make this bread… and this cup…' and the rest of the prayer, and so you finish."

"The prayer I know," he answered. "It's even written in the book. But I can't."

---

2. That is, on the other side of the iconostasis.

"Why can't you, our Father? Forgive us, it's easy! Just say the prayer and seal the Precious Gifts, and then we can finish."

"It's not that easy. For there is fire round about the Table, and I am not able. I say the prayer up to a certain point, but suddenly I behold fire around the Table—two, even three yards high, and I am unable to enter into the fire to seal the Precious Gifts. There is fear and terror then, and I don't know what to do. I fall down prostrate, I weep, I sigh, I beseech the Father of Lights, my sweet Jesus, the All-holy Spirit. I cry out, 'Lord and Master of my life! My Fashioner and God! Spare Thy creature, and take away these flames so that I can approach and seal the Precious Gifts.' I then lift up my eyes and gaze towards the Holy Table. If the flames have ceased, I get up and seal the Gifts. If not, then I pray again and beseech with tears and deep sighs until either the fire ceases, or a way is found that I might be able to enter into the veil of fire without being burned. Sometimes the fire ceases and everything is as it was before. At other times the flames divide to one side and the other, and become like an arch, and thus trembling I enter and dare to stretch out my hand and seal the Precious Gifts."

Hearing such astonishing things, they didn't bother Father John any more about the length of the *epiclesis*.

This Father John was so reverent and filled with compunction during the Divine Liturgy that many Christians came from other villages in the neighborhood of Kelveri, sometimes many hours' distance, to attend Liturgy. On occasion a thousand or more people—men, women, and children—attended Liturgy when Father John served. All of them came to contrition and wept even as the celebrant did. When the Liturgy was over and the faithful departed, the floor of the church without fail would be drenched, as if one had splashed water on it—so much did the people wet the floor with their tears.

For some this might seem unbelievable, but I, wretched as I am, when I heard it, immediately remembered my Hadji Yiayia—

Macrina the pilgrimess—and other Cappadocian refugee women in the United States where I was born.[3] These blessed souls would gather at Hadji Yiayia's house (even as others visit and chat all sorts of nonsense *about winds and waters,* as they say in Greek, or *tourlou tourlou* as they say in Turkish), and setting in their midst an icon of the burial of our Saviour, they would begin a lament—the Lamentations at the Tomb—with weeping and wailing.[4] Their eyes became fountains and their tears ran in rivers. Such was their lament and mourning then, such their compunction and noetic prayer, that they were absent from this world, and were found at Golgotha where Jesus, the Son of the Virgin, was being taken down from the Cross, and at the all-holy Tomb for His burial. On such occasions, you could easily enter the room where they were gathered and take whatever you like, and leave, and those blessed myrrh-bearers would not notice anything, as if no one entered and exited the place, such was the compunction and concentration they had in their mourning and prayer.

Since I have mentioned Hadji Yiayia, I should say this also. In the course of one of my visits the Elder asked me, "You, being a young man from America, how is it that you came to Greece and became a monk?"

I answered him with reverence, "In America where I was born and reared, from a tender age I had a certain Hadji Yiayia, and she would always speak to me about the blessed Ascetics and Saints of our Church. She was a compunctionate soul and always wept, and she told me that the world was false and to flee from it and become a monk."

---

3. *Hadji*—from the Arabic *hajj*—one who has made the pilgrimage to Jerusalem. *Yiayia:* grandmother.
4. Actually the icon was a silk antimension that a monk from the Holy Mountain had given to Hadji Yiayia. She did not know what an antimension was, and framed it. It was kept among her many icons in her icon corner. The icon is found today in the sanctuary of the Holy Transfiguration Monastery. See the photograph on page 287.

Hadji Yiayia Macrina.

"What was her name?" he asked me, "And where was she from?"
"Macrina pilgrimess," I answered him, "and she was from Ürgüp—Procopion—in Cappadocia. There were many other women also, compatriots from Ürgüp, Nev Sehir, Sinasos, and other parts

Ürgüp—called Procopion in Byzantine times—in Cappadocia, c. 1911.
Here Saint John the Russian (✝1733) lived out his captivity as a slave to a Turkish cavalry officer and was sanctified.

Antimension used by Yiayia Macrina as an Icon of the Lamentations at the Tomb.

of Anatolia. We also had a priest with the Old Calendar, Papa Agathangelos, from Andaval, Nigde, who was also an iconographer."

"I knew your Yiayia," said the Elder. "After the war (World War II) she came to Greece—to Tabouria of Piraeus—and I went and we met, and we spoke about spiritual matters, in Turkish, since she didn't know Greek. As for Papa Agathangelos, even though he was my compatriot, I didn't know him. He was older than I. But in our church of Saint Gregory in Kelveri, we had icons 'by the hand of Papa Agathangelos.' I heard much concerning him, but I didn't know him. Then came the destruction of Asia Minor and the Exchange of Populations—he went to America (he had relatives there), I came here to Greece. Since you grew up with compatriots

Father Agathangelos of Andaval, Nigde, in Cappadocia, a married priest who emigrated to America and served in Ann Arbor and Detroit, Michigan.

of mine, now I understand how you became a monk. For the greater part of them were all pious people. They fasted; they prayed with tears; they struggled to be saved. When we came to Greece after the Exchange, we were deeply scandalized. We didn't know if the people here were even Christians at all. They swore, they sang worldly songs, they didn't fast, they didn't keep vigils, they didn't dress modestly. *Aman! Aman!* we said. Where did we come to? If it were possible we would all immediately return to our homeland Anatolia. But where was Anatolia to be found? It did not exist any longer for the Christians. We left without any possibility of returning. Compared to things here, all our villages in Cappadocia were like monasteries. Everybody fasted, prayed, ran to church. Nowhere would you hear worldly songs in the streets or in Christian homes. If one of the young people dared to sing a worldly song, you immediately heard the older ones say, "Sin! Sin! *Shaytanlar!* [*Devils!*]" and they would begin to chant. The older folk had composed certain hymns in Turkish in the form of songs with a religious content—for example, the life of Saint Alexis the Man of God, the Sacrifice of Abraham—which would be chanted to the melody of "On the Sea of Tiberias" or "That which came to pass in thee." Thus, the girls, when they did housework or wove rugs, chanted these compunctionate hymns, and instead of imagining improper and worldly things, they would think of those things which are unto the salvation of the soul. Nowhere would you see women with uncovered heads and short sleeves. And now when we say these things to the natives here, they think that we're telling stories."

While the Elder was saying these things, I remembered the Greeks from Asia Minor I had known in America when I was young, and especially the compunctionate hymns about Saint Alexis the Man of God, which the women would chant, and weep. Of a truth, the destruction of Asia Minor in 1922 was a great calamity for the nation and the Church. For that most Christian civilization of Cappadocia and Pontus and the whole region of Anatolia was snuffed out. Snuffed out were the seven lamps of the Book of Revelation, and for this reason we have the present winter and darkness which has engulfed all.

T HE ELDER was a grace-filled man, and his speech had wisdom. He was deep and alert, and being an Anatolian, he often spoke in parables. If there happened to be a theologian among his visitors, and this was told him, he would turn to the theologian and say, "If you are a theologian, then you know letters. But if you have no fear of God, then you only have a trade."

In other words, if you are a graduate of theology, then certainly you are educated; you have read many books. But if you do not also have the fear of God and keep His commandments, then you possess a profession only and not the mystery of Theology.

He often said to his visitor, "Are you satisfied with yourself?"

If the listener didn't know what to answer, or if he hesitated, or if he answered in the affirmative, he heard the Elder say, "I am not satisfied with myself. I have much to correct." Hearing this, you would involuntarily sigh, censured by your conscience.

If someone told the Elder that so-and-so was good, without fail he would hear, "Yes, he is good. But he can be better. To reach from good to best there are many steps to climb. Yes—we can always be better."

The Elder was always careful when he spoke. His every word was measured, weighed, and with seriousness. He never spoke lightly or without thinking. He therefore desired his listeners to be so also, and he continually enjoined us to be circumspect.

Once, someone said in the Elder's presence that so-and-so (he had already departed this life) was a Saint.

"And you, are you God?" retorted the Elder immediately. "Only God knows who is holy. As for you, do not say so easily that this one or that one is holy. You don't know the hidden things of the heart. If he is a Saint, God will reveal it, when and if He wills it. As for you, do not say this."

"Forgive me, Elder. It is because the departed was a virtuous man and an ascetic (he had been a virtuous monk of the Holy Mountain) who had a good end: that's why I said he was a Saint. I meant it relatively—that compared to us, he was a Saint."

"Listen. Relatively is one thing and reality is something else. Therefore, do not say that somebody is a Saint. God has the say. He will judge who is a Saint and who is not."

As for his appearance, the Elder was always dressed with patched clothes and slippers, ungroomed and unkempt. He had made a vow, he told us, not to wear new clothes, but only used and patched ones.

"When I was young, I was very poor," he told me. "Especially in Jerusalem, where I stayed for a while, and here in Aegina, when I first came as a refugee after the exchange of populations. In Jerusalem, because I was from Asia Minor and my pronunciation was Anatolian, they didn't allow me to serve at the shrines as a deacon, and sometimes I was in want even of my daily bread. Often I opened my handkerchief and begged in the street so that I wouldn't perish from hunger."

As he was saying this, he opened his handkerchief which he always had in his hand, and he wept as if he were begging that very moment.

"Poverty is good. It teaches humility. Whenever I give something, be it a little leaf, a blade of grass, my ego goes before it. But when I am constrained to beg and stretch out my hand to receive from another, then I am humbled."

How can one forget such words of the Elder's? For the words he spoke to us were not abstract things, but were taken from experience, and when one meets them in life, they remain indelible in the heart.

Later in life, a little before the Second World War, when he left the hospital of Aegina where he first resided as a refugee and came to the hermitage of the Annunciation where he lived until his end, he espoused voluntary poverty. It was then that he made the vow never to wear new clothes. In his food also he was very frugal and plain. In all things he applied the teachings and admonitions of Abba Isaac the Syrian, whom he loved exceedingly.

One could rightly say that the Elder Ieronymos of Aegina was the incarnation of the words of Abba Isaac, to such a degree had he embraced the teachings of this great Saint and Father of stillness. The Elder was unable to speak without referring, either directly or indirectly, to the teaching and sayings of Saint Abba Isaac. Saint Isaac had become his life and his breath. It was for this reason that when you visited the Elder, you thought you were looking on one of those blessed Abbas of the desert of the first centuries of monasticism. In the Elder Ieronymos was fulfilled the saying of Saint John Chrysostom, "Not the place, but the way of life," makes the Christian or the monk. For although he did not live the greater part of his life in the deserts of Palestine, Egypt, Syria, or Mesopotamia, nor even of his own beloved Cappadocia, but rather on the island of Aegina, yet in his heart and in his mind he remained a dweller of the desert, alone with God alone, face to face.

The Elder was so unkempt in appearance that he often had caked mucus in the corners of his eyes. This did not bother him in the least, nor was he even conscious of it. Once when I was visiting him, an illustrious person came to see him. Mother Eupraxia, who served him, began to do what she could to make him appear as presentable as possible to the exalted visitor. First of all she took away his crumpled handkerchief that he always held in his hand and gave him a clean, freshly ironed one. With the boldness she had, she undertook to clean the mucus from his eyes with the old handkerchief, even as a mother does with her little ones. But the

Elder protested, saying, "Nun, does that bother you? It doesn't bother me. Leave it alone! Leave it alone!"

Then he turned to me and said, "The nun wishes to make me pretty. She doesn't understand. She is a woman. She wants the outside to be beautiful. But I want the inside to be beautiful. We should beautify the soul, the inner man. The body is of no profit."

THE ELDER had a great gift for imparting his meaning to others, and with his characteristic simplicity he would find original ways to get it across to them. With these ingenious means, he would indelibly imprint in us the message he wanted to communicate. Occasionally, while he was speaking, he would take his ever-present handkerchief and, holding it by one end, dangled it in the face of his listeners. If the "nun" happened to be close by, she would run in terror, the poor creature, to find a clean handkerchief to give him, so that we wouldn't be seeing the soiled one. She would snatch the old one and give him the clean one, scolding him because he displayed his soiled handkerchief to the visitors in such a demonstrative manner. The blessed Elder would remain unperturbed, and after displaying it before us, he let go and it fell to the floor.

"Of course," one of the visitors would always say; "since you let go, it fell."

"Thus also is it with us. If the strong right hand of the Most High does not hold us, we fall on our faces. No one stands on his own! No one is saved! If the grace of God leaves us, we all fall headlong. Let no one pride himself on his knowledge, on his cleverness. Let no one hope in his own strength. Some trust in chariots and some in horses, but we will call upon the Name of the Lord and shall be saved (cf. Psalm 19:7). It is not of him that willeth, nor of him that runneth, but of God Who in His good pleasure showeth mercy (cf. Romans 9:16). Without God we can do nothing. In vain do the builders build, in vain do the watchers watch, if the Lord our God does not build the house and keep watch (cf. Psalm 126). With God the impossible is possible. Yea, if we let go of the handkerchief, it falls. Yea, of a truth, if the sweet grace of our Saviour lets go of us, we are lost. Then no one is saved. We should always gaze up unto our heavenly Father. We should always hold on to the mighty right hand of our Christ. Then He will verily hold us up also."

I once related to a bishop this anecdote about the handkerchief, and it made such an impression on him that for some time whenever we met, he would take out his handkerchief and holding it, he showed it to me and said, "Without God we can do nothing."

Once when visiting the Elder with Mother Maria of Oinoussai, in the course of a conversation with Mother Maria we heard the Elder emphatically exclaim, *"Mou!"* He repeated it a few times— *"Mou! Mou! Mou!"* Both Mother and I were perplexed. What in the world was the Elder trying to say, mooing like that? Did he have a stomach-ache or something? Of course, in Greek, *mou* means *my*. Whereupon we heard him saying to Mother Maria, "How is it that you speak of our Lord and Saviour saying, 'Jesus said'? Who is this Jesus? Is He not our Christ? When you speak about your husband, your son, your daughter, do you not say MY husband, MY son, MY daughter? Never speak therefore of our Saviour without the *mou* [*my*] or *our*."

This observation made an impression on me. Since my early youth I would always say "our Saviour," "our Lord Jesus the Christ." I was born, reared, and lived among believing Orthodox Christians, and this was the way that they thought and spoke. The Anatolian Greeks would always say in Turkish, *Tatli Iesoum, Effendi,* i.e., My most Sweet Jesus Master. They would never speak of our Saviour in a cold impersonal manner. As a boy I would be bothered if someone, even a clergyman, said "Jesus said" even as one might say "Socrates said," "Confucius said," "Einstein said."

Our Saviour and Lord Jesus Christ was not just someone down the street—not one of many—but the God-man Lord Jesus. One therefore never spoke of Him in an impersonal or casual manner. That was rude if not irreverent. Mother Maria never forgot this incident of the "Mou" at the Elder's. She lived another forty-some years after this and would always prefix "my" or "our" before the all-holy Name of our Saviour.

On one of my trips to Greece I stayed for a few days in a house close to the center of Athens. The couple in whose house I stayed were pious and always offered hospitality to clergymen and monastics from all parts of Greece. The week before, a spiritual father from the Holy Mountain had come and stayed in the same home. The lady of the house said to me, "What can I tell you, Father? How great a thing spiritual love is. Neither children nor blood relatives are able to have so much and such strong love as spiritual people have. Just last week such-and-such an Elder from the Holy Mountain was staying with us, and a few days after his arrival he received a letter from his spiritual son, who wrote to him that from the day that he left, everything was gloomy in the kellion. It was as if the sun had been eclipsed. Everything was dark and gloomy. He couldn't wait to see him back. He wrote his Elder that for him, he was his spiritual oxygen, and that without him he couldn't even breathe, and to hurry back, and many other things. I marvelled at what great love spiritual people have. We who are in the world don't see such love and yearning even from our own children. As soon as the Elder received the letter, he read it to us for our profit, and because we liked it he gave it to us. Let me go and fetch it so you can read it yourself."

She went to the icon corner of her house where she kept it and brought it to me. Out of respect, I read it. The praises seemed to me somewhat exaggerated, but I reproached myself that I was not spiritual and that was why they did not move me so. Then again I said in my mind, that I grew up in another part of the world, and there must be a difference in the way of thinking and manner of expression between Greece and the United States, which was why the whole thing did not enthuse me. But I didn't say anything to the lady of the house in order not to scandalize her.

A few days later I went to Aegina like a thirsty deer to see the Elder. Having gone first to Saint Nectarius to worship, I went immediately to the hermitage to stay a few hours and then return to Athens. You would think that the Elder was waiting for me. As soon as I greeted him and kissed his hand, he said to me right off, "Once, when I still lived in Asia Minor, I went to Constantinople for the first time. I was a deacon then—my name was Basil. I went to the Patriarchate, I worshipped the Pammakaristos Mother of God, the holy relics of Saint Euphemia and Saint Solomone, I went to the holy spring of Blachernae, to many churches, and to the Life-giving Spring. I saw many marvellous things. I said to myself that now, here in Constantinople, I would be able to find experienced spiritual fathers to learn things I never knew. For, I supposed, if we in the depths of Anatolia, in Cappadocia, knowing Greek either not well or not at all, without patristic books and ecclesiastical education, still had some kind of spiritual knowledge and experience, how much more here—in the center of things, where they have the Patriarchate and the national schools, where they know the language well and read the Fathers in the original— would they have an advanced spiritual state, much more advanced than ours. I went here, I went there, wherever I heard the report that there was a spiritual man somewhere, I searched, I asked— *aman!* I found no one even to come close to those people that we had in my country. Some even misunderstood me and looked at me strangely, as if I were deluded for inquiring about prayer of the heart and spiritual states. I was bitterly disappointed, my soul pained me. I sat and with tears I wrote to my spiritual mentor Misael at Kelveri. I described to him all that I had seen and worshipped in Constantinople. Patriarchal liturgies with bishops of the Synod, superb chanting, Patriarchal protocol, holy springs, churches, and so forth. I wrote to him also that as a panting hart, I sought a man to speak with of spiritual things and found none. There where I thought that I would find highly spiritual persons, I did not find even one. I wrote to him, 'A man like you I did not find to benefit me.' After a while I received an answer. He had someone write to me in Turkish, since he was illiterate: 'My beloved child, Deacon Basil, from my eyes to your eyes I greet you. I received your precious letter. You, my son, endeavored to hurl me headlong into the abyss of destruction, but I set before me all my sins and was not shaken, I did not fall. If ever again you write to me that you have not found another man like me, I will not write to you again, nor shall I pray for you anymore, and even your memory I will efface from my heart.' That is what the men of old were like. They were vigilant, they were watchful, they guarded themselves against pride, they were austere and serious. Today spiritual fathers rejoice and delight in praises and flattery. They take pride and get puffed up when you praise them. They have forgotten that which is written, 'He who praises a monk surrenders him to the devil.' I wrote one innocent thought to my spiritual guide Misael, to express the pain of my soul and my disappointment, and he, to protect himself from pride, immediately brought to mind all his sins. By his answer he made me careful to avoid soul-corrupting pride and boasting. How could anyone forget such fathers and guides?"

Saying these things, the Elder wept, remembering his blessed spiritual guide Misael. I was astonished. I hadn't said anything to the Elder about the letter I had read a few days ago in Athens. There was no need for me to tell him anything because he knew it all. Verily he had been awaiting me in order to relate to me this episode from his life, and so make me careful for the rest of my life against praises and pride. How then, on my part, could I forget such a father and guide!

Once when I was with the Elder there came a young man with his wife for a visit. From the conversation that ensued, it became evident that the young man was already an acquaintance of the Elder's and had lately gotten married. He was bringing his wife to meet the Elder for the first time and to receive his blessing. It was summer and quite hot. The young man wore short sleeves and his wife likewise, but otherwise both were dressed modestly. After they had greeted one another and kissed the Elder's hand, the Elder said to the young man, "It is evident that your wife loves you very much."

"From what do you infer this, Elder?" asked the young man.

"I behold short sleeves on you, short sleeves on your wife also. From the great love that she has for you, she does whatever you do, she imitates you."

Both of them blushed. The young man said, "But it's summertime, Elder. It's very hot."

"It's summer for me, too, but I don't take off my clothes, I don't wear short sleeves. You're the head, you are the instructor in your house. If you are modest, then she will be modest also. You govern. As you wish, so it is."

The Elder was amazing. There was nothing that he left unobserved, that he did not comment on. But he always made his observations with love and wisdom and on occasion with humor.

Afterwards he said to the couple, "I do not wish to grieve you. I don't want you to depart with sadness, but as a spiritual father it is my duty to tell you what is right, what is profitable to your souls."

Then he gave them many beautiful admonitions. The nun brought them treats and so they departed. On this occasion the Elder did not tell me to go to the chapel or to sit in the courtyard until he had seen the newlyweds. I surmise that he kept me close to him for me to hear all that was said so that I might have it as instruction. As for the young man and his wife, I doubt they ever forgot the Elder's admonitions.

ONCE I WENT to the Elder with two novices of our synodia. He said to the one who didn't know Greek, "Who is your Elder?"

The other novice translated it for him into English. Then the novice pointed to me, and the Elder said to him, "Is he, or do you have him?"

The young novice said to him through the interpreter that he didn't understand what he meant. To tell the truth, even I didn't readily understand what the Elder meant.

He therefore asked him a second time, "Who is your Elder?"

Again the novice pointed to me, and again he heard, "Is he, or do you have him?"

Then I understood what the Elder meant to say in his Cappadocian manner of expression—is he really your elder, or do you just have him to point him out as such? The novice again did not understand and he said this to him. Then the Elder, waving his hand, said, "Let be! Let be!" and didn't speak with the novice any further. Most of those present took no note of this in the midst of so many things that the Elder told us, and forgot about it. But I noted it mentally, for the Elder never said anything at random without meaning. Time passed; the young man showed zeal in his monastic calling and in the work he had as an obedience. But from time to time I observed a certain self-will and obstinacy, and this troubled me. The three years of the novitiate passed and it was time for him to be tonsured a monk. To this very day, no one in our synodia has become a monk without at least three years of trial, and oftentimes four and five years, and more, if necessary. Finally, when the three years had passed, I mentioned to the senior fathers my hesitation concerning the tonsure. They said to me, "He's good. We all have our faults. He's young and is overzealous. He'll mature with time. The Fathers teach us not to seek the priesthood, but as for the monastic tonsure, to seek it persistently. The brother therefore is applying this dictum in insisting on becoming a monk." Wherefore the tonsure took place, the years passed; but from time to time I saw disquieting signs and I remembered the Elder's words. Some twelve years passed after the repose of the Elder, and the brother left without a blessing. He wanted us to have him ordained a clergyman, but we would not accept this in any way. He went far away, was ordained a priest, and became abbot of himself as he had been from the beginning.

Many things that many of us heard from the Elder appeared improbable or even inconceivable when we heard them, but with time even the most improbable came to pass. It has been almost twenty years since the Elder's repose, and things he told us are still being fulfilled so that we might know that he had the gift of prophecy.

As a monastic community, we here in America have been profited and benefited in a very great way by the Elder Ieronymos, even though he never came to the States. One of these benefactions is that we have Father Isaac as a member of our synodia. Born of Greek parents in Utah, Father Isaac came as a nineteen-year-old to Holy Cross Theological School in Boston. As a youth he had never heard of monasticism, nor knew that our Church even had monks. As soon as he learned of this upon coming to Boston, he desired to become a monk. I hindered him at the time, on one hand because he was only nineteen years old, whereas legal age at that time was twenty-one, and on the other because I knew from experience that his parents, as well as the ecclesiastical authorities, would be against it, and they would accuse our monastery of taking students from the school, and so on and so forth. I told him then that his first obedience in becoming a novice was to finish the seminary, which took seven years, whereupon he would have also reached legal age and no one would be able to hinder him. I also told him not to tell anyone his thoughts about monasticism because it would only elicit all manner of comments and remarks without profit. I gave him spiritual books to read, such as volumes of the collected lives of the Saints and the sayings of the Fathers.

Nearly four years passed, and in the end the young man was expelled with another six students from the school because they would not consent to eat fish and dairy products during the Great Fast and to kneel at the Liturgy on Sunday, which are both prohibited by the sacred canons of the Church. In the meantime, his mother was stricken with cancer, and his parents wanted them all to go together to Crete to see their relatives. I then told the young man that since he was not yet dressed in black, to tell his parents that he would accept to accompany them before he entered the monastery, but with the stipulation that they would first go to Jerusalem to worship the all-holy Sepulchre and the other shrines, and that after he had gone to Crete and seen his grandmother and relatives, he would go to stay on the Holy Mountain with the Fathers of our synodia at New Skete for a few months. At the end of the summer I would also come with one other brother, and we would all meet at the Holy Mountain.

And thus it came to pass. He flew from Boston to Athens with his parents; they went to Crete, he to Mount Athos, where he spent Holy Week and Pascha. Shortly after Pascha he rejoined his parents in Crete and together they made the pilgrimage to Jerusalem. Then they returned to Greece, and before his parents made a second trip to Crete before returning to the U.S., they all went together to Aegina and worshipped at Saint Nectarius. But apparently his parents were tired, so they returned with a relative to Athens. The young man remained on Aegina to visit the Elder Ieronymos and return later. It was his first visit to the Elder; though he had never met him, he had heard many things from me and had great reverence for him.

Here I should add that the young man had also heard from me many good things about the Holy Mountain and the fathers there. At times he had thoughts that it might be better to stay there, instead of returning to the U.S. When he went, therefore, and spent Pascha on the Holy Mountain and made the acquaintance of Papou-Arsenios (this is how we referred to the Elder Arsenios of our synodia) and the other fathers, he had already decided to stay with them on the Holy Mountain rather than returning to Boston, though he had not told his thought to anyone. The other thought he had not mentioned to anyone was never to accept ordination; since he had attended seminary, it had occurred to him that upon entering the monastic life he might be asked to become a priest, which he had decided he would refuse to do.

He finally reached the hermitage of the Elder Ieronymos. He knocked on the door and shortly the Eldress Eupraxia opened. After she had taken him to the Elder and he had kissed his hand, the Elder said to him, "I am old and ill. At the moment I'm tired. You come from afar. The nun will offer you something to eat, and I will rest a little. Afterwards we can speak."

So the Eldress prepared the table and set a dish with dolmades for the young man, and the Elder "rested." Fifteen to twenty minutes later, the Elder opened the door of his cell and received him. He looked at him intently, asked him where he came from; then he asked him if he had any problems with the monastery in Boston. When the young man answered that he did not, the Elder told him three things:

"One: Father Panteleimon is sufficient for your salvation. Two: Do not ask to receive the priesthood. If Father Panteleimon proposes this to you, do not refuse it. Three: Do not look at women. Much care is needed."

These things he said, and nothing more. Sending him off with prayers and blessings, he dismissed him so that he would not be late for the ferryboat.

From the beginning the Elder loved and esteemed the young man. His joy was great from the first meeting, and he would always mention this to the nun Eupraxia. When the Elder and I met later, he told me many things in detail concerning this young man and how much he loved him. When he had first met the Elder, being too overawed by his presence to be able to speak, he had not said anything to him of his intention to remain on Mount Athos for good; but after the three things the Elder told him, he understood that the Elder had been declaring to him the will of God, and he decided to return to the monastery in Boston instead. "When he spoke to me," said Father Isaac later, "I understood that he spoke with authority, and there was no room for gainsaying or discussion. When you saw the Elder, you understood that he was not an ordinary person, but rather a man of God, and that God spoke through him."

Three years later, at his tonsure, the young man received the name of the Elder's beloved Saint. Years later when he reached canonical age, we gave him the obedience of receiving the priesthood; when, according to the decision he had made years before, he wished to refuse, we reminded him of the injunction of the Elder Ieronymos, and he could not do otherwise than accept; and today he is a great comfort to our synodia.

The Elder considered the priesthood a very exalted office and heavy ministry, and rarely encouraged anyone to receive it. He himself, after he was ordained, served a very short time as a priest (according to some, only forty days) before he resigned from the priesthood. He saw something during the time of the Liturgy and was affrighted, and he resigned. But he continued to hear confessions. Years later he lost his left arm from the elbow, after which, even if he wished it, he could no longer serve the Liturgy. He told me once, "When I was ordained priest, I put a ribbon of fire around my neck. People would come to confession, and whatever they told me during the day, the demons would come by night and play me replays. *Aman!* I said, heavy is the *epitrachelion*."

Once when I visited him, the Elder said to me, "So-and-so whom you sent to me some years ago wanted to become a clergyman. Did he or not?"

"He was ordained," I replied, "and is already serving as a priest."

Then the Elder sighed and said, "If he is able to pick up Aegina on his back, he did well. If not, then he did badly."

When I heard this I was terrified, and I began to sigh myself. The nun Eupraxia said to him, "How is it that you always say such things and terrify people? Should men then not be ordained priests? How would the churches then be liturgized? How would the Christians receive Communion?"

The Elder turned and said to her, "Nun! I have spoken, and it is even so, as I said it!"

Then he turned to me and said, "Heavy is the priesthood! Very heavy, for him that has a mind and understands!"

The Elder was wont to say that there are seven impediments for ordination to the priesthood (I do not know where he got the number seven). "Yet," he said, "there's an eighth impediment—the greatest—and that is 'I want.'"

Once he said to me out of the blue, "Whom do you commemorate?"

"Metropolitan Philaret of the Russian Synod Abroad," I replied.

"Well! You do well! And so do!" I heard him tell me.

This made an impression on me, for I knew for a fact that a certain few had complained to him because I did not commemorate a Greek Old Calendarist bishop, but rather a Russian. What impressed me was the absence of any phyletism, which is rarely absent even among spiritual people in that part of the world.

On another occasion he said to me, "The world is burning! Both here and abroad a great conflagration has been lit. The whole world, the whole planet, has become a great furnace. Everything is on fire. Blessed art thou and those with thee! For as the Three Children in the fiery furnace, so are the true monks and Christians today. Only hold fast well to the things of the monastic estate. For even as the Three Children were preserved whole and unharmed in the midst of the flames, thus you also will be preserved by the grace of our Christ and God-man Jesus."

The Elder loved monasticism greatly and with discretion he encouraged many, both men and women, to embrace this mode of life. I often heard him tell a visitor, "You are good. I should have made your acquaintance some time before. I would have made you a monk. Now you're married, it cannot be. But even so, do not leave off prayer. God loves all. Attend to your salvation. Be diligent! Fearful is indolence. A great thing is diligence."[5]

During the last years of the Elder's life, much was heard in the ecclesiastical and secular press concerning bishops and other clergymen. Some were exalted, others were hurled down. (It was the time when the Archbishop of the State Church was forced out of office, following mass protests.) I never heard the Elder comment in any way on any of these doings. It was as if he did not live on this planet, as if he not only had no opinion, but not even any cognizance of what was being said and done outside in society. One always heard spiritual words from his mouth. And if anyone ventured to say something from the "news" of the world, the Elder pretended not to understand what was said to him, and immediately turned the conversation to examination and censure of self, whereupon the visitor would become embarrassed and understand his mistake. Only once did I hear the Elder break his silence and say something about a current event. This was when Patriarch Athenagoras prayed with the Pope in Jerusalem, and one year later lifted the Anathemas of 1054. I then heard the Elder say, "Many evils will come forth from that head, many afflictions for the Church." Kyr Eleftherios Koumbis, who is still living,[6] was also present on that occasion.

Many who knew the Elder have observed that rarely, if ever, did he speak on matters of faith, or concerning the calendar issue, or

---
5. An allusion to one of the Praises hymns for Holy and Great Wednesday.
6. Mr. Koumbis reposed some years after this was written in 1985.

anything relating to Church politics. I had observed this also, even while the Elder was yet alive. Later I observed the same thing in Archbishop Andrew of Spring Valley of blessed memory, who reposed on June 29, 1978, the feast of Saints Peter and Paul. He had evident gifts of the Holy Spirit, especially that of foreknowledge and clairvoyance. Once a certain clergyman of the Greek Archdiocese, knowing that Archbishop Andrew was the spiritual father of our monastery, asked me to intercede with the Archbishop that he might receive him as a visitor in order to discuss some matter with him. Archbishop Andrew was already on in years and not able to receive visitors every day. I telephoned his residence at the convent and asked his cell attendant, Prince Dimitri, if it were possible for the clergyman to visit. He asked the Archbishop and the answer was: If the person wished to discuss some personal matter, he was welcome; but if it was concerning ecclesiastical matters, then to go to Metropolitan Philaret in New York or to Father George Grabbe, the secretary of the Synod, who also spoke English, since Archbishop Andrew for some years now did not read ecclesiastical periodicals and therefore did not know what was happening in the ecclesiastical world.

This did not mean that these two contemporary fathers (Father Ieronymos and Archbishop Andrew) had nothing to say, especially on matters of faith, but they applied the saying of Abba Isaac the Syrian, "Flee from discussions on dogma as from an unruly lion… either with those raised in the Church, or with strangers" (Homily Seventeen); and, "Confute those who would strive to dispute with you by the strength of your virtues and not by the persuasions of your words" (Homily Four); and yet another, "Do not provoke any man or vie zealously with him, either for the sake of the Faith, or on account of his evil deeds" (Homily Five). This I ascertained in both these fathers. In the instance of Father Ieronymos, I was present once when a certain pious woman (presently a nun) who celebrated the church feasts according to both calendars (when she could), informed the Elder that she had decided henceforth to celebrate only according to the old reckoning.

The Elder said to her, "Did I ever speak to you about the old and the new?"

"No, Elder."

"Now you yourself on your own have resolved it and made a promise?"

"Yes, I myself vow."

"Take care now! To God and not to man do you promise. You can no longer celebrate now and again according to the new reckoning also. No one compelled you. Of yourself you have understood what is right, and make a promise. Tomorrow if your son or grandson says to you, 'Mother, today it's Christmas' or a nameday—and it's according to the new—what will you answer? Surely—No my son, it is not yet the Nativity of our Saviour, neither the feast of Saint John or Saint Nicholas. The Church does not celebrate now. From the beginning it has known only one calendar, without corrections, without additions or subtractions. Besides, it was according to this reckoning that we were born and which we have received. This then is the one that is right."

The Elder, knowing that there is no profit, nor end, to theological discussions and disputes, kept his peace, spending his time in prayer and fasting. For there would only be fruitless debating for the other person and loss for himself, with the sole outcome that he would lose his peace. Rarely, if he discerned that one had a good volition and would profit, he broke his silence and quietly guided such a one in matters of faith. Except for these rare occasions, the Elder endeavored with admonitions and exhortations rather to awaken in his listener a thirst for Christ, Who is truth itself, and then each one on his own, if he was honorable and sincere with himself, would come to a conclusion concerning ecclesiastical matters. But then again, there could be no greater witness, lesson, and preaching than his own utterly immovable steadfastness in piety. In matters of faith, the Elder taught and strengthened us by his silence and example more than by words and demonstrations. Yet there are from time to time certain disputers of this age who wish to convince us that the Elder Ieronymos and grace-filled people like him are outside the Church, because they are not in communion with World Orthodoxy. Our answer is this—may our sweet Saviour Jesus number us sinners with these Fathers, and it more than suffices us.

Once Dostoevsky, writing to a French lady, said that when he was an exile in Siberia as a revolutionist, he made a friend, and he found such friendship and love in his friend, and he came to love him so greatly and continues so to love him, that if one were able to demonstrate that truth was found outside of his friend, and his friend outside of truth, he would choose to remain with his friend rather than with truth—and his friend was Christ. Of course the truths and proofs of the world (and they are many and varied) are a self-deception. It is also recorded in the Acts of the Apostles that when the Apostle Paul preached for the last time to the Jews in Rome, they said to him, "We neither received letters out of Judea concerning thee, neither any of the brethren that came showed or spake any harm of thee. But we desire to hear of thee what thou thinkest: for as concerning this sect, we know that everywhere it is spoken against." (Acts 28:21–23)

Well, better that we be found in the "sect" of the Apostle Paul and have communion with him and the other Apostles and the multitude of Fathers and Teachers of our Faith, than to be found with the world-acclaimed and official "synagogue" which communicates in the world heresy of this age.

O<small>NCE THE ELDER</small> said to me, "I'm going to ask you a question. Are you a Cappadocian or not?"

"I, Elder, was born in America. My parents were from the Peloponnesus. My father of blessed memory was from Philiatra of Messenia and my mother is from Mani, from the villages of Mount Taygetos. But I grew up amongst Cappadocian refugees in my childhood. After the destruction of Asia Minor many refugees were found in the city in which I was born. From a young age, I learned their ways, their customs and foods. If I'm a monk today, I owe much of it to their piety, to their example, and their instructions. In my soul, therefore, I am a Cappadocian."

Then the Elder smiled and said—somewhat altering the saying—"What is in the soul is on the face." That is, since you are a Cappadocian in soul, you are also a Cappadocian in appearance.

Later I learned that he had a contention with Mother Eupraxia. The Elder said that I was a Cappadocian and that was why I had a Hadji grandmother from Ürgüp. But the Eldress, who had diligently examined me, said that I was not a Cappadocian, but simply referred to Hadji Macrina from Ürgüp as grandmother. But the Elder insisted that I was a Cappadocian, saying, "even his appearance and his speech betray him that he is a Cappadocian." Thus the contention. This made a great impression on me, for I verified once again something that I had observed concerning the gift of clairvoyance—that is, that God reveals what is needed and not everything. For example in the case of Prophet Elisseus, he knew what the Syrians were speaking in their secret chambers and passed it on to the King of Israel, whereas the death of the child of the Shummanite woman, God hid from him. Similarly the great Abba John, surnamed the Prophet, the fellow ascetic of the great Abba Barsanuphius, who knew the secret things of the hearts of men, did not know about the end of Abba Seridus, "On the seventh day after Abba Seridus, I depart… If Abba Seridus had remained, I would have remained another five years. But, because God hid this from me and took him, neither do I remain…" (Answer 124).

Thus was it with the Elder Ieronymos also. My thoughts were

known to him, he gave me answers to questions which I had mentally without opening my mouth to ask, and yet my descent he knew not. If the power he had was not from God but from the enemy, then the opposite would have been the case: he would not have known my thoughts, but he would have known my descent, for the demons do not know our thoughts, but they know external events.

The blessed Elder was wont to say, "The day that passes and you do not find Jesus in your heart, in your mind, by prayer—that day you have lost. It will not return again. Every day find the immaculate feet of Jesus. Take hold of them and lave them with your tears. The day that passes and you do not encounter Jesus, you harvest loss, you gather injury, you remain hungry."

He often said, "Do not take me, O my Christ, my sweet Jesus, until I become wholly Thine." On occasion he went so far as to say, to the horror of some, "Cancer has come out of Paradise. It is a blessing for the believing man. It prepares him. It gives him time to reflect, to repent. It does not take you out of this life suddenly. The Fathers call a sudden death an evil death. I pray, 'My most sweet Saviour, Lord Jesus, give me a painful cancer before I die, that I may be cleansed. Then take me.'" And the Lord, Who hearkens to the prayers of the righteous, granted this petition to the Elder. He suffered very much in the end, for some months, with lung cancer. I was young when I heard this, some thirty years old. Now many years later I pray the same prayer, but sinner that I am I have no assurance that our Saviour will hearken to my prayer.

"Thieves!" the Elder would say to the astonishment of his hearers. "Learn how to become thieves. There are twenty-four hours in the day. How many hours we work, we sleep, we eat, we rest, we occupy ourselves with sundry matters. Can we not find one hour—half an hour—to pray? Learn how to steal time for prayer, for spiritual reading, for *hesychia* (stillness)."

A young maiden, who was a university student, often visited the

The well in the courtyard of the Elder's Hermitage.

Elder without her mother's knowledge, lest her mother get nervous that she wanted to become a nun. He would say to her, "Every day, every evening, find time to pray, to read Abba Isaac, to be quiet. Say to your mother, 'Mother, tomorrow I have an important exam and I need to study.' Shut yourself in your bedroom and pray. Another day, tell her, 'Mother, I have a splitting headache. I have to be in a dark and quiet room' and withdraw. And again some other day, say, 'I'm very tired. I want to retire early today.' Go to your room, get into your bed. Draw the covers over your head and don't sleep—say your prayers in bed. If we can make 'excuses in sin,' can we not make excuses to be quiet and pray?"

Again he would say, "When you want to dig a well, you don't just dig a little and leave off. Rather, you labor and dig deeper day by day, until you find water. Thus it is with prayer also. We will labor every day, we will dig—Lord Jesus Christ, Son of God, have mercy on me. Lord Jesus Christ, Son of God, have mercy on me. Lord Jesus Christ, Son of God, have mercy on me. With the spade of our mind we will dig in the heart, until we find the source—the living water springing up unto life everlasting."

In 1966, as if I knew that the end of the Elder was drawing nigh, I visited him many times that summer, alone and with others. On one of my visits he asked me, "Do you have a staff?"

"I do, Elder, it's a Holy Mountain stick which a certain zealot monk made for me, but since I'm young I don't carry it. But when I go to the Holy Mountain and walk long distances I use it."

In fact I needed a walking-stick, for I had a great deal of pain, but in 1966 I didn't know what ailed me, since I avoided doctors. Later, I found out that I had osteomyelitis in my left hip and disk problems of long standing. (I was operated on for both in 1974.) But since I was young, I was embarrassed to use a walking-stick. My thought told me that men would say that being young I carried a stick out of pride. The Elder said to me, "Take mine. I give it to you."

Embarrassed to deprive him of his stick, I said, "I thank you, Elder, but I wouldn't want you to be left without it."

"I no longer have need of it. Besides, I have another one. You need it."

I thus received the Elder's staff from his own hand as a great blessing. We have it to this day as a treasure, together with the little stick of Papa Nicholas Planas, kept in the sanctuary of our monastery, along with other blessings. His other stick he gave to Peter Botsis whom he loved greatly.

ONCE THE ELDER was visited by a certain lay preacher who has since passed away. He was a bibliophile and collector of old editions. He heard of the Elder and went to see him. The Elder began to speak of prayer and other spiritual subjects. The preacher was not paying much attention, but was looking about the Elder's little cell to see what books he had and was reading. It could be he hoped to find some rare and hard-to-find book, or some first edition of an old book. He knew that during the exchange of populations of 1924 the refugees had brought ecclesiastical books with them. It was also known that the Old Calendarists had a great reverence for old editions of spiritual books. Close by where the Elder sat, he had the *Homilies* of his beloved Abba Isaac the Syrian, an edition by Archimandrite Joachim Spetsieris printed at the beginning of this century.[7] Interrupting the Elder in mid-sentence, the preacher said, "Elder, this edition has many typographical errors. You must surely be aware of the first edition by Nikephoros Theotokis printed in Leipzig. It's much better."

The Elder continued what he was saying as if he hadn't heard. But not much time passed before the preacher burst out again. He repeated his observation to the Elder, considering that the Elder's hearing was not very good. Whereupon he heard the Elder telling him somewhat austerely, "This edition is enough for me, even if it has many errors. If I could put into practice even one small part of what is written without errors in this book, even if but one homily —even with errors—it suffices me."

The preacher immediately understood his mistake and asked forgiveness. This was told me by the preacher himself when once we met in Athens. By saying this, the Elder did not mean that he approved of faulty editions; he himself was a zealot of exactness and desired that which was genuine and whole; he wished to draw the preacher's attention to the fact that there would be no profit for him in collecting rare editions of spiritual books, if he did not apply—even if imperfectly—the things written therein.[8]

The Elder often used to tell his visitors the patristic saying, "There is nothing more fearful than the changeableness of man." And he not only said this, but with living illustrations he gave you

---

7. That is, the twentieth.
8. The preacher was the late Demetrios Panagopoulos of Athens.

to grasp the height, the depth, and the breadth of the mutability of our fallen nature.

He said, for example, "I get up in the morning and everything is bright. The sun is shining within and without, I have peace in my heart. I love everything and everybody. I glorify and thank our good God for everything. Comes the noon, and it begins to get cloudy. I find fault with this, that, and the other. This bothers me; that bothers me. Comes the evening, and everything is darkness. Everything and everybody bothers me. When at last night comes, then I fall into despair and hopelessness. All things are gloomy and dismal. Nothing and nobody pleases me. I don't love anything or anybody. I have turmoil within me. And all this in one day! Yes, man is changeable, very changeable. He is easily altered. The space of a day is enough to turn him all the way around. And why do I say the space of a day—in the space of an hour a man can make a complete about-face. Man changes from minute to minute. In truth, nothing is more fearful than the changeableness of man."

Nevertheless, if the Elder saw that the visitor listening to him was unsettled or saddened (since each one saw within him the strength and truth of the Elder's observation in his own experiences), then he said to him, "I don't want you to go away grieved. I want you to have courage. Listen! Only the Angels never fall or change for the worse. Nor do the demons humble themselves or repent. But men fall and repent—we both sin, and we repent. Abba Isaac the Syrian says that in this imperfect life, there is no perfectness. All things change, all things are mutable. There is no stable and unvarying state. Nevertheless, be of good cheer! For if man can change for the worse, he can also change for the better. He can come to his senses, can humble himself, can repent. If a wheel turns downward, it nonetheless also turns up. As we will, it comes to pass. It's in our hands. In my homeland we say, *Ashkolsoun tchivirineh*.[9] Well done, therefore, to him who turns the

---

9. Lit., *Bravo to him who turns* [i.e., the wheel, as the Elder has just explained].

wheel upward. Beside that, we Christians have our Creator and tenderly loving God as helper. We have the Angels, our Panagia, All Saints for our help. Therefore let no man despair. Let no one lose his courage. Let us all hope in God and be saved."

O NCE the Elder said to me, "I go into the country to buy some fish or for some other need and I return to my cell. Along the way I have thoughts—sometimes even harmful ones—for, 'from my youth do many passions war against me.'[10] I say the Creed and immediately all the thoughts perish. Do thou likewise."

When I heard that counsel from the Elder I noted it well. Before that meeting, when I had thoughts, I said the prayer "Lord, Jesus Christ..." or "Let God arise, and let His enemies be scattered... (Psalm 67:1)" with greater force—as my Elders on the Holy Mountain had taught me—and I found help. But after the Elder's "Do thou likewise," I began in obedience to say the Creed; and although so many years have passed, as many times as I have said the Creed with attention when assailed by thoughts, the thoughts have been immediately cut off as with a sword. Evidently the Creed is an exceedingly powerful prayer, and not simply an exposition of what we believe; therefore it bothers the demons a great deal, as a confession of the Orthodox Faith.

Once some of us were with the Elder and he said to us, "From time to time a certain pious Christian comes by—a woman from Aegina—to hear the word of God. She usually doesn't speak; she just listens and leaves. Then she goes home and tries to apply the things she hears. After a certain length of time she comes to me and says, 'I'm not doing well, Elder, I'm sick.'

"I say to her, 'Tell me, where does it hurt? What are the symptoms of your ailment, so that we can find a medicine to heal you?'

"'No,' she says, 'You don't understand, Elder, my body doesn't

10. From the Hymns of Ascent in Fourth Tone.

hurt. My ailment is of another kind. I don't know what to tell you to try to get it across to you. The problem isn't that I'm in pain. Something has changed inside me. I'm not the same. I'm not doing well.'

"I say to her, 'If you can't describe your ailment to me, how am I going to help you?'"

"The woman says, 'Well, it used to be that when I looked at my husband, my child, I felt longing—I wept for joy. Something leapt inside me. My joy was to cook, to get their clothes ready, to take care of them. Now, everything has changed. I look at my husband, my son—I don't get a feeling of longing, I don't skip for joy. I'm not moved as I was before. I've suffered something. Something has changed. I haven't stopped taking care of them. I continue to attend to my responsibilities. I love them; but I don't feel any yearning for them when I think of them or see them. I would much rather just be by myself.'

"'When you're by yourself, where is your mind found? What are you thinking?'

"'I find myself at Golgotha, at the Anointing Stone, and I weep with our Panagia and the Myrrh-bearing Women.'

"'Listen, my sister, that's a good ailment you have there. Whoever has heartfelt pain for our Jesus, whoever thirsts, hungers for God —he will be filled to the full with everlasting life. Death will never touch him. From henceforth he will find himself in Paradise.'"

Hearing these things from the Elder, I considered myself wretched and wept, calling that woman blessed who in her simplicity said that she wasn't doing well. I remembered the blessed Elder Joseph of the Holy Mountain, who used to say, "I'm sick! I pain!" When you asked him what his sickness was called, he answered, "God." Of a truth, such a pain is good, and it works a man's salvation. Would that we all had that sickness.

I again remembered my Hadji Yiayia in America. Even as she sat quietly there on her sofa, you could hear coming out of her,

"*Vakh, Pana! Tatli Iesoum, Effendi! Amani, Amani! Validim Soultan Panagia!*"[11] And then, as from two fountains, her eyes began to flow with tears. Anybody who didn't know her interior activity would have said within himself, "What on earth is wrong with this little old lady for her to start crying and mourning like that right out of the blue?" Blessed are they who mourn now, for they shall be comforted. Blessed are they who sow in tears, for they shall reap with rejoicing in that day. *Thou hast smitten me with yearning, O Christ, and by Thy divine love hast Thou changed me.*[12]

Now I will write something I heard concerning a visit to the Elder. I had hoped that he who visited him would write it himself, but since he was pardoned (that is, reposed) a year ago, I have undertaken to write it as I heard it.

After the visit of the publisher Alexander Papademetriou and his wife Maria, as was mentioned above, he was so impressed that he would tell others to go to visit the Elder. At the time Dr. Alexander Kalomiros had come from Thessalonica to visit Athens (the Papademetriou couple were the God-parents of one of the Doctor's children), and they urged him to go with them to the Elder. And so it happened. The Doctor had already heard about the Elder, and, as he himself later told me, he had a desire to question him on five subjects. While on the way on the ferryboat, the Papademetriou couple were continually talking to the Doctor about the Elder. But the Doctor, as he related to me later, was thinking of the subjects that he wished to ask about, and he decided not to bother the Elder about all five of them, so as not to tire him, but only to ask about two, and to save the other three for another visit.

---

11. *Woe is me, O most sweet Jesus, Lord! Aman, aman! O Mother of the King, Panagia!*
12. From Ode Nine of the second Canon of the Feast of our Lord's Transfiguration on August 6; also used as one of the prayers before Holy Communion.

When they reached Aegina, they first went and venerated Saint Nectarius, then immediately afterward went down to the Elder's. Mother Eupraxia received them with kindness and informed the Elder about the visitors, all three of whom he received in his little cell at the same time. Having entered and kissed his hand, Kyr Papademetriou said to the Elder, "This is Dr. Kalomiros." The Elder looked them over well and said, "Not Kalomiros [*fortunate*], but Kakomiros [*ill-fated*]." All three of them froze. Mrs. Papademetriou said in her mind, "What has happened to the blessed one that he would say such a thing? How much it must have wounded the poor Doctor. *Po! po!* what was this?"

The Doctor said nothing. He only looked at the Elder closely. The Elder then said a few words to Kyr Papademetriou, and kept only the Doctor with him so they could speak between them privately. Whereupon, the Elder, without pausing, spoke to the Doctor concerning all five subjects that he had initially had it in mind to inquire about, without the Doctor's ever opening his mouth. And the marvellous thing is that the Elder spoke about the five subjects in the order and according to the priority that the Doctor had planned to ask him before coming and before losing his courage to ask about all five, mentally telling himself he would only ask about two.

When the visit ended, the Elder bid them farewell with the prayer, "Go with the blessing of our Christ and the Panagia," as he was wont to say, and they departed for Athens. The Doctor was astonished and awe-struck. On the return trip by ferryboat to Piraeus, Mrs. Papademetriou, who had not yet recovered from the Elder's first words, *Not Kalomiros, but Kakomiros,* said to the Doctor, "You know, Doctor, the Elder is from Asia Minor and he doesn't hear well. So don't be offended by what he said to you when we first greeted him. The way that the Anatolians express themselves is different from ours. For this reason, it often happens that they wish to say one thing, and something else comes out."

The Doctor answered, "I was not offended in the least by what the Elder said to me. On the contrary, I understood from his very first words to what great degree he has the gift of clairvoyance, and a certain awe and divine fear seized me."

Whereupon the Doctor explained that his last name was Kakomiros and he had changed it to Kalomiros. Originally it had not even been Kakomiros. Kakomiros was a nickname that had been given to his grandfather when he was quite young. The occasion was this. When his grandfather was a child, he was playing once with other children and they climbed a tree. Later, the other children came down, and he remained alone up in the tree. The other children shouted at him to jump and come down, but he was afraid to jump because the height was not small. The other children therefore began to make fun of him, shouting up at him to jump and saying that they had all jumped down and none of them was hurt. But he began to cry and bemoaned himself, saying, "O the ill-fated one [*kakomiros*] that I am! O the ill-fated one that I am!" After that, the nickname Kakomiros stuck, and in time became his surname.

When the Doctor was young, the other children at school taunted him that his name was Kakomiros—ill-fated—and he would plead with his father to have their name officially changed from Kakomiros to Kalomiros. And his father, after much pleading, was persuaded, and he had it changed. But all this was unknown to the Papademetriou couple, even though they had such a close relationship with Dr. Kalomiros. To the Elder, nothing was unknown, on account of the gift of clairvoyance that he had, even when seeing the Doctor for the first time in his life.

ONCE THE ELDER came to Athens—something very rare. Our good God provided that I also should be in Greece, having come from abroad. I was at the house of the blessed monk, Xenophon (in the world Panagos Diamantis Pateras), which is at Psychico. I was staying in the basement where they had the cell of the blessed daughter of the family, the nun Irene Myrtidiotissa. They came and announced to me that the Elder Ieronymos was upstairs in the enclosed porch. This seemed unbelievable to me. I made haste and went up and what should I see? I behold the Elder with the Eldress Eupraxia sitting in the porch. O, what joy! What a blessing! Then came also the lady of the house, Mrs. Katingo (presently Mother Maria Myrtidiotissa, nun).[13] We heard the Elder saying, "I came to Athens, and told the Eldress that we should come and see you. I love you. Besides, I am indebted."

After the usual treats, we took him through the grand dining room to the parlor (*müsafir onta*, as they say in Asia Minor) and by the central stairway up to the second floor, where the chapel of the Annunciation was found. In every room we passed there was a giant icon—in the dining room, the Hospitality of Abraham; in the parlor, the Vladimir Mother of God with an icon lamp. He observed everything. In front of the icons he made the sign of the Cross and he showed that he was pleased, whereas with everything else he was rather displeased.

"I do not laud, I do not laud!" he said. "Too much extravagance! It's a sin. What is the profit?"

"You're right, Elder," answered the hostess, "but when we built the house we didn't know better. If we were building it today, we would do otherwise."

Finally, we reached the second floor where the chapel was. As soon as he entered, his face lit up. His eyes smiled like those of a little child when he sees toys and games. Although the chapel was small, it was delightful. It was wholly frescoed by the blessed Kyr Photi Kontoglou, the iconographer. The icons of the iconostasis were by the same master also. Immediately we heard the Elder say, "I laud! I laud! I greatly laud!"

13. Mother Maria reposed on Holy Ascension, 2005, at the age of 94.

I made haste and opened the beautiful gate. He saw the Communion of the Apostles in the small apse (it is reproduced in the book *Ekphrasis*). Mrs. Katingo invited him to enter the tiny sanctuary. The Elder, for some reason, did not want to enter. She began to plead with him, and with her customary boldness, she almost pushed him in. Then I heard the Elder tell her, "You want me to enter as a blessing. Yet can there be any greater blessing than that our very Christ, the Great High Priest, He Who offers and is offered, He Who sanctifies and is sanctified for our salvation, stands in person Himself at every Liturgy?"

The Elder caught and knew all things, whatever one had in his mind, without our even opening our mouths.

Finally, the Elder entered the sanctuary and kissed the Holy Gospel, the Cross, and the Holy Table. He then said playfully, "For this reason did Katina want me to enter the sanctuary, so that I would see the gold Gospel she has, and the gold Cross."

"Why, no, Elder, that wasn't the reason. Such a thing didn't even cross my mind," said Mrs. Katingo.

"Good, good," said the Elder. "I laud! I laud! Now I laud very much. The house I do not laud. Too much pride, fantasy, too much expense to no purpose. But the chapel I laud very much. Our Christ is worthy of the best. Whatever man has that is better, that is very precious, it is to God that he should offer it. In the Church all things should be gold and silver. All should shine and sparkle. Our Byzantine forefathers had great love for God (the Elder used the word *eros* here). For this reason they raised up so many churches and monasteries, and they adorned them with mosaics and costly offerings. They had great love and zeal for the divine."

Then he turned to the Eldress Eupraxia and said, "Nun, let's chant 'It is Truly Meet' to our Panagia."

Whereupon he began to chant in the usual compunctionate Anatolian manner *It is Truly Meet* in Second Tone with the Eldress holding ison. Oh, what a melody that was! What compunction!

He chanted every word clearly, accenting and coloring the words according to the text and the unutterable sighs of the heart. He stood in the presence of the icon of our Panagia on the iconostasis, and as long as he was chanting, his eyes were running with tears. All of us present wept and were wishing that it would never end. Wretched as I am, I remembered Papa Agathangelos who was in the States, in the city that I was born. He was a compatriot of the Elder's and chanted in the same manner, slowly, without hurrying, sorrowfully, with compunction. Beholding and hearing the Elder chant to our Theotokos, the *Sultana Validedoullah*[14] as they addressed her in Anatolia, you understood that at that moment not before an icon was he standing and chanting, but rather before our Panagia herself in person. This was why he chanted in such a manner, with all his soul and "all that is within" him to our *Pantanassa Despina* [*Lady Queen of All*].

When the Elder finished chanting, we went down to the basement, to the cell of our blessed Mother Irene Myrtidiotissa. The Elder beamed again—he rejoiced in spirit. Everything was "with propriety and order." Two, three little cells, a little refectory, a little kitchen, and a little library filled with spiritual books, icons, analogion...

After sitting for a short while, the Elder arose and we went next door to the house of the eldest daughter of the Pateras family, Calliope Hadjipateras (who has also since fallen asleep). It wasn't necessary to go out into the street, since at the time the two houses were connected by a garden. Some went before and some remained behind, and so I was alone with the Elder. While we were going, the Elder had a little difficulty caused by old age, and it seems that his illness had already begun from which he later reposed. He had his walking-stick, but I gave him my arm also on which he rested what remained of his left arm. As we walked, I wanted to pose a question to him, but from reverence and awe, I

14. *Sovereign Lady Mother of God.*

couldn't find enough boldness to say anything. I said it earnestly, only in my mind, without opening my mouth. At a certain moment, while we were walking along, the Elder stopped, and looking at me, gave me the answer to my question, as if I had asked him out loud. I was astounded!

We finally reached Calliope's house. We went straight to the icon corner. We prayed and afterwards the Elder sat on a chair in the kitchen while they made him some Turkish coffee. The Elder loved Calliope very much and always grieved for her, because she had many sorrows. He spoke to her with tears. The coffee only touched his mouth. He drank very little of it; he spilled most of it on his long, thick beard. Fortunately, they had put a large napkin on him like a bib, and thus his *rasso* was not stained.

The Elder was wont to say that once the camel was asked why her back was crooked. The camel answered, "Why do you behold that my back is crooked? My neck also is crooked, and my legs are crooked, and my nose, and my snout and my whole form! Everything is crooked. Is there anything about me which is not crooked and ugly? So why are you picking on my hump?"

And the Elder would ask, "Is there anything straight and comely about us? Is there anyone without his hump? He who is able to understand, let him understand."

THE SUMMER OF 1966 I was in Greece. Of the many times that I went and saw the Elder, on one occasion there were ten, twelve, possibly even more of us, I cannot remember now after so many years. But I remember well that the Eldress Martha, the disciple of Papa Nicholas Planas, and Basilaki Lepouras were in the group. The Eldress Martha had often heard about the Elder, but by now she was quite old, and it was with difficulty that she ever went out of her little house, on Tsimiske Street, in the center of Athens. I had also told her about the Elder, and had promised her that once I would come from America and take her with her brother, Papou Nicholas, to visit the Elder. It was fortunate that we went in the summer of 1966, since in October of the same year the Elder reposed.

Basilaki Lepouras, together with a young man who helped him with his wheelchair, since he was paralyzed, came on the same trip. I often told Basilaki about the Elder, and he also desired to meet him. In the same group was Father Neketas Palassis of Seattle, Washington, who happened to be in Athens, having gone on a pilgrimage to Jerusalem and to the Holy Mountain. I knew him well from the United States. We were also accompanied by a student of theology, another acquaintance of mine from the States, Panagiotis Tsamperas, presently a priest of the Greek Archdiocese. Deacon Mark (presently a Priestmonk) of the Athenian newspaper *Orthodoxos Typos* and another two of our synodia from the States were included. I do not remember who else was with us. We all departed from Piraeus by ferryboat for Aegina. Mother Martha was hard of hearing, her brother Nicholas was almost blind, Basilaki was in his wheelchair. One with a walking-stick, another being led, one helping the other, pulling one, lifting another.

We were a whole band, like the pilgrims of old who went in caravans to Jerusalem. Mother Martha was holding a bunch of candles to light at Saint Nectarius's, and a little bundle of "holy things" (dried flowers from the *Epitaphios* of Great Friday, holy oils, candle stubs, little pieces of cotton from Unction services, and the like) to throw overboard into the sea, in a "clean place," as she put it. One held a large candle, another held a prayer rope. All in all, we were a sight and report most marvellous—a spectacle to Angels and to men. Everybody was stopping and looking at us with curiosity. Later, when Kyr Aleko Papademetriou, the publisher of Astir House, heard of it, he said to me, "I wish, my Pantelaki, that I had known it. I would have left the factory and come to Piraeus just to see you all and admire you. Oh, if blessed Photis (Kontoglou) were still alive and had seen such a sight! He would have rejoiced. He would have immortalized you on canvas. Truly there was fulfilled the popular proverb—all the blind and lame go to Saint Panteleimon. Oh, if only I could have been there to see such a sight!"

We finally reached the island of Aegina. We took taxis and went up to Saint Nectarius. We worshipped and came down to the Elder's. What joy we all had, what tears, what compunction. The Eldress Martha skipped for joy, like another Anna the Prophetess, the daughter of Phanuel of the tribe of Asher. As for the Elder, like another Symeon the Ancient, he exulted. Mother Martha entered his cell and went to confession. She could not hear. She shouted herself, the Elder shouted also. All of us who were out in the courtyard could hear everything. But the Eldress being such an innocent soul, and advanced in years as she was, what sins could she have? Finally, the Elder came out of his cell, since the entrance was quite narrow, and Basilaki's wheelchair could not pass through. Besides, we were too many to fit in his little cell.

What joy the Elder had in meeting Basilaki. Like a little child clapping its hands, thus was the Elder—except that he didn't have two hands.

He told Basilaki, "I envy you! If it were possible I would give you my body and would take yours. What a crown our Christ is plaiting for you! Just be patient like Job and render thanks for all things to our sweet Jesus."

Then he turned to us and said, "Whosoever carries him, the Angels will carry in that day."

There followed words of consolation and instruction for all of us—clergy, monastics, laity. All wept, all rejoiced, all came to compunction. At the end the Elder read a prayer over us and thus we left.

In the boat on our return trip, sometimes we chanted softly, and sometimes we reminisced about our visit and what we had seen and heard, giving thanks and glorifying our sweet Creator and God, Who deemed us worthy in such times to see and hear such an Elder as those of ancient times.

This visit was in the summer of 1966. I saw the Elder one more time before I left for the United States. Thus, that summer I saw him four times. In October I received a notice that on the third of the month—the memorial of Saint Dionysius the Areopagite—the Elder fell asleep in the apartment of Kyr Eleftherios Koumbis in Athens. I had been notified earlier that the Elder was terminally ill and that he was hospitalized in the Alexandra Clinic, but I didn't expect that he would have reposed so quickly. Even as he had desired and had asked in prayer, he had cancer, he suffered greatly, and so he fell asleep. As gold in the furnace was he cleansed in the end, and departed for the mansions on high.

Some who visited him in the clinic told me that he was in great pain, and that even though he was given morphine shots, he was still in pain. From time to time, he would cry out in the midst of his many sufferings, "Mommy! My Mother!" and Mother Eupraxia, who was always close by, said in her thoughts that whoever heard him would think that he was calling his mother, just like little children, who when they feel the slightest discomfort immediately cry out for their mother. "What will they be saying," thought the Eldress, "everybody who hears him—an elderly clergyman crying out 'Mommy' like a little child." Whereupon the Elder opened his eyes, and looking at her, he said, "Nun, it is our Panagia that I am calling upon, Our Mother, the *Pantanassa* [*Queen of All*], not my mother in the flesh."

As soon as we heard in the U.S. the report of the Elder's repose, we immediately served *trisagia* and *pannikhidas,* (on the third day, the ninth day, the forty-day memorial, and the appointed prayer rope every night). Every day—except Sunday—we served a *trisagion* after the Divine Liturgy. When the forty days were fulfilled, we started after the Liturgy to chant the memorial service.

We reached the *evlogeitaria,* and while we were chanting, all the icon lamps in the church of our monastery began to swing of themselves, without anyone even touching them. First the hanging lamp of the Holy Table, then the lamp over the Beautiful Gate, and following that, those of the iconostasis, of the *proskynetarion* of Saint Nicholas—all the lamps quietly, without any sound or noise, began to swing from the right to the left, even as we swing them for the chanting of the *Polyeleos* during vigils. All of us that were present beheld it and are witnesses. I was censing at the time and quietly chanting the *evlogeitaria* together with the Fathers. It seemed as if the Elder were present. Without seeing him, of course, we felt his presence, as if he wished to thank us, and at the same time to inform us that his soul had found Him Whom he desired, and consequently was skipping with joy and exultation, even as the icon lamps were swinging joyously. At first the lamps began to swing slightly, but by the time the *evlogeitaria* were finished they were swinging fully from side to side, even as when we chant the *Polyeleos* and doxologies and we swing them by hand.

WHEN THE ELDER was living and I used to go to see him, I was never able to visit him without weeping. I usually had a tissue in hand and would wipe my eyes—sometimes I used the sleeves of my *rasso* when I didn't have a tissue. I often mentally told myself, even before I left the States for Greece, or when I was on the ferryboat going to Aegina, that this time I was not going to weep in the Elder's presence. I would make an effort and withhold my tears. At times others were with me when I went to see the Elder. What must they have thought seeing a monk crying? But no matter how much I tried, I was not able even once not to weep. As soon as I saw the Elder's compunctionate face, straightway I began to weep. And as soon as he said something compunctionate, I would cry inconsolably. For this reason I was always wiping my eyes, or even covered them with my hands. Once the Elder said to the Eldress Eupraxia, "What's the matter with him? Why is he always rubbing his eyes?"

And she, the blessed one, answered him, "His eyes bother him, Elder, and that is why he's always rubbing them."

Whereupon he turned towards me and said with sympathy, "We know a good ophthalmologist in Athens. You must go and be examined. You are still young and have need of your eyes. I am old now, I don't hear well, I don't see well, but then I don't need to anymore. What I can hear and see is enough for me. From time to time I hear so many things from those who visit me, that I call blessed as many as are deaf and blind these days, for they hear not and see not the sounds and sights of this age."

The Elder fell asleep, and coming to Greece I went with Mother Maria Myrtidiotissa to Aegina to visit his grave and see his little cell again. I said in my mind—This time since I will not see the Elder's grace-filled face, I won't weep.

When we reached the Elder's hermitage we knocked and the Eldress opened. As soon as she saw us she began to weep and say, "Where now is the Elder who loved you? He departed, and I'm left behind all by myself to light his lamp."

Mother Maria also started to cry as soon as she heard the Eldress Eupraxia's words. But I constrained myself and did not cry. We went immediately to the Elder's grave. As soon as I saw the Cross and the marble slab that covered the grave, then I could no longer hold myself back and straightway began to cry uncontrollably. I began a lament, weeping inconsolably as Hadji Yiayia Macrina the pilgrimess did when I was little. I felt the presence of the Elder so strongly as never before—even when he was living upon the earth. I fell upon the marble slab, as upon the Elder's neck, and wept uncontrollably. Then I sat opposite the grave and sent up a lament without end. I was crying so much that for a moment the two nuns feared I would have a heart attack. Whereupon they stopped their crying and began to scold me that I should not weep so much. They began to pull at me to get up and go to the cell of the Elder. Finally, after some time I got up and went to the courtyard where the Elder's cell and the chapel were located. The tireless Eldress Eupraxia brought refreshments—*to forgive the departed*, as the Greek pious say—and the two nuns began to reminisce. Sinner that I am, it was like the first time that I visited the Elder. I couldn't take anything of the treats. There was a lump in my throat. I just sat there as though dazed and heard as if from afar the voices of the two nuns conversing, and from time to time I wiped my eyes. Thus, I was not able even once to visit the Elder—either when he was alive or after he departed this world—and not come to compunction and weep.

When the Elder was living (I mean in the present life, because "the righteous live unto the ages and death doth not touch them" [cf. Wisdom of Solomon 5:15]), I often said to myself that I would ask him this or that. But when I came into his presence, then all my thoughts would perish, and either I was not able to remember what I was going to ask him, or out of awe and compunction I was unable to open my mouth and articulate even a word. Because of this, when the Elder first reposed, I regretted that I had not asked him this or that. But now I have peace and joy, that all that I heard from his mouth was of his own choosing and as the Holy Spirit provided for my profit, without my own will entering in. The subjects on which he spoke to me when I visited him and the exhortations he gave me were as our sweet God illumined him, and not because I sought or asked about them. I only listened like Moses and the Israelites at the God-trodden Mountain of Sinai. And as many things as he spoke to me remain indelibly in my mind and in my heart and I have a well-spring from which all these years now I have been able to draw up, and apply to many and various instances in my life. Without asking, I continuously have answers to many questions, because the words of the Elder were words of wisdom, words of prudence, taken from life (in other words, from experience), salted with the grace of the All-holy Spirit. Such words never fail, but rather continuously water the soul and make joyous the heart of whoever hears them with faith and simplicity. This is the good seed which our sweet Christ speaks of in His Gospel, and whosoever receives this blessed seed in his heart, in time it bears fruit, and thus he has provisions of life in this path which we walk.

RARE ARE THE PEOPLE like the Elder Ieronymos. Saint Abba Isaac the Syrian writes somewhere, "Just as among ten thousand men scarcely one will be found who has fulfilled the commandments and what pertains to the Law with but a small deficiency, and who has attained to limpid purity of soul, so only one man among thousands will be found who after much vigilance has been accounted worthy to attain to pure prayer." As for that which is found beyond pure prayer, which Saint Isaac calls a mystery ("and gain experience of that mystery"), scarcely is there to be found a man "who by God's grace has attained thereto" from generation to generation (Homily 23, p. 117). Of these most rare of men was the Elder Ieronymos.

Many ask me if I ever see the Elder in dreams. I answer, No. I thank God that I rarely see a holy person in dreams. I was taught by my spiritual fathers not to desire to see dreams, but rather to pray to our Heavenly Father to keep me from dreams and visions.

But, often—while awake—I will see something, or hear, or read something in spiritual books, and I will remember the blessed Elder Ieronymos. This happens almost daily. Rarely does a day pass that an occasion is not given for the Elder to come to mind. But often at night also, when all is quiet and I am alone, I remember the blessed Elder. Then in my mind I see him most clearly, and in my heart I hear again his wise and comforting exhortations. This happens especially when I have a tribulation or sorrow, or I am found at the hermitage of the Holy Apostles on the Atlantic, one and a half hours by car from our monastery. I surmise that, since I have the Elder continuously in my mind and heart, even though twenty-five whole years have passed since the day that I met him, it is as yesterday that is past. For this reason are his memory and his words so strongly with me. But even if another twenty-five years pass, if I live, I do not think that this memory will diminish or be wiped out from within me.

From time to time, besides this living memory of the Elder, I experience his presence very strongly—without, of course, any image or form: a tangible presence within me, which comforts and encourages me in the adversities of life. This presence and consolation I attribute to the grace of the Paraclete. Our Sweet Lord and Master Jesus promised us that He would not leave us orphans. And on the holy and great day of Pentecost He sent forth the All-holy Spirit and fulfilled His promise. Since then our Sweet Christ, the Saviour of the world, is with us either through the Eucharist and other Mysteries, or through prayer, or through the holy icons, and so many other ways and means. He again is the Treasury of all the Saints and Righteous, according to the Old Testament saying, "The souls of the righteous are in the hand of God" [Wisdom of Solomon 3:1]. And on the night that He gave Himself up for the salvation of the world, He asked of the Heavenly Father that all the Apostles, and as many as believed through their preaching, be united with Him, and that where He is they might be also—"that they may be one even as We are," "…those whom Thou hast given Me, I will that where I am they also be with Me" [Cf. St. John, Chapter 17]. This prayer of our Lord has been fulfilled. That is why the presence of our Saints is so strong in the life of the Church. Because through our God-man Jesus Who is present, they are present also. That is why the presence of the Elder Ieronymos for those who knew him and call upon him, and for those who have heard about him and call upon him, is so perceptible.

May our Sweet Jesus, through the prayers of the righteous Elder, always grant us this presence, and through the Faith may He keep us in unity with Him and with one another. Amen.

Archimandrite Panteleimon,
Abbot of the Holy Transfiguration Monastery, Boston
Summer, 1985

Miracles of the Elder Ieronymos

IN THE YEAR 1953 I had a problem with my health. Around my armpit some forty pimples had appeared, which today would be called small tumors or warts. The doctor told me that I had to be operated on to clean out the area.

But we went to the Elder.

After we told him of the problem and showed him the infected area, he used a certain salve and a little pin with which he pierced the primary tumor, having whispered certain words. When he took out the pin, he said to me, "Daughter, do not eat fish or meat for three days. On these days go also and bathe in the sea."

When I fulfilled all that the Elder had told me, even from the first day I saw that the wounds began to diminish and by the third day they had vanished.

WHEN I WAS LIVING in Germany, my sister in Greece was with child and I was anxious about her state and how she would give birth.

One Saturday night I saw the Elder in my sleep. As soon as I saw him appear at the door, I said to him, "Elder, you're here?" He said to me, "Daughter, why are you worrying? Your sister has given birth and has had a delightful little girl." And in fact, the next day they telephoned and informed me that just a half an hour ago she had given birth to a girl.

I, of course, had learned of it a day earlier...

From my acquaintance with the family of the Elder's nephew, George Apostolides, I had heard of him, but had never met him.

One morning when I went to Athens, I saw an elder and an eldress weighed down with bags. The Elder had a knapsack, and one of his arms was missing. They were waiting to take the bus to Eleusina where his brother lived.

I then approached him and said, "Elder, are you from Aegina?" "Yes. And who are you?" Having explained to him who I was, I found a taxi and paid the driver to take them to Eleusina.

Then he said, "Eldress, do you see? God doesn't abandon anyone. This daughter appeared and now we are going by taxi."

In the year 1968 I was a patient in the orthopedic hospital in Voula, since I had a serious problem in the lower back, especially at the third vertebra at the waistline. I suffered from a disc problem.

All the doctors had told me that I would be paralyzed, and for them to operate, I had to give my signature for it.

It was then that an acquaintance of mine telephoned, and I asked her to bring me a small icon of the Elder. I had not slept for a year and a half, even though they were giving me strong pain medicines and sleeping pills. But as soon as I hung the little icon of the Elder on the bed, I fell asleep. In the morning when the doctors came and found me asleep, they were amazed.

That night in my sleep I saw three women who stood close to my bed and said to me, "What are you worrying about?" I told them, "They told me that I would be paralyzed." They answered, "Don't worry, because you have the Elder Ieronymos above your bed."

When the operation was over, eight and a half hours later, and the doctors came out of the operating room, my mother asked them if I was paralyzed. They answered her, "No, but someone must have helped her, because as soon as we applied the lancet, the whole tumor that was on her spine came out, and we didn't touch anything, so that she wouldn't be paralyzed."

A VERY CHARMING EXAMPLE of the assistance given after the Elder's repose is the following. Father Ieronymos was a very compassionate and almsgiving person while in this life. The courtyard outside the little chapel of his hermitage was always filled with little tables and benches with boxes of tools and parts of wall clocks and alarm clocks. He knew how to repair clocks and would either repair old clocks or put one together out of parts of others, and gave them as gifts to the inhabitants of Aegina, who were mostly poor.

In his lifetime he had given a wall clock to a family down the road from his kellion, and shortly after his blessed repose, the clock stopped working. The man of the house said, "Where are you now, Elder, to repair the clock? You've left us, and I have no money to get a new clock."

That night during his sleep he saw the Elder, who said to him, "Why are you grieved? Get up and I'll show you how to repair the clock." Whereupon he took a pen knife and opened the clock from the back and said to him, "Look well at what I'm doing," and he proceeded to repair the clock.

Upon awakening, the man got up and did as he had been instructed, and the clock began working again.

This is reminiscent of that charming miracle worked by Saint Seraphim of Sarov recorded in his life:

> Once Saint Seraphim appeared in a dream to a shop-keeper's wife of Shatsk who had known him in his lifetime and deeply respected him, and he said, "During the night thieves broke into your son's shop, but I took a broom and began to sweep near the shop, and they went away."
>
> And actually, in the morning all the locks were found torn off, but the shop was intact and untouched.

At the cell of the Elder Ieronymos on Aegina, a ledger is kept wherein are recorded many miracles of healing and assistance through the Elder's prayers, but we have been unable to obtain a copy. His holy relics are found in the little church of the Annunciation at his kellion. His head is treasured in a beautiful silver case, a gift of the Monastery and Convent in Boston and the Convent of the Mother of God Sfalagiotissa of Lemesos in Cyprus.

East Door to the Church of the Annunciation as it looks today.

Service to the Elder Ieronymos of Aegina
Whose Memory is Kept on October 3

VESPERS

After the Proemial Psalm, we chant Blessed is the man. *For* Lord, I have cried, *we allow for six verses and chant the following Stichera, repeating them all:*

Fourth Tone. As one valiant

WITH a singular vehemence,* righteous Father Hieronymus,* thou didst love thy neighbour with all thy strength of soul; * and by thy love, thou didst draw men unto Him Who is love itself. * For thy very countenance * shone with grace from that other world, * where thou dwellest now, * interceding with Him Who hath received thy many labours for His Name's sake, * that they who honour thee may be saved. (*Twice*)

WITH the simplest of parables, * which were taken from earthly life, * thou didst show the myst'ries of Heaven unto men, * revealing thoughts of the heart, the hidden truth, and the mind of God. * What an awesome mystery! * that a mortal of dust and clay * was the mouth of God. * Yet because of thy lowliness of heart and strong desire for men's salvation, * such gifts were freely bestowed on thee. (*Twice*)

As a new Elder Symeon, * being great in humility, * thou didst plead with God that thou mightest not see death * till thou

© Copyright 2007, Holy Transfiguration Monastery, Brookline, MA
A full service has been printed in Greek by the accomplished hymnographer Haralampos Bousias.

hadst seen His salvation and wast truly and wholly His; * and the Lord, Who heard thy prayer, * crowned thy long life with sufferings * which increased the joy * that in part thou hast even now received as thou dost pray for our salvation, * thrice-blessed Father Hieronymus. (*Twice*)

Glory. *Plagal of Second Tone*

Passing thy childhood in the rock-carved caves of Cappadocia, thou foundest the Pearl of Great Price even in thy youth, O our righteous Father Hieronymus; and guarding this treasure thy whole life long through voluntary poverty, unwearying acts of mercy to the suffering, diligent detachment from all earthly things, and rigorous attachment to unceasing prayer, thou didst attain to the stature of the great God-bearers of ancient times, being a marvel and a vision to all. Wherefore, as thou keepest company with the Saints in the many mansions, earnestly implore Christ to save us who keep thy memorial with joy.

Both now. *Theotokion*

Who would not call thee blest, O all-holy Virgin? Who would not praise thine untravailing giving of birth? For the Only-begotten Son, Who shone forth from the Father timelessly, hath come forth from thee, the pure one, having become ineffably incarnate, being God by nature and becoming man by nature for our sake; not that He was divided into two persons, but that He is known in two unmingled natures. Him do thou beseech, O august and all-blessed one, to have mercy on our souls.

Then the Entrance, O Joyous Light, *the Prokeimenon of the day, and the Readings.*

For the Entreaty. First Tone

Let us go in spirit to Aegina; for there, where Dionysius and Nectarius shine as her two great lights, a third is now risen of equal brightness. With fiery rays of clairvoyance, he pierced the mists of forgetfulness, showing men their sins; and with Christ-like compassion, he healed the hidden wound. And he receiveth with love all who cry to him with faith: O our righteous Father Hieronymus, intercede that our souls be saved.

Same Tone

O EAGLE of Anatolia, that madest thine eyrie in Aegina, O initiate of the everlasting revelation, and friend of Christ; O teacher of godliness, and stream of grace healing hearts withered in sin; O champion of holy tradition, and unerring guide to God: O God-bearing Hieronymus, intercede that our souls be saved.

Third Tone

IN the hills of Cappadocia, in churches cut out of the rock, thou didst engrave the image of prayer in the purity of thy heart; and living a life of self-denial out of love for God, thou wast filled with His grace and becamest the saving pledge and surety of mercy for the repentant. Wherefore, take us also into thy fatherly affections, O God-inspired Hieronymus, heal the ailments of our souls and bodies, and make us heirs of the Kingdom of God.

Glory. *Plagal of Fourth Tone*

THROUGH thine unrelenting struggles of self-sacrifice and prayer, O God-bearing Father, thou wast completely filled with the Holy Spirit. The sight of thee brought men to the fear of God; the sound of thy voice pierced hearts with compunction; thy words enlightened souls to cast off the slumber of negligence and to seek God with diligence. Thy life was the life of Christ, and while dying a painful bodily death, thou didst heal the souls of them that ministered to thee. And now, as thou standest at the throne of God in glory and boldness, O marvellous Hieronymus, importune Him to save us who honour thee.

Both now. *Theotokion*

LADY, do thou receive the supplications of thy slaves, and deliver us from every affliction and necessity.

For the Aposticha, the following Stichera:

Plagal of First Tone. Rejoice

REJOICE, inspired Apostle of prayer, * making the love and fear of God known to sinful souls; * rejoice, balsam and astringent that sharply stingeth the wound * then applieth healing with assuaging words; * the Prophet and hesychast, showing men their remove from God * and present suff'rings as the fruit of forgotten sins, * tearing off the veil of oblivion from their minds. * In thee, O great Hieronymus, the Prophets of Israel * walked once again on the earth and directed men with inspired rebuke * and skilfully led them * to the love of the omnipotent Saviour of our souls.

Verse: Precious in the sight of the Lord is the death of His saint.

THOU who hadst built a house for the sick * with mighty labours of compassion and sacrifice * didst after regret the time taken from the doing of prayer, * when thou hadst discerned the treasures hid therein. * Yet, growing more great in prayer, and increasing in grace divine, * thyself wast healing for the sick and distressed of soul, * being unto all a great spiritual hospital. * Wherefore, we also bring to thee our ailments and sufferings * and we beseech thee with fervour to show thy sympathy unto us * by making entreaty * to the Lord to heal us also in body and in soul.

Verse: Blessed is the man that feareth the Lord.

REJOICE, who through denial of self * becamest great in love of God and for suff'ring man, * thou mountain retreat and fastness exalting passion-bound souls * from the world's disturbance to the peace of God. * Though love of the Crucified once espoused thee to poverty, * there are no patches on the garment thou wearest now, * woven seamlessly out of love, prayer, and sacrifice. * Now is the vindication of thy life of humility, * as thou art raised to the Heavens arrayed in glory and holiness, * extolling thy Master, * and imploring Him for all who observe thy memory.

Glory. *Plagal of Fourth Tone*

Having wondrous Misael the Cappadocian as thy guide to Christ in thy youth, and Abba Isaac the Syrian in thine age, thou becamest a singular master of the art of prayer; with the holy Unmercenaries as thy friends and guardians, thou also wast a healer of both souls and bodies, giving comfort to all in distress; and having a love for thy Lord's all-holy Mother that surpassed all men on earth, thou becamest a genuine brother of her Son. Intercede with Him, O God-bearing Hieronymus, to forgive us our failings and to save our souls.

Both now. *Theotokion*

O unwedded Virgin, who didst inexpressibly conceive God in the flesh, O Mother of the Most High God: Receive the petitions of thy servants, O all-blameless one. O thou who grantest unto all purification from offences, do thou now receive our entreaties, and beseech that we all be saved.

DISMISSAL HYMN
Plagal of First Tone. Let us worship the Word

Reaching forth with thy whole soul unto the Lord thy God, * thou didst attain to the stature of the great Fathers of old, * striving after their humility and love for God; * and as a sharer in their grace, * thou dost cover with thy prayers the faithful that seek thy succour. * Hence ever pray to the Saviour, O blest Hieronymus, that we be saved.

Glory; both now. *Theotokion*

O impassable gate of the Lord Most High, rejoice. * Rejoice, O rampart and shelter for them that hasten to thee. * Tranquil haven and pure Maiden who didst not know man * and who didst give birth in the flesh * to thy Maker and thy God, rejoice; and cease not to pray Him, * making entreaty for them that worship and praise Him that was born of thee.

And the Dismissal.

MATINS

After the First Reading from the Psalter, the following Sessional Hymn:

Plagal of First Tone. Let us worship the Word

As a prince of compunction and prayer and fear of God, * thou, being clothed with divine grace as a most fair purple robe, * wast invested with full power in thy blessed soul * to banish demons and disease, * to drive sicknesses from men and guide sinners to salvation. * Be our protector now also, O mighty Saint, O great Hieronymus.

Glory. *Repeat the Same.*

Both now. *Theotokion*

REJOICE, O God-trodden mountain divinely sanctified. * Rejoice, O soul-endowed bush that was unconsumed though aflame. * O thou only bridge that leadeth from this world to God, * conveying mortals to the heights, * unto everlasting life: Rejoice, pure and spotless Maiden, * who never knowing a man, yet didst bring forth Him Who doth redeem our souls.

After the Second Reading from the Psalter, the following Sessional Hymn:

Plagal of Fourth Tone. Thou, as the Life of all

THE exile on the earth, who by prayer dwelt in Heaven, * the pauper clothed in rags, wearing God as a mantle, * he who with all his power * loved God and neighbour more than he loved himself, * he of whom our pure Lady * said: No man loveth me like Hieronymus, * the same now maketh bold and ceaseless prayer for them that keep his feast-day.

Glory. *Repeat the Same.*

Both now. *Theotokion*

THOU gavest birth to God, our Creator and Saviour, * Who out of Adam's stock chose thee out as the greatest: * stronger than Heaven's Angels * in spotless diligent never-ceasing prayer; * peerless in Godlike longing * that all be saved and united unto God, * the which, O Lady, earnestly implore for us who sing thy praises.

We say the Canon of the Theotokos, I shall open my mouth, *and the following of the Saint. Before the Troparia, we say,* O Saint of God, intercede in our behalf.

Plagal of Fourth Tone
ODE ONE
The charioteer of Pharaoh

COME, let us honour with our songs Hieronymus, the man of marvellous love, * the prince of compunction, * and the Cappadocian horseman tightly reining in his heart, * who, not letting it wander amidst the wastes of the world's delights, * spurred it to the heights of the love of Christ.

THIS festal day doth shine and shout with joy to laud the Saint revealed in our times, * the peer of the ancients, * that true oracle of Aegina who prophesied by Christ, * whose pronouncements admitted of neither gainsay nor disbelief, * coming from the Father of Lights on high.

O FATHER, open up to us the door of thy beloved cell once again; * receive our petitions * and admit us to thy fatherly affections great with love; * and as no man departed from thy compassion left unconsoled, * neither leave us sinners without thy help.

Theotokion

THE fall of Adam and the universal woe of our departure from God, * the wall of division, * was undone, O holy Virgin, and our ruin was reversed * when our infant Artificer was contained in thy blessed womb, * joining God to man with a saving bond.

ODE THREE
In the beginning

THOSE lofty fortresses of prayer, * eyries of God-seeking eagles, * the spiring cones of Cappadocia the blessed, * nurtured great God-bearing Saints, the giants of unceasing prayer, * of whom the last to fly forth * was the high-soaring Hieronymus.

THY patrimony to thy sons * was not estates and possessions, * but thy zeal-kindling example of virtue, * dauntless diligence in prayer, humility before the Lord, * and never-shaken patience, * with faith that God doth direct our ways.

TODAY our feast doth have as host * him that had no earthly riches, * the provider of the orphans and widows, * and the refugee in whom all men found refuge for their souls, * the haven of great mercy, * the Heaven-reaching Hieronymus.

Theotokion

A PILGRIM homeless on the earth, * thou hadst thy mind in the Heavens, * bravely practising detachment from all things; * exiled far from Kelveri, thou daily wast at Calvary, * where, with His Virgin Mother, * thou drewest strength from thy Master's Cross.

SESSIONAL HYMN
Plagal of Fourth Tone. By conceiving the Wisdom

LIKE that Hannah who poured out her soul in prayer, * thy good mother enkindled thee with her zeal * and as her young Samuel * dedicated thee to the Lord; * and through diligent working of virtue didst thou wax great * in the grace of clairvoyance and wondrous prophetic gifts. * Wherefore, as a judge unto God's people, thou spakest * the oracles from on high, * turning all to the love of Christ, * O God-inspired Hieronymus. * Intercede with Christ our God * that forgiveness of all their transgressions be * granted to them that with longing * keep thy holy memory.

Glory; both now. *Theotokion*

THEE do all generations of mankind bless * as the Virgin and only in womankind * who seedlessly brought to birth * God incarnate upon the earth. * For in thee is the fire of the Godhead come down to dwell, * and thou sucklest the Maker and Lord as a little babe. * Wherefore, we, the race of man, with all of the Angels, * befittingly glorify * the All-holy Child born of thee, * and with one voice we cry to thee: * Entreat thy Son and God that He grant * the forgiveness of transgressions unto them * that sing the praise of thy glory * as is meet, O spotless Maid.

ODE FOUR
I have hearkened and heard

WITH a needle, a walking-stick, * with a blade of grass, with a crumpled handkerchief, * thou didst raise men's minds to things on high, * using earthly things to ravish from the earth.

LIKE an eastern-grown apricot, * thou at once wast tart with thy sharp rebukes for sin * but most sweet with strong consoling words, * strength'ning souls on comfort tempered with reproof.

AS a man of great enterprise, * thou didst trade for profit in every circumstance, * that all things might bring thee greater gain, * making thee more rich in love for God and man.

Theotokion

THOU didst run to the Holy Land, * thirsting for the places that God had sanctified * when He walked the earth arrayed in flesh * taken from the Virgin prophesied of yore.

ODE FIVE
Wherefore hast Thou deprived me

LEARNING prayer from thy mother, * thou wast nourished more on her tears than upon her milk; * and her great compunction * formed thy soul in its image from tender youth, * so that she was mother * both of thy soul and of thy body, * educating thee early in godliness.

Daily diligent digging, * op'ning up a deep-springing source of abundant grace, * made thee an oasis * for the world-weary wand'ring the wilderness, * who in thee found guidance * and new provisions for the journey * to the Land of the Living, our Saviour Christ.

Sorrows, poverty, sickness, * every earthly woe from which men flee with all their might, * thou didst reckon favour * from a merciful Providence saving us; * nor was it a wonder * that he who saw God's hand in all things * took the loss of an arm so courageously.

Theotokion

To a virgin's detachment * and complete dispassion towards earthly and carnal things, * thou dost join a mother's * strong and binding affection and tender love * for all of her children * and longest after our salvation * more than we ourselves seek it, O Full of Grace.

ODE SIX
O Lord, be gracious to me

The bee-hive cones celled with caves * of Anatolian Kelveri * brought forth this honeybee who with stings of the conscience roused repentance in sleeping souls, * whom he also sweetened * with the honey of paternal care.

The Saints have all had the grace * to pierce the hearts of those seeing them; * but thou, O Father, dost move with wondrous compunction them that only have heard of thee, * as a living presence * in the souls that saw not, yet believe.

Now the Thebaïd is glad, * and desert Syria singeth praise, * as they behold a new sun that shineth as bright as did the Fathers of ancient times, * Aegina's ascetic, * Anatolian Hieronymus.

Theotokion

WHAT testimony so great, * what praise could equal the blessedness, * as for the Virgin to say: No man on earth loveth me like Father Hieronymus: * next to such a witness, * what is all the world's magnificence?

KONTAKION
Fourth Tone. Be quick to anticipate

LIKE Moses, thou spakest face to face with God as a friend, * and thou wast thyself a fiery pillar of ceaseless prayer, O Father Hieronymus; * wherefore do thou lead us from the Egypt of passions, * out of thickest darkness to the light of salvation; * for thou possessest boldness with Christ, Who was well pleased in thee.

OIKOS

DAILY thou bentest thy knees on the ground, and sentest thy mind speeding to the heights, lifting up thy hands to Heaven, and drawing down the grace of God. And now, O Father Hieronymus, seeing Christ hath lifted thee up to wondrous heights, we implore thee to bend down to us in our tribulation and mightily come unto our aid; for thou possessest boldness with Christ, Who was well pleased in thee.

SYNAXARION

☦ On the third of this month we commemorate our righteous and God-bearing Father Hieronymus of Cappadocia, who reposed in peace on the island of Aegina in the year 1966.

Verses

Cappadocia, which gave us Gregory and Basil,
Giveth us Hieronymus as her last oblation.
Asia Minor's major glory rested on the third.

By his holy intercessions, O God, have mercy and save us. Amen.

ODE SEVEN
Once from out of Judea

Thou didst labour at virtue * as a craftsman perfecting his art to greater heights; * and virtue richly gave thee * the love-engendered boldness * of a Saint crying mightily: * O God of our Fathers, blessed art Thou.

Thou beheldest the glory * of the Unbloody Sacrifice and with boundless fear * withdrewest from the priesthood * but drewest all the nearer * unto Christ through prayer, crying out: * O God of our Fathers, blessed art Thou.

Though the Lord showed thee secrets * of men's past and their future to guide and comfort them, * He showed thee not the danger * that smote thee down with suff'rings; * yet with faith unmoved, thou didst cry: * O God of our Fathers, blessed art Thou.

Theotokion

Thou art come from the Father * as forgiveness and mercy and everlasting life, * redeeming them that honour * Thine ever-virgin Mother, * in whose shelter we shout to Thee: * O God of our Fathers, blessed art Thou.

ODE EIGHT
Let us ever extol

Those who scorned thine unkempt outward appearance * soon thereafter were stunned * when thou with piercing wisdom * didst show to them their squalid and dishevelled souls, * yet with such compassion * that their haughty hardness * was turned to awed compunction.

Let the eye of the needle be made spacious * and the camel made small, * and I might see the Kingdom; * or plead for me with Christ, O kind Hieronymus, * and what men find hopeless * for the Lord is easy, * entreated by His servant.

Though thy holy and awe-inspiring presence * struck men's mouths dumb with fear, * yet thou didst fully answer * the deepest thoughts concealed within their inmost heart, * which to thee lay open * in the Holy Spirit, * Who richly dwelt within thee.

Theotokion

As a father constrained by his affection, * in the hour of my death * come quickly stand beside me * and, saving me from them that prey on parting souls, * lead me in thy mercy * with the Virgin Mother * to Him Who gave me being.

ODE NINE
The heavens were astonished

Alas, for our Elias is taken up, * leaving no Elisseus behind with double share of grace; * yet, as grace-filled mantle to those on earth, * he freely doth bestow on all * his consoling presence within the heart, * forsaking none that love him, * but guiding them through sorrows * to Christ, Whose love hath overcome the world.

With Gregory, thy neighbour from Kelveri, * Amphilochius, Basil, and all thy Cappadocian friends, * Isaac thy beloved ascetic guide, * the newly-shown Nectarius * and great Dionysius of Aegina, * and all the Saints in Heaven, * make ardent intercession * that we find mercy with you in that day.

Thy faith transformed the cutting-off of thine arm * to the greater extension of reach of soul in prayer to God, * bartering things earthly for heavenly, * committing thy whole self to Christ, * soul and body, time and eternity; * and Christ received the off'ring * presented so completely, * and hath completely made thee His on high.

Theotokion

The instrument of mercy for Adam-kind, * the compassion of God, the bright quenchless hope of fallen souls, * and the more-than-Mother consoling all, * the flesh and blood that God assumed * for the full recovery of our race, * the Virgin ever standeth * in tireless intercession * for all who run to her with childlike faith.

EXAPOSTILARION
Third Tone. Thou Who, as God, adornest

Having as bright examples * the mighty Misael and John, * thou wast arrayed in the breastplate * of ceaseless prayer, compunction, love, * whence all the darts of the demons * fell back as arrows of infants.

Theotokion

No man on earth doth love me * as doth divine Hieronymus, * didst thou declare in a vision * to his disciple in her doubts. * On his account, gracious Lady, * show mercy unto us also.

For the Praises we allow for four verses and chant the following Stichera:
Plagal of Fourth Tone. O strange wonder

O strange wonder! In these latter times * a star of light riseth up * shining mightily on the Church * with the never-setting beams * of the righteous of ancient times. * He hath the prayer of the desert-dwelling Saints, * prophetic gifts, seeing secrets deeply hid, * and holy love of God * for the sake of which he spared no pain or toil, * till he reached the stature of the great God-bearers of old.

Rejoice, fair child of Anatolia, * and Cappadocia's bright bloom, * sweet with scents of celestial prayer, * watered with the streams of tears * pouring forth from a heart afire. * With fasting, vigil, and sighs unutt'rable, * thou hast arrived at the Angels' state on high, * which thou didst daily seek * with astonishing intenseness of desire, * O divine Hieronymus, thou joy and wonder of all.

Love was thy labour, thy food and drink, * thy meditation, thy life, * and our Lady herself declared * that no man upon the earth * had a love that was like to thine. * For while abiding in unrelenting prayer, * thou wentest everywhere, searching out the poor, * that not a single day * pass without the acts of mercy outwardly * and within, a conflict unto blood to find God in prayer.

In thy breast thou hadst the love of Christ * burning away earthly thorns * and enlight'ning thy mind with grace, * making thee a guide of souls * and a Prophet of mighty speech. * As we extol thee with ardour and desire, * worker of wonders, all-wise Hieronymus, * warmly implore the Lord * with the fervour that blazed in thee all thy life, * that He grant His mercy and His kingdom unto us.

Glory. *Plagal of First Tone*

As an image of the wisdom of the Holy Fathers, and a living monument of the Fathers' love, thou hast been pleasing unto God and men in thy words and deeds, O all-famed Hieronymus. For shining out like a pillar of virtue reaching unto Heaven, thou didst illuminate them that were in darkness, and didst warm souls that had been frozen with ignorance and sin. Wherefore, as we celebrate thy memorial today, and embrace the chest of thy holy relics, we also seek thine entreaties with the Lord, Whom thou hast loved.

Both now. *Theotokion*

We the faithful bless thee, O Virgin Theotokos, and we glorify thee, as is meet and proper: O unshaken city, impregnable battlement, invincible protection, and sheltering refuge of our souls.

The Great Doxology, and the remainder of Matins.

MEGALYNARION

Unto thee, O Father, the hearts of men, * like a book, lay open, * where thou readest their secret thoughts. * Wherefore, we acclaim thee, Hieronymus our Father, * who wast like a great Prophet, * guiding new Israel.

The Elder Ieronymos of Aegina

was typeset in Font Bureau Miller by the Holy Transfiguration
Monastery and printed in an edition of 5000 copies
by Edwards Brothers, Inc., in Ann Arbor,
Michigan, on Mohawk Superfine,
an acid-free paper of proven
durability and of the
highest quality.

GLORY BE TO GOD FOR ALL THINGS. AMEN.